Spaced Out:
Policy, Difference and the Challenge of
Inclusive Education

by

FELICITY ARMSTRONG

Institute of Education,
University of London, U.K.

KLUWER ACADEMIC PUBLISHERS
DORDRECHT / BOSTON / LONDON

A C.I.P. Catalogue record for this book is available from the Library of Congress.

ISBN 1-4020-1261-6 (HB)
ISBN 1-4020-1263-2 (PB)

Published by Kluwer Academic Publishers,
P.O. Box 17, 3300 AA Dordrecht, The Netherlands.

Sold and distributed in North, Central and South America
by Kluwer Academic Publishers,
101 Philip Drive, Norwell, MA 02061, U.S.A.

In all other countries, sold and distributed
by Kluwer Academic Publishers,
P.O. Box 322, 3300 AH Dordrecht, The Netherlands.

Printed on acid-free paper

Printed in the Netherlands.

CONTENTS

SERIES EDITORS' FOREWORD

This is an extremely important book containing a wealth of ideas and insights and raising important questions for discussion and further exploration. In a lucid and cogently argued analysis, the author both challenges dominant ideas and interpretations and provides some alternative innovatory perspectives. These include, the making and meaning of policy; the varied and complex ways in which inclusion and exclusion can be understood; the nature and function of categorisation, labelling and discursive practices within official discourse and procedures and the position and relationship between space, place and identities in relation to the experience of marginalized people including disabled children and young people.

Drawing on concepts and insights from social and cultural geography Armstrong is able to seriously examine and discuss daily activities within institutional and social settings in England and France from several different angles. In sensitive, thoughtful and imaginative ways the micro-politics of social settings and encounters are explored through a process of deconstruction and reconstruction. Subtle, overt and contradictory features of interactions are carefully identified and critically discussed. This covers how meanings, decisions and outcomes of such encounters are developed, challenged and changed.

Both in relation to discussions of the history of special education and her critical self-reflections on the research process, the author challenges homogeneous conceptions and sanitized accounts of what, she argues, is an essentially messy process. It is the unevenness, discontinuities and contradictions of social conditions and relations that are depicted in insightful and disturbing ways.

One of the most challenging aspects of the book is the analysis of the social construction of difference and its contingent relations with the broader socio-political, cultural context. Armstrong is particularly interested in how categorizations of difference are transformed into deviance through the activities of significant professionals and institutional conditions and relations. Thus, the focus of attention is directed towards spatializing processes and discourses. The complex, overt, subtle ways in which space is used and what Armstrong calls 'segregated space' and its impact on social relations, identities and opportunities, provide a series of alternative questions, insights and understandings that make this such an exciting and significant book.

Whilst the explorations of particular social settings are in England and France, the author both clearly demonstrates the difficulties of cross cultural research and maintains that this is not a comparative study. These two contexts are quite different and this impacts on how language is used, categories defined and policies developed, experienced and changed. The author is therefore particularly interested in raising questions and identifying issues which emerge from both contexts.

The stories that are presented are not from the position of an uncommitted, neutral observer. Armstrong is passionately concerned with issues of democracy, equality and social justice and as she contends, 'with what the broader picture means in terms of the lives of individuals and what those relationships mean in terms of issues of equity and inclusion, which are important' (p. 169) This has motivated her to place the voices of particular people to the centre stage of consideration. It is about the lives, experiences, feelings of real people that this book is about.

In this book the reader is able to recognise the complex exploration that the author undertakes of ideas, issues and understandings with regard to the topic under examination. The quality of the book has been enhanced by the lucid, readable, informative and thought-provoking style of the writing. It is a major piece of work which provides a wealth of issues and questions requiring further investigations and as such, will be of importance in encouraging debate and dialogue over these fundamentally important concerns.

Len Barton
Marcia Rioux
January 2003

ACKNOWLEDGEMENTS

Although there are numerous references to the work of other people in this book, it is difficult to provide formal acknowledgement for ideas which float to the surface as a result of conversations which take place on tops of buses, over dinner, in the chat which follows a seminar, a visit to the cinema or on a train journey. These ideas emerge often after years of lying fallow and are hard to place once they become 'your own'. So I want to thank all the friends, family members and colleagues who have provided me with ideas and encouragement in so many different ways and at different stages over a number years. I have borrowed ideas from you, sometimes ill-digested, re-moulded them, and reintroduced them in different contexts and from different perspectives.

In particular, I would like to thank the following people for generously sharing their ideas through discussion, argument, their writing, paintings or photographs, and suggestions for reading:

Alan Alcock, Derrick Armstrong, Phil Armstrong, Zoë Armstrong, Len Barton, Nathalie Bélanger, Brigitte Belmont, Tom Billington, Patrice Blougorn, Tony Booth, Andrew Brighton, Catherine Brighton, Shane Brighton, Henry Brighton, Melissa Clarke, Peter Clough, Barbara Cole, Robert Doré, John Ferguson, Nicholas Garant, Andrew Glyn, Danny Goodley, Suzy Harris, David Hyatt, Claire Tregaskis, Judy Mabro, Gary McCulloch, Alison Meyric Hughes, Henry Meyric Hughes, Michele Moore, Darren Murphy, Selena Murphy, Jon Nixon, Moises Pedraza, Helen Phtiaka, Eric Plaisance, Pam Poppleton, Patricia Potts, Sharon Rustemier, Nel Saumont, David Sibley, Bob Sutcliffe, Aliette Verillon, David Walsh, Chris Winter.

My thanks and gratitude also go to Roger Slee and Jenny Corbett for commenting on my work and encouraging me to develop it at a crucial stage.

I thank Len Barton for taking an interest in my work, sharing ideas and encouraging me over the past nine years. He has made a major contribution to the development of this book.

I thank Phil Armstrong for his gargantuan contribution in terms of the amount of time, patience and energy he has given in reading, commenting on, proof reading and setting out this book, and for encouraging me for so long.

I thank the following organisations for allowing me to try out and discuss ideas relating to this book in lectures and seminars: The Centre for Educational Research, Canterbury Christchurch University College; The Centre for Inclusive Education, University of Sheffield; Centre de Recherche sur le Liens Sociaux

(CERLIS) Université de Paris V; Centre de Recherche sur l'Éducation Spécialisée et l'Adaptation Scolaire, Institut National de Recherche Pédagogique, Paris; Centres Nationaux de l'Adaptation et de l'Integration, Suresnes, France; Institut d'Études Pédagogiques de l'Ontario, Centre de Recherches en Éducation Franco-Ontari-enne, University of Toronto (Canada); Département des Sciences de l'Éducation, Université du Québec at Montréal (Canada); University of Cyprus; University of Edinburgh; The British Educational Research Association (Annual Conference)

I wish to thank Astrid Noordemeer-Zandee and Tamara Welschot from Kluwer Academic Publishers for contributing their support, enthusiasm and detailed work to the process of producing this book.

I thank Len Barton (again) and Marcia Rioux for inviting me to contribute to this series on *Inclusive Education: Cross-Cultural Perspectives*

Finally I thank all those – in England and in France – who generously gave up their time to discuss issues with me and be interviewed, or who allowed me to observe meetings, or visit their work setting and come into their classrooms. Without this help, I would not have been able to carry out the research which forms the basis for this book.

Chapter 4 of this book is a revised version of the following paper:
Armstrong, F. (2002) The historical development of special education: humanitar-ian rationality or 'wild profusion of entangled events'?, in *History of Education*, Vol. 31:5, 437–456.

Some of the material discussed in Chapter Seven is discussed from a different perspective in a forthcoming article:
Armstrong, F. (2003) Difference, discourse and democracy: the making and break-ing of policy in the market place, in *International Journal of Inclusive Education*, Vol: 7.

Felicity Armstrong
2003

CHAPTER 1

RESEARCHING THE PRACTICES AND PROCESSES OF POLICY MAKING

INTRODUCTION

This book explores the relationship between space, place and identity and multiple processes of policy making in education. It's main purpose is to try and understand these processes in terms of the values and principles which work through policy making in relation to 'provision'. By 'provision' I am referring to the structures, places, assessment procedures, allocation of resources, curricula and ways of naming made in relation to disabled children and young people, and other learners at risk of exclusion in education systems. Possible alternative ways of understanding how policy processes create, or contribute to, exclusions in education are explored through a number of different lenses as a means of teasing out some of the contradictory or obscured mechanisms at work which produce particular constructions of difference and 'needs'. Legislation has been both slow and weak in counteracting exclusions and reducing discrimination; in fact, policies which are presented as being concerned with widening participation in some areas may strengthen forms of marginalisation in others. This book seeks to contribute to an understanding of the ways in which policies are made and interpreted and to explore some possible implications for social justice.

useful expression of my thoughts.

Although there is a focus on spatialization and policy making in relation to disability and learning difficulty in education, the ideas and arguments put forward are connected to other forms of exclusion and inclusion. The kinds of approaches used to examine policy making in education – theories of space and place borrowed from social and cultural geography, critical historical enquiry and discourse analysis – could also be applied in relation to other groups such as girls and women, or boys and men, in particular education or work settings and career structures. They could be applied to an exploration of policy making in relation to the experience of young asylum seekers in education systems. They can be connected to values and practices informing decisions about planning in towns or rural communities and local economies, as well as in terms of the role and location of different schools, public transport systems, the design of buildings and opportunities for communities to develop and flourish. These are inseparable from issues relating to inclusion and exclusion in education which are about local, national and global policy developments relating to social and economic change, as well as about the making of education policies. As Bill Morris (General Secretary of the Transport and General Workers Union, UK) pointed out in commenting on the proposal to set up detention camps contained in the Nationality, Immigration and Asylum Bill in October 2002:

> Let's get one thing clear: these centres are not for accommodation; they are for detention. Founded on the socially repugnant objective of separating refugees and their children from society ... they will be a constant reminder that, in 2002, this country legislated in order to discriminate ...
>
> In perhaps the most graphic example of discrimination inherent in this policy, the children of asylum seekers will be barred from local schools and educated apart from the children of this country. In doing this, the Government is not only in clear breach of UN guidance on the rights of the child, it is also sending out a dreadful message about the value our society places on these children. (Morris, B., 2002)

The social, political and economic changes taking place internationally, therefore, and their ramifications at the macro and micro levels of social life in different parts of the world, have an impact on the kinds of issues we face in terms of overcoming barriers to inclusive education. These issues extend to the whole of society and cannot be confined to a narrow interpretation of inclusion as being concerned with disabled children and those described as having 'special educational needs'. This is not to argue that the processes of stereotyping and discrimination take the same form or are experienced in uniform ways across all marginalised groups.

Re-read.

At this point, I am already stumbling over the language of 'marginalization' and 'marginalized groups'. Marginalization only has meaning in particular social, temporal and spatial locations. There is a real danger in identifying groups as excluded based on the familiar paradigms of ethnicity, gender, class or disability, and of actually contributing to the processes of exclusion by positioning some groups as *naturally* the subject of marginalization. In later chapters we shall examine some of these issues in relation to language and the creation of identities.

INCLUSION: PRINCIPLES, DISCOURSES AND PRACTICES

When I set out to write this book, my original purpose was to examine policy making relating to inclusion and exclusion in education. I was interested in how policies are interpreted and work their way through to changes in the educational and social lives of children and communities, especially in a historical period in which 'inclusion' has become an everyday discourse of governance. At the same time the notion of inclusion can be interpreted in ways which challenge exclusionary and unjust values and practices.

useful.

In the context of this book, my interpretation of inclusion refers to a set of principles, values and practices which involve the social transformation of education systems and communities. It does not refer to a fixed state or set of criteria to be used as a blue-print, but seeks to challenge deficit thinking and practice which are 'still deeply ingrained' and too often lead 'many to believe that some pupils have to be dealt with in a separate way' (Ainscow, 1999, p. 8). In the following chapters,

I will try to explore ways in which spatialized and disabling discursive practices take place through the technical and bureaucratic procedures of categorization, labelling and placing and how these processes and procedures may be absorbed and absolved within official versions of inclusion itself. Roger Slee raises disturbing questions which challenge dominant interpretations of the notion and practice of inclusion in which:

> ... discursive practices form an alliance that pursues an assimilationist agenda described in a language of 'inclusion'. In other words, residual professional interests of those working in the field of special education have necessitated resilience over changing political imperatives. Predominantly unchanged practices are described in new terms. Inclusion is practised, in traditional ways, by those who presided over exclusion. The aim is to have 'othered' children fit the schools we provide with a minimum of fuss and without disrupting the institutional equilibrium. This is assimilation. Inclusive education ought to suggest a process of cultural reconstruction. (Slee, 1999, p. 127)

This cultural reconstruction has to be situated within a critical appraisal of the discourses and values articulated through the physical environment and the use of space as well as of the discourses used in relation to students, curricula, schools and communities.

What is needed is a close examination of the multiple levels and conduits through which exclusions take place. Inclusion, then, is concerned with cultural change in all areas of social, personal and political life (Armstrong *et al.*, 2000a; Booth, 2000; Corbett, 2001; Potts, 2003a). In this study inclusion is seen as a process or set of processes involving a re-evaluation of the premises on which education systems are based. As Barton explains:

> Inclusive education is not merely about providing access into mainstream school for pupils who have previously been excluded. It is not about closing down an unacceptable system of segregated provision and dumping those pupils in an unchanged mainstream system. Existing school systems in terms of physical factors, curriculum aspects, teaching expectations and styles, leadership roles, will have to change. This is because inclusive education is about the participation of *all* children and young people and the removal of *all* forms of exclusionary practice. (Barton, 1998, pp. 84–5)

A friend recently complained to me that 'the disability movement has high-jacked the inclusion agenda, and other groups and issues relating to race, gender, sexuality and class are being pushed aside in the debate'. I would argue that, on the contrary, the rights of disabled children to attend their local school have been consistently denied and ignored in debates about education and inclusion until very recently, but this comment does emphasise the dangers of compartmentalizing groups and their perceived interests. It is a contradiction to see the struggle for inclusion as taking place – and being lost or won – in relation to the discrimination, or levels of participation, experienced by particular groups. (This is illustrated by the hypothetical example of a disabled person gaining physical access to a local school or college, only to find themselves discriminated against because of practices and attitudes relating to, say, Travellers, asylum seekers, class, race or gender). Inclusion is concerned with countering oppressive and marginalizing values and with understanding how these connect to practices and polices wherever they take place and in whatever form. There is a real danger of fragmenting the struggle and mirroring divisive and deficit-driven policies and practices which position particular groups as weak or needy and requiring special treatment because of *their* problems. The failure to make connections between wider issues of inequality relating to whole communities, class, economic, social, political or national status, race, gender, sexuality – categories which cut through each other horizontally and vertically, now merging with each other, now becoming distinctive – allows the separation and segmentation of struggles for social justice to be weakened and dispersed. It allows institutions to respond to the introduction of new legislation defensively, with a focus on meeting the minimum legal requirements relating to particular groups, rather than interpreting their obligations in terms of human rights and principles of equality. For these reasons while much of the discussion in the following chapters relates to disability issues, there is no intention of disconnecting this discussion from wider issues of exclusion and inequality.

BACKGROUND TO THE STUDY

In the late nineteen nineties a particular opportunity to research policies relating to processes of exclusion and inclusion presented itself in a city Local Education Authority (LEA). A special school, designated 'for' physically disabled children and young people was to be closed down as part of the LEA's policy to reduce the number of special schools and increase participation in ordinary education. I decided to follow the story of the closure of this particular school – referred to in my study as Freelands School – in an attempt to understand the ways in which policies are made and re-worked. By studying policy making surrounding the closure of one school, I thought I had found a particularly neat and manageable focus for my research.

Another on-going research interest since the early 1990s has been education policies and exclusion in France. I have been interested in policies and process of segregation both within the education system itself and as part of the wider social structures of health and welfare. Among other things, this has included the gathering of material in a small number of segregated institutions designated 'for' disabled children and young people. This, I thought, would provide an opportunity to do a comparative study of policy making and provision focusing on two settings, one in France and one in England. At the time my notes read:

> I shall look at how and where education policy is made in France and England in relation to disabled pupils, and the ways in which it impedes, or promotes, their inclusion in ordinary schools. I will also critically evaluate the cross-cultural research process, drawing on the experience of carrying out this enquiry.
>
> My 'hunch' is that *educational opportunities for disabled young people*

are shaped and structured in complex and sometimes contradictory ways by
different policy making interests, structures, procedures and practices which
disregard equality and human rights issues. My study will investigate the
relationships between these different areas and the roles they play in producing and reproducing inequalities, in the context of two specialist institutions,
one in France and one in the UK.

As my research developed I became increasingly aware of the possible pitfalls
and issues raised by attempting to 'make comparisons' between two different
cultural settings. An early attempt to match the research settings in terms of finding schools which were similar in size, purpose and community, was abandoned
when confronted by the simple and – with hindsight – obvious fact that different
contexts do not produce the same social categories, structures, and practices. Nor
could I possibly expect to discover a policy-in-the-making situation in France which
could be compared with the one which presented itself in England. Leaving aside
the linguistic complexities and difficulties involved in comparing meanings in
two different countries with their own cultural, historical and political contexts, it
became clear very quickly that the idea of comparing two environments, matched
and controlled for their likeness to each other, had to be ruled out. It then seemed
more interesting to explore aspects of the contexts themselves and their particulari-
ties, their unique differences, histories and practices in terms of policy making
processes and outcomes. This study, then, is not 'comparative' because there is no
attempt to treat the material from the different settings as comparable. The nature
and level of detail of the material drawn from the two countries is very different,
but I hope that the questions and issues which emerge from considering two quite
distinctive contexts will be illuminating.

POLICY, SPACE AND PLACE

One of the theoretical frameworks used in this study is influenced by Fulcher's
work on policy (1999). Fulcher argues that:

> Policy is the product, whether written (laws, reports, regulations), stated or
> enacted (for example, pedagogic practice), of the outcome of political states
> of play in various arenas. (Fulcher, 1999, p. 11)

Rather than referring to a simple top-down process, policy needs to be understood
in the wider social context in which it occurs and in terms of its relationship to
people's lives. It is not something made by government and handed down through
government agencies ready-made. Policy is paradoxical, the product of struggles
and contradictions. It is made at many levels in society through legislation, social
and political structures, institutional and institutionalized practices and discourses
and through the struggles which take place in classrooms, staff rooms, meetings of
governors, parents and trades unions, the media – all are arenas in which policies
are made, re-interpreted and transmitted.

This enquiry will broadly examine the relationship between the use of space, the erection of boundaries, the creation of places for particular purposes and the construction of identities, as a means of enhancing understanding of policy making and practices in education, and processes of exclusion and inclusion of disabled children and young people.

In the process of my enquiry into policy making in England – beginning with interviews with teachers – a particularly distinctive set of issues began to emerge which gradually formed themselves into a number of questions concerning the relationship between the ways in which space is used and its impact on social relations. As I studied my interview material, I was struck by the frequency with which implicit references to spaces, boundaries and places were made. I became increasingly aware of the importance of these issues at all levels of debate around inclusion and exclusion. At a concrete level, teachers in special schools and ordinary schools expressed concern about 'having enough room' or of having 'their' space taken over by others. At a more abstract level, the struggle over the control of space by different groups represented profound political struggles surrounding conflicting interests and different perceptions of rights. At yet another level, was a complex merging of identity of people with places. Thus, both children and teachers were assigned identities attached to the schools they belonged to. Special schools were segregated places whose communities were defined as 'other'. Links between spatiality in its many complex forms and policy making at multiple levels became increasingly evident, leading to the formulation of a set of questions:

- What is the explanatory power of theories of space and place in understanding processes involved in the exclusion of children and young people from ordinary schools?
- To what extent do assumptions and beliefs concerning place and identity inform perceptions of disabled students?
- How do discourses of space and place inform the processes and practices of policy making?
- What light do these questions throw on the traditional historical accounts of special education?

These questions run through this study, overlapping, and constantly re-emerging in different places and guises. There is no attempt to try to provide solutions to problems, only to 'draw attention to, and challenge the assumptions informing policy …'. and to contribute to knowledge about how 'injustices and inequalities are produced, reproduced and sustained … [and to]… provide a basis for the development of social transformation.' (Ozga and Gewirtz, 1994, p. 122).

THE STRUCTURE OF THE BOOK

Chapter 2 begins to build an analytical framework for discussing education policy making with reference to issues of inclusion and exclusion. I draw on theories relating to space, place and policy to create a number of vantage points from which to think about issues of inclusion and exclusion in relation to education.

Chapter 3 introduces some research issues which have arisen during this enquiry in relation to the nature and processes of policy making and the challenges and possibilities opened up by cross-cultural research. There is a critical discussion of the methodological approaches developed in response to the unfolding research scenario, and some of the dilemmas which were encountered along the way.

Chapter 4 critically reviews some traditional accounts of the historical development of special education in England and France and Chapter 5 explores some possible alternative approaches to understanding the past and its relationship to contemporary issues and questions concerning inclusion.

Chapter 6 presents case studies relating to particular settings in England and France. It focuses on policy making in one Local Education Authority in England, particularly concerning the proposed closure of a special school. It looks at policy making in France through three different settings: a hospital based school, and a Lycée in which around 70% of students are disabled, and a segregated centre médico-pédagogique under the control of the Ministry of Health and Social Affairs. I discuss some of the difficulties associated with the construction of case studies by researchers and try to offset some of these by drawing on insider accounts as far as possible.

In Chapters 7 and 8 I discuss material gathered during my fieldwork, drawing on ideas and questions presented in Chapter 2. Chapter 7 examines the material in the light of a range of discursive practices identified during interviews and meetings in the English setting which reflect wider struggles relating to inclusion and exclusion. Chapter 8 looks at some of the structures and processes of spatialization in the broader French context which produce and reproduce segregation in education.

Chapter 9 returns to questions which have arisen in earlier chapters and considers these in the light of some of the theoretical ideas put forward and the analysis of the material gathered during the field work in England and France.

Some of the material discussed in the chapters relates to fieldwork carried out in settings in England and in France between 1995 and 1999. The issues raised in this discussion are urgently relevant to the challenges we currently face in overcoming discrimination and marginalisation in education. In spite of a small decrease in the numbers of children attending segregated schools in certain Local Education Authorities in England (CSIE, 2002) and while the UK government has published policy documents which purport to widen participation in education, other policies have led to the sharpening of selection procedures and competition between schools and students which have had exclusionary effects. In her exploration of selection, schooling and community based on the city of Birmingham, Potts has found that:

> There is widespread selection by attainment, gender, wealth and religion
> into hierarchies of independent, foundation, voluntary aided and state (or
> 'community') mainstream and special schools ... (Potts, 2003b, p. 25)

Segregated schooling is still very much a feature of education systems, but while the issues relating to the marginalisation of disabled children remain largely comparable to those of the late 1990s, there has been a change in the language

What do Eritreans mean by inclusion — forms a question to research this. What, for example, were we talking about in the workshops — I often had a sense of talking at cross purposes, both within the core team from ATE? & ourselves — ref. to my stressing the importance of language — see

notes from Wk1 or Wk2 to provide an example.

used to talk about them. While the term 'integration' was still common currency in the late 1990s, teachers and policy makers are far more likely today to use the term 'inclusion' in relation to a range of practices, many of which may have little to do with the transformation of school cultures. Very often, the terms are used interchangeably, reflecting contradictions in government policy and confusion about who 'inclusion' is *for* and what it means in terms of values and changing practice. The term 'exclusion' has been used in France for many years in relation to social and economic marginalisation and discrimination; it has been increasingly applied to structures and practices in education and the notion of 'inclusion' is becoming part of the discourse used in debates on widening participation in education as well as in disability studies.

There is often an assumption that inclusion is concerned with increasing opportunities for participation for those who have traditionally been excluded, such as disabled children, and particular 'minority' groups, or for sections of the population who are economically and socially disadvantaged. While this is certainly an important aspect of developing inclusive practices, inclusive education is concerned with transforming *all* schools in terms of their cultures and practices in ways which involve all their members and their local communities. In the Index for Inclusion (CSIE, 2002) an inclusive school is seen as concerned with:

> ... all aspects of schools, in staffrooms, classrooms and playgrounds, and in relationships within and between all staff and students and between schools, parents/carers and other members of surrounding communities. (Booth, 2003 p. 11)

The Index has encouraged the development of a:

> ... new way of thinking about educational difficulties and ways to overcome them that avoids the language of 'special educational needs'. The notion of special educational needs is replaced by the concept of barriers to learning and participation. Whereas 'special educational needs' directs attention at the deficits of students as the cause of educational difficulties, barriers to learning and participation are seen to arise in all aspects of schools and communities, and at all levels of the system. (Booth, 2003, p. 12)

read pt.

The research underpinning this book is based on a similar interpretation of inclusive education but seeks, in particular, to explore the barriers to inclusion which can arise in policy making processes in which the 'deficits of students' are often the focus for debate and decision making, rather than the structures, procedures and cultures of policy making processes themselves. What are the hidden, or unexplored, mechanisms and attitudes at work in policy making which create challenges for inclusion? To what extent do these contribute to the creation of relationships between people in places and spaces which are both productive and reproductive of cultural practices, stereotypes, exclusions and inclusions? These are the questions which are explored in the following chapters.

The names of towns, schools and those interviewed have been changed in the book in order to respect confidentiality.

CHAPTER 2

SPACE, PLACE AND POLICY MAKING:
DEVELOPING A THEORETICAL FRAMEWORK

INTRODUCTION

This chapter explores some possible theoretical frameworks which could provide a starting point for discussing policy processes. This will involve a critical engagement with some ideas from different disciplines concerning notions of space and place, especially as they relate to discourse and the making of education policy. In this context the term 'critical engagement' is concerned with a commitment to social justice and to joining with the work of others in different fields to contribute to the same ends as that described by Dutton for architecture:

> An architecture of social responsibility (worthy of the name) resists dominant social trends in order to promote social justice and 'radical democracy' and works towards liberation by helping groups achieve a spatial voice in new forms of community and solidarity, conceived within difference. (Dutton, 1996, p. 159)

Could the research process itself provide an arena in which the voices of others, those involved in, or affected by, the issues being explored, would find a space? What would it mean to promote social justice and 'radical democracy' through the research process, or would it be enough to explore these issues through the research questions, data collection and analysis? I cannot claim to have shared power in the design and process of the research and the voices of children and young people are rarely heard. What I have tried to do is to make visible some of the obscured processes through which decisions are made about where some children go to school, and to raise questions about these in relation to issues of democracy, transparency and equality. This has involved borrowing ideas and terminology from different disciplines, and using them to provide fresh vantage points from which to explore familiar issues.

Terminology

Some of the terminology used in this and later chapters is more usually associated with social and cultural geography or with other disciplines, but – of course – as in any discipline, geographers themselves don't all use terminology in a uniform way. Some of the sharpest struggles within individual disciplines are about language and meanings. I make no claims for my use of borrowed terms, or for their linguistic or disciplinary legitimacy, except that they have extended the vocabulary at my disposal and made it possible to think and write about everyday issues from a number of different angles. As soon as you begin to use words like 'boundary' or 'place' in ways which are both physical and political in relation to schools, for example, you have a new set of concepts with which to critically evaluate political or historical accounts and rationales applied to education.

Here, and in later chapters. I use the term **landscape** to refer to the shape, the history, the practices and the constant changes associated with particular spaces or contexts. This use of the term encompasses temporal, spatial and cultural qualities as well as the attitudes, memories and associations of communities and individuals. The term **space** is used to refer to amorphous areas – metaphorical and literal – in which, and through which, places, practices and identities are formed and reformed. The terms **place** and **site**, used interchangeably, are defined by 'specific social activities with a culturally given identity (name) and image' (Shields, 1991, p. 30). Spaces and places are known by their physical shapes and appearance, as well as by their purpose, history and reputation. Place identities, as well as being shaped by consensual, public meanings, also connect to individual autobiographies and associations.

The term **arena**, in the context of the discussions which follow in later chapters, is distinguished from *place* and *site* in that it is used to refer specifically to areas in which policies are advanced, opposed, made and mediated through practice and discourse – or '... wherever there is debate and decisions are made' (Fulcher, 1999). There are stable, permanent, or semi-permanent arenas such as parliamentary or council meetings, and meetings of parent-teacher associations or trade union members – and more informal, but none the less regular, arenas such as gatherings of parents at the school gates at the end of the school day. There are also arenas which are created bureaucratically, such as task forces, focus groups or think tanks, with the specific purpose of controlling the selection of participants and defining agendas. Bodies such as these give the appearance of democracy and consultation often without actually being invested with any power to decide on their own composition, what may and what may not be discussed, or on the kinds of recommendations which can be made.

Arenas, like places, may also be created by **events** –or suddenly emerge out of situations. An example comes to mind of the occupation of a nursery school by parents and members of the local community in South Oxford in the 1970s. Through their actions the protesters created or transformed a place (the nursery school) into an arena for political debate and struggle. This transformation involved the emergence of new, if transient, democratic and political practices and discourses in which those involved deployed the language of struggle – that of values, commitment, roles and discipline. The notion of arenas, then, is associated with the processes and discourses of policy making. Of course, different sites – or places – are always characterized by particular discourses and ways of talking, but these are not necessarily connected with making policy though they may well be essential in maintaining existing policies and power relations.

The notion of the **state**, in the context of these chapters, refers to structures and apparatuses (institutions of government such as parliament and local councils, and structures through which government policies are disseminated such as schools, job centres, benefits offices, social services offices, hospital trusts) as well as the processes, practices and discourses which both inform and reflect the management of power relations in society. But the state is located in the world, and operates and is operated on, in complex and less visible ways than might be suggested by listing its offices and practices. Whitty argues that:

> ...current changes in education policy are themselves linked to a redefinition of the nature of the state and a reworking of the relations between state and civil society. (Whitty, 2002, p. 86)

> ...as education appears to be devolved from the state to an increasingly marketised civil society, consumer rights will prevail over citizen's rights. This will reduce the opportunities for democratic debate and collective action. (Whitty, 2002, p. 87)

Later, in Chapter 7 some examples of policy making processes are explored in which democratic debate becomes sidelined and fragmented through the orchestration of 'consultation' procedures and the more powerful claims – in terms of their effectiveness – of economic rationality and market forces working through the education system.

The state is not one thing, but many, and it is constantly changing. In England the move away from the kind of welfare state which followed the Second World War and the Beveridge Report, has ushered in a state which is overtly committed to a market culture (Harris, 2003), in which the old state machinery and its servants have been replaced by a slicker market driven version of policy making and implementation and in which 'democracy' has been rationalised to serve the needs of efficiency. This affects the ways in which individuals and communities are involved in policy making and the ways in which the state is managed. As Gewirtz explains:

> In the **post-welfarist** era the formal commitments to Keynesian economics and distributive justice were dropped and replaced by formal commitments to market 'democracy' and competitive individualism. Key welfarist orthodoxies were challenged, in particular the view that welfare was best provided within bureaucratic organisational formations. Now welfare bureaucrats and professionals were held to be the source of major problems rather than the source of solutions. (Gewirtz, 2002, p. 2–3)

Welfare rights have become reinterpreted as being linked to notions of deservingness as measured by social usefulness and participation in productivity (Armstrong, 2002), rather than being founded on a commitment to a shared social project of welfare for all. 'Social' areas such as crime, health and housing have been partially privatized as a means of increasing efficiency and decreasing government expenditure as well as undermining the foundations of welfarism as an ideology and as a financial responsibility of government.

The 'welfare state' project was only partially and unevenly fulfilled and could, of course, never deal with all aspects of the 'unacceptable face' of capitalism. Post-welfarism, however, is paradigmatically different in that it represents a decoupling of the state from principles of social justice because state support (however inadequate that may have been) for the right of all to benefit from social goods such as health care and education, regardless of wealth, has been withdrawn. The introduction of wealth-led policies in relation to access to higher education is only one example of this paradigm shift.

References to the state in these chapters and to representatives of the state and government, such as LEA officers, are based on a recognition of the complex and shifting nature of the way policies are made and implemented and the means by which society is managed.

SPACE, DISCOURSE AND VALUES

In England, the majority of schools are still not physically accessible to all. Education was excluded from requirements laid down in Part 3 of the Disability Discrimination Act (DDA) (1995) which in theory introduced 'new rights of access' to 'goods, facilities and services' in 1996 (DfEE, 1995; DfEE, 1997) to be extended 'over the coming years'. The Special Educational Needs and Disability Act arising out of the final report of the Disability Rights Task Force (DfEE, 1999b), seeks to ensure that disabled students are 'treated fairly' by schools and LEAs and to introduce new rights for improved access to further, higher and adult education. The setting up of the Disability Rights Commission which started work in April 2000 and the implementation of the Special Educational Needs and Disabilities Act from September 2002 are potentially important elements in the struggle over spaces and boundaries at the formal level of policy making. However, the policy struggles which are taking place in different local authorities over school access or closure and in relation to the placing of children indicate that the interpretation and implementation of policies are more complex than is suggested in the legislation itself. Far more is involved in interpreting policy or translating formal policy into practice than can be read from the wording of policy documents themselves, including struggles over different values, spaces and identities.

The location of schools in relation to different communities and social, economic and geographical areas is fundamental in defining their role and purpose. Traditionally, special schools have been situated on the outskirts of towns and cities. There are many possible reasons for this, including, for example, the belief that 'fresh air' in a setting away from the hustle and bustle of urban life was beneficial for 'delicate' children (Wilmot and Saul, 1998). But people and groups who are deemed disturbing or seen as not fitting in, have been removed to the margins of community life in many societies. Removal has been a fundamental response towards people who are regarded as useless, dangerous, a drain on resources, 'out of place' or in need of care or protection.

As Imrie argues, social relations are 'constituted in and by space': 'the built environment is essentially a social and cultural product' (Imrie, 1996). Urban land-scapes change before our eyes; psychiatric hospitals, set up as asylums in Victorian times and closed down in the 1980s and 1990s as part of 'care in the community' policies, are transformed into luxury flats. Car factories are closed and replaced by hypermarkets. Detention centres rise up in rural areas of England to confine and process asylum seekers. As landscapes change, so do the characteristics and patterns of social exchange of the different populations who move in or out of them; they, in turn, transform the meanings and mythologies associated with these landscapes. But the attitudes and positions taken up by the 'already there' population towards the 'incomers' is as much part of this transformation as the arrival of outsiders. The character of the small French seaside town of Sangatte has – claims the media – changed beyond recognition. Jon Sopel's piece on Sangatte in the BBC's News Front Page on December 5th 2002 catches the paradoxical relationship between place, history and identity:

> By the end of December, Sangatte will be no more. Of course, Sangatte the small seaside town near Calais will continue to exist – it's just the building which has given it unwanted worldwide fame that will cease to be.
>   A one-time anonymous hangar for storing drilling equipment when the Channel Tunnel was under construction, the Sangatte refugee camp has for three years been a magnet for the dispossessed and desperate from the world's trouble spots who believe that Britain is the promised land. (BBCi, 5.12.02)

It is doubtful that Sangatte could ever return to what it was before. The 'build-ing' which Sopel refers to did not contain the event of Sangatte whose meanings and mythology are embedded in the place and the positions taken up by local residents, commentators, politicians and civil rights activists nationally and internationally.

Potts (2003a) and the team involved in the study of the different social dimen-sions of inclusion and exclusion in Birmingham have emphasized the relationship between policies in education and the wider 'social fabric of cities' (Booth, 2003) and the impact of outcomes of this relationship on processes of inclusion and exclusion. Their study is perhaps unique in making connections between the many levels at which social and education policy and the social and cultural geography of cities interact and produce change. Some of the arguments put forward challenge commonly held assumptions about, for example, the positive outcomes of 'spatial stability/immobility', suggesting that fluidity and mobility can be more conducive to developing inclusion and that 'staying put' is by no means a taken-for-granted factor in improving attainment in education (Potts, 2003b). This is rather disturb-ing in terms of challenging common sense assumptions about the desirability of stability and permanence, and suggests that largely unexplored social-geographical factors as they intersect with education, communities and issues of inclusion and exclusion, are of fundamental importance.

An integral characteristic of the emergence of separate and separating sites has been the development of particular discourses, different sets of practices and particular relations of separation with the wider community at all levels. Discourse plays an important role in anchoring spatial organization in cultural practices and values. An example is the way in which the status and power of professionals in special education has traditionally been recognized and legitimated by the peculiar, supposedly 'scientific' language of their assumed 'expertise' and this is rooted in the medical model of disability and learning difficulty. The terminology used by professionals in relation to the children and young people with whom they work marks out a particular, exoticising and separating space which authenticates segregation. This terminology has increasingly become an arena in which conflicts and values are being struggled over, especially in an era of heightened awareness of the power of discourse. But discourses and attitudes are not ephemeral, but rooted in material conditions and practices. One argument commonly put forward in the English context by some teachers and professionals is that labels are necessary because the identification of a specific category of impairment is the mechanism through which financial resources are released to support individual children experiencing difficulties. Any discussion about the values and effects of labelling children, therefore, must make connections with the complexities of the world in which labels are used, but this is a further example of the effects of a finance-driven ethos on social relations in which people become commodities. Children who experience difficulties may have a 'credit value' in terms of attracting additional funding but this may be offset by what is regarded as their possible negative effects on a school's performance in the league tables. Schools sometimes present 'shopping lists' (including items such as 'new science laboratories') to LEAs as part of negotiations over the possible arrival of a group of disabled students or the setting up of a unit or centre which will provide some kind of specialist provision. (In my experience, such attempts to 'get something' in exchange for a group of disabled students as a kind of 'sweetener' are likely to be rebuffed.)

For Foucault, the key to understanding how society is ordered was to study how 'human beings are made subjects' (Foucault, 1982, p. 208) through the deployment of discourses and practices and the ways in which these transform human beings into 'subjects of a particular kind'. Foucault charted the eighteenth century 'projects of docility' such as the development of systems of incarceration (asylums, prisons, hospitals) and the emergence of a new 'political anatomy', which, Foucault explained:

> defined how one may have a hold over others' bodies, not only so they may do what one wishes, but so that they may operate as one wishes, with the techniques, the speed and the efficiency that one determines. Thus discipline produces subjected and practised bodies, 'docile' bodies. (Foucault, 1977 p. 138)

The control and ordering of human beings and their differentiation into 'subjects of particular kinds' is achieved through social practices and discourses, through, for example, the conceptualization and management of the built environment. Thus architecture and urbanism became integrally related to group differentiation and social relations. In Chapter Four this argument will be mentioned, particularly in relation to the design and organization of the nineteenth century workhouse as a vehicle of social control and productivity. But it would be a mistake to interpret such a position as being simply about oppression. The design of buildings and urban spaces has the capacity for expressing egalitarian values which take into account the experience and aspirations of the users in ways which are empowering and creative. A study of the history of the architecture of school buildings, for example, bears this out in accounts of the design of school buildings following the Second World War. As Saint explains:

> What the Herts architects did was to start from the perceptions of the child. They thought of lighting and colour together, as stimuli. In infant classes, the educationists and teachers told them, the child was learning how to see, how to interpret shapes and colours in two and three dimensions, how to make out letters, how to identify trees and birds and bushes outside the window. The architects solicited the aid of the technologists in easing these tasks and making them as exciting as possible. (Saint, 1987, p. 87)

Another related idea which will be explored relates to the notion of 'landscape as text' which is an important theme in cultural geography. Cosgrove refers to '... the metaphor of landscape as 'text' to be read or interpreted as a social document ...' (Cosgrove, 1987, p. 95). The notion of landscape as 'a social document' can be expanded to open up possibilities in which, by drawing on a number of disciplines and representations, we can try to understand better the relationship between spatial repartitions, a sense of place, social values and processes of exclusion. This may help to uncover the symbolic qualities of boundaries in the construction of images, roles and stereotypes. In Chapter Five, these ideas are discussed particularly in relation to architecture as a spatializing discourse and the potential contribution that a study of buildings and paintings from different historical periods might make in terms of raising questions concerning social responses to difference.

The adoption of historical and cross-disciplinary approaches, drawing on different kinds of materials and representations (paintings, novels, architecture, for example), also raises questions about the routine merging of the notion of the *contemporary* with the idea of *progress*. Dominant accounts which are based on assumptions that there has been a historically smooth and linear progressive development in policy making and attitudes towards greater enlightenment, humanitarianism and democracy (based on western values) need to be critically evaluated. Thomson argues:

> It is only through supplementing the study of legislative politics with analysis at the point of provision that we can fully assess the nature of policy (Thomson, 1996, p. 207)

Among the thousands of possible 'points of provision' in relation to responses to difference in society during any particular historical period, hospitals, asylums, work houses and schools are particularly visible and concrete realizations of policy.

Along with maps, paintings, public notices, displays and other forms of public representation, these are all part of the broad social and physical landscape of policy making, informing and reflecting dominant values and perceptions. They both perform as, and bear witness to, frontiers of exclusion in society. As Kitchin argues:

> We live and interact in spaces that are ascribed meaning and convey meaning. A city is not just a set of buildings, roads, parks and other infrastructure, a city is also a (cultural) text which we read and react to (Donald, 1992). Spatial structures and places within the landscape provide a set of cultural signifiers that tell us if we are 'out of place' (Cresswell, 1996, p. 349). (Kitchen, 1998, p. 349)

'Space' and 'spatialization' are ideas which have become the focus of attention across a number of disciplines in recent years, including social geography, cultural studies, architecture, sociology and philosophy. One problem, remarks Massey, is that writers from different disciplines are using the term 'space' in a multiplicity of ways and '... each assumes that their meaning is clear and uncontested' (Massey, 1994. p. 250). In the context of my study, the most relevant and important debate is over the meaning of space and spatialization in relation to political struggles. Massey observes that dominant definitions of space ' ... effectively de-politicize the realm of the spatial.' (Massey, 1994. p. 250)

She argues that 'space is constituted through social relations and material social practices' and that:

> ... the social is spatially constructed too, and that makes a difference. In other words, and in its broadest formulation, society is necessarily constructed spatially, and that fact – the spatial organization of society – makes a differ-ence to how it works. (Massey, 1994, p. 254)

As Massey points out, this is not a new idea. Lefebvre (1972) argued that the functions of the appropriation and allocation of space through the identification of place, function and social purpose are political and ideological in producing and reproducing values and social relations. This is illuminating in terms of the struggles which emerge over the proposed closure of special schools, for example, or the construction of detention centres in particular localities to facilitate the removal and dispersal of asylum seekers from urban spaces.

For Lefebvre space is both 'out there' and observable and hence can be measured, divided up, named, represented in maps and charts and is, at the same time, 'subjective' in that it is defined by human experience, emotion and identities. Particular meanings, become attached to places and practices, both at the individual level and in ways which are collective and shared by communities as 'culture'. While space is physical and observable, it is socially constructed and experienced at the individual and at the collective level of social life. Space also has symbolic meaning in that an apparently 'empty' area can carry layers of history, struggles and meanings (such as 'no man's land' or 'unoccupied territory', the space of the school playground or the space around a prison wall).

In the context of education in England and Wales, we can argue that education is spatialized at a number of levels, including at the level of geographical location, the shape, design and designation of buildings (i.e. schools, colleges and other institutions), culture (both in the terms the content of curricula and values and practices of the institution), and at the level of a highly differentiated labour force (Harris, 1992; Harris, 1999) (teachers, other professionals and pupils) who are distributed between physical spaces (schools) and cultural spaces (curricula and school ethos). Special schools provide examples of the ways in which conflicts and contradictions play themselves out in social practices, as do all schools which are differentiated in terms of physical position in relation to different communities, origins of pupils and staff, curricula, cultures and teaching styles.

MOBILITY, SPACE AND SOCIAL PRACTICE

The creation and differentiation of separated spaces and sites allow for particular specialized behaviours and practices, made possible or manageable by their seclusion. Indeed, this is an argument sometimes put forward in support of the continued existence of segregated special schools on the grounds that disabled pupils need particular therapies, treatments, curricula and levels of care. Thrift argues that the fragmentation of social life is also part and parcel of the homogenization of different practices:

> Space is increasingly created as a series of commodified enclaves (mobility is crucial in differentiating these spaces), within which at least parts of everyday life can be carried on by one social group in isolation from other social groups. (Thrift, 1996, p. 83)

Middleton highlights potential dangers of residential care for disabled children in which:

> Some disabled children are cared for away from home in what are euphemistically called 52-week placements which as 'educational placements' can legally operate without the safeguards which would accrue to a non-disabled child whose family were not the primary carers. (Middleton, 1999, p. 131)

In support of her arguments Middleton cites the Utting Report (1997) and Morris (1995) who was highly critical of standards she uncovered in 'thinly disguised residential care'. The placement of disabled children in institutions away from their families and communities, is an example of the 'commodified enclaves' described by Thrift, which function out of sight of ordinary social life. Historically, the rationale for this is that the children they 'care for' are so out of the ordinary and the treatments and activities required so specialised that they must take place in a separate place from the lives of other people. [These kinds of statements can provoke offence, hurt and consternation among parents, teachers and other professionals, and especially voluntary bodies who run residential homes. But it is surely not too much to expect that, in the words of Arendt, we at least 'do nothing more than think what we are doing'(Arendt, 1959, p. 5).]

DN's isolation hospital for 9 months? Interview him.

*Historical context
of "space" control.
useful ref.*

Segregation and estrangement

*vivid
pt.*

The *removal* of awkward, non-conforming, weak and non productive others to places
on the margins of ordinary life is a powerful example of the multiple processes
and mechanisms of spatialization in western societies which have been characterized by the categorisation and compartmentalisation of groups of human beings.
The processes referred to here can be related to what Giddens called 'greedy'
institutions such as prisons and asylums which, like the massive institutions of
commodity production, emerged during the nineteenth century. They were part of a
new industry of care, control and segregation which were connected with '... new
modes of controlling miscreants in large urban spaces, where the more informal
sanctioning procedures could no longer apply' (Giddens, 1981, p. 172).

The segregated places of correction, referred to by Giddens were part of a
wider growth in institutions of all kinds. In the nineteenth century hospitals and
health services also proliferated in an attempt to maintain a healthy productive
work-force and protect society in general from diseases – such as cholera, TB and
typhus – which spread so rapidly in the hazardous new urban environments with
their poor and crowded living conditions and dangerous sanitation.

The control of spaces in the new industrial towns and cities became part of the
burgeoning state machinery of surveillance and submission of the body. Although
there had been institutions which looked after sick and destitute people for hundreds
of years, these were mainly religious. After the 1830s a piecemeal infrastructure
of 'medical or quasi-medical functionaries and of institutions ...' began to emerge
(Porter, 1987, p. 57). The New Poor Law made the workhouse the statutory
mechanism for the control of paupers and set up Poor Law infirmaries alongside
them for the control and segregation of disease. Disabled and sick children made
up an important part of the workhouse population, but they were also placed in
asylums for the insane.

Imrie argues that:

> ... the advent of the special institution, of segregated spaces to deal with the
> 'peculiarities' of the disabled, precipitated spatial markers which somehow
> set them apart, socially estranged and outside the mainstream of society, ef-
> fectively ghettoized. Such an inscription was especially evident in the context
> of the nineteenth century mental asylums, the propagation of particular moral
> spaces, or places that the dominant socio-institutional practices defined as
> the 'appropriate' spaces by which to avert the gazes of the disabled. These
> ranged from the special schools segregated in particular parts of the cities, to
> the asylums purpose built to both control and 'hide away' those that society
> deemed 'mad' and 'uncontrollable'. ... the segregated 'solution' was critically
> related to spatially shifting 'the problem' ... (Imrie, 1996, p. 15)

A number of key ideas are introduced here. The first is the notion of 'spatial
markers' which 'set apart'. Sites are powerful mechanisms and indicators for marking out insiders and outsiders, exemplified by special education and segregated
schools which create particular identities and 'knowledge' about those who attend

them. Particular areas in cities and housing estates serve the same function. 'Spatial markers' do not have uniform recognition and interpretation. The same site may serve as a positive or negative spatial marker, depending upon local culture and the values and situation of the interpreter. Accent, appearance, food and social practices are also examples of spatial markers. The identities associated with particular spatial markers may be internalized as a kind of self-knowledge by those they set apart. In the research discussed in later chapters, teachers and students from the special school in the English context sometimes expressed views that suggested that special schools and their own exclusion from 'the mainstream of society' were somehow 'natural' and appropriate. These views mirrored the dominant view expressed by teachers and governors of the ordinary school where I carried out my fieldwork.

'Social estrangement' – like the spatializing mechanisms which produce it – works in complex ways. Thus, some students who attend special schools, and their parents, express contentment with the support provided by the community of the special school, and some anxiety about the possible social estrangement they might experience in a 'mainstream' environment. Paradoxically sites which 'set apart' may be experienced as providing arenas in which members feel 'included'. In the context of my research, I found that this view was frequently expressed, both by members of 'mainstream society' on behalf of excluded others ('They're much better off being together') and by those attached to segregated school ('Our students support each other. They understand each other's problems'). This is absolutely not to argue in favour of the retention of special schools, but to highlight the deep-rootedness and complexity of some of the attitudes and assumptions associated with segregated schooling. (There is, surely, no rational reason why all schools should not be involved in a project of transformation in which 'being together' and 'understanding each other's problems' concerns everybody.)

Policies concerning disabled children and young people cannot be separated from policy making relating to the broad system of education. While a policy may appear to be, or be presented as, relating to a particular group based on an impairment led model or 'SEN' model – all such policy making is related to the wider education system. All schools and colleges are affected, for example, by a policy which allows for the segregation of any group, and one reason for this is that such a policy prevents them from establishing fully inclusive communities, cultures and practices. In addition, by presenting policies as attached to particular groups, however vaguely defined, such as 'pupils with SEN', the idea of separation as a consequence of difference is reinforced.

Linked to the notion of 'spatial markers' is the idea of 'appropriate spaces' and the processes by which 'the problem' is spatially shifted. Reference to, and belief in, the notion of 'appropriacy' is deeply ingrained in the education systems in England and France. It is frequently used as a criterion which is applied to children for acceptance into the mainstream; such criteria are implicitly underpinned by a socially constructed idea of what is 'appropriate' which is concerned with the general efficiency of the system and the maintenance of an idealized and externally imposed set of 'academic standards'.

As a 'belief' the idea of appropriacy underpins many of the procedures and processes of selection and the creation of excluded others, acting in the guise of a 'common sense' rationality. What is 'appropriate' is a fundamental part of a power discourse which hides its main purpose – that of managing extradition – under a mantle of liberal humanitarianism and rationality. It serves as a bench mark against which children and young people are deemed to be worthy of inclusion, or deemed to be candidates for 'spatial shifting' on the grounds that 'they would not benefit ...' or 'it would be inappropriate ...'

Spatializing discourses

Discourse plays a crucial role in the creation of the 'place myth' of institutions and perceptions about the lives and characteristics of those who occupy them. One approach to developing an understanding of the history of special education would be to trace the emergence of highly specialized and localizing discourses relating to 'conditions' or 'impairments', 'expertise' and 'treatments'. These discourses are deeply embedded in the processes and characteristics of the making of myths attached to special schools and institutions. The way, for example, that children and young people are talked about, the language adopted to discuss their difficulties and the assumptions made through discourses about the origins and possible responses to these difficulties conspire with the language of different fields of expertise to create the 'place myth' of the special school.

Discourse is not just about naming and describing, it is also about syntax, stress and intonation. In one meeting I attended, a parent governor who had been silent, suddenly offered the following:

> I've been up there and *seen* them. They're not like *our* kids. It's not just a question of limbs ... (fade out)

The spatializing effect of using pronouns and prepositions ('there' and 'them'), rather than naming the place and group concerned, the use of emphasis to strengthen implicit meaning and of 'our kids' as a way of distinguishing and distancing children who attend an ordinary school from those who attend a special school, achieves a powerful spatializing effect in which the imagination is allowed free play in conjuring up myths concerning both places, people and their characteristics. This is an example of the use of discourse being deployed '... as tactic ... to persuade others to the speaker's view' and as 'an instrument of power' (Fulcher, 1999, p. 4). The role of discourse in policy making and as a part and instrument of segregation is discussed in Chapter Seven in which the deployment of discourses used in various arenas in the context of the proposed closure of Freelands special school is analysed.

PLACING AND SPACING THE OTHER

One argument which emerges from the previous sections is that put forward by Massey that 'the social and spatial are inseparable' (Massey, 1994, p. 254). This section considers how this relationship is made material in the defining of places through human experience, social practice and struggle.

Social history is embedded in landscapes, representing both historical and contemporary social and economic development (Hayden, 1996). While the dividing up of space into marked off areas, fulfilling different social and economic functions is itself a social act:

> Social constructions of space and time are not wrought out of thin air, but shaped out of the various forms of space and time which human beings encounter in their struggle for material survival. (Harvey, 1996, p. 210)

As part of this struggle the organization of space and time produces and reproduces particular power relationships of class, ownership of capital, gender, cultural group and difference. These are represented in the creation of places – such as special schools, factories or army barracks – which are the domains for particular groups, practices and cultures. Harvey argues that concepts of space and time:

> ... affect the way we understand the world to be. And they also provide a reference system by means of which we locate ourselves (or define our 'situatedness' and 'positionality' ...) with respect to that world. It is therefore impossible to proceed far with a discussion of space or time without invoking the term 'place'. (Harvey, 1996, p. 208)

Places are both externally identifiable as part of a social landscape, and individually constructed through personal experience. Thus, the notion of 'prison' or 'factory' is both public and private. Places take on mythological statuses which grow up around perceptions and beliefs concerning people and practices associated with them. At the same time 'places' endow those connected to them with identities derived from perceptions – often based on mythologies – about their characteristics and practices. Importantly, places are closely associated with the construction of identities of others and of stereotypes, and the construction of self. The notion of 'otherness' or 'the other' is integral to the political and social meaning of 'place'. As Hetherington explains:

> Otherness is provided through a relationship of difference with other sites ... providing an unsettling of spatial and social relations or an alternative (subversive or threatening?) representation of spatial and social relations ... Otherness can mean a number of things, prominent among which are: *something without* (defined as different to the norm either within a culture or between cultures; see Said 1991), *something excessive* or *something incongruous*, a hybrid combination of the incongruous. (Hetherington, 1997, p. 8)

Otherness can be marked out or signalled by spatial demarcations and social practices such as processes of identification and categorization, and the ordering of groups in society by filtering procedures and exclusions. The construction of some groups as outsiders or 'others' is a function of particular social practices belonging to specific historical contexts. Thus, in medieval Italy and seventeenth century Spain, the lives of people who might be excluded on the grounds of physical difference in another historical period or place, were present in representations of the time such as the woodcut from *De Balneis*, Venice (1553) which shows a public baths in a health resort (reproduced in Guthrie, 1945) in which disabled people are clearly identifiable among the bathers. The painting *The club-footed boy*, by José de Ribera Jativa, painted in 1642, depicts a confident, ebullient child, his face is lit up and looks out of the picture with a roguish grin. This is a portrait of a child who is in his social world, not a portrayal of physical impairment or of an othered person. It would be hard to find an equivalent picture painted in today's world, although, for me, David Hevey's photographic portraits which are discussed in Chapter 5 have a remarkably similar feel to the picture of *The club-footed boy* which hangs in The Louvre.

The notion of otherness is well described by Bailey, writing about how she found her identity equated with the institution where she was placed by powerful professionals:

> So I came and went as best I could. In the local shops, no one asked where I lived. They knew I came from 'that place'. I no longer had the pleasure of being just a stranger, a pleasure as a disabled person I had fought so hard to get ... No one looked at my face. No one looked at any of our faces. We were all the same ... We were enclosed in thick grey walls to separate us from 'the community'. Walls 'the community' cemented with their fear of our differentness, greyness they painted to make our unique selves and our unique souls indistinguishable. (Bailey, 1994, p. 33)

Places are externally visible or recognisable through the erection of boundaries, the posting of signs or the evidence of a particular activity which defines a place such as a farm, church or factory or hospital. They are internally constructed through personal history, culture and experience.

Places, boundaries and spatialized identities

As I have argued earlier in this chapter, policy making relating to any groups of children or young people effects all educational settings, regardless of type of school or college or the group involved. This supports Sibley's argument that 'exclusion is inevitably concerned with inclusion – with what is considered "normal" as well as what is considered "deviant"' and involves '... processes of boundary erection by groups in society who consider themselves to be normal or mainstream', and '... the curious practices of this majority, the oddness of the ordinary' (Sibley, 1995, p. xv).

A fundamental requirement of boundary maintenance and the creation of separate and separating places, argues Sibley, is the production of stereotypes:

> 'Others' disturb the observer's world view, but the stereotype removes them from the scene in the sense that others are distinct from the world of everyday experience. Because there is little or no interaction with 'others', the stereotyped image, whether 'good' or 'bad', is not challenged. (Sibley, 1995, p. 18).

This observation is borne out by some of the debates and the discourses deployed around inclusion in education in England and Wales. Behind much of the rhetoric, lies a continued commitment to forms of segregation on the part of many policy makers at all levels. This partially explains the apparent sticking power of special schools – in spite of a slight decrease in the numbers of children attending special schools in England in recent years (Norwich, 2002) – and the persistent use of medically based labels, or that differentiating super-category 'having special educational needs', to describe children.

Goffman (1968) argued that the recognition of social identity is an important part of gate-keeping practices. Sometimes, in situations such as job interviews, to simplify processes of selection or de-selection, dress codes are applied or people are treated differentially on the basis of such characteristics as skin colour, accent, gender, job, marital status or home address. The spatialization of identity is particularly important in the processes of cognitive recognition. Questions such as 'where are you from?', 'what school did you go to?' and 'where do you work?' are far from disinterested examples of small-talk but important and every-day devices for 'placing' people and assigning them social identities.

This is particularly evident in the example of perceptions of people who are connected to institutions or 'special' places such as special schools, Children's Homes or day centres. In England, children and young people 'in public care' (or 'being looked after' to coin a recent euphemism) may perceive themselves as having identities assigned to them as a consequence of being *removed from* the ordinary setting of 'ones own' family to a residential institution – euphemistically described as 'a home' to distinguish it discursively from just 'home' – or to a 'foster' family (Morgan-Klein, 1985; Armstrong *et al.*, 1995). They become spatialized others.

The use of labels is an important mechanism through which individuals are homogenized into groups, facilitating their management. Slack debates the consequences of labels for disabled people:

> To deny the individual experience is to deny the human expression of a reality which faces disabled people every day of their lives. There is the internal self and the external self – that applies to all human beings. It is no different for disabled people. The difference as I understand it lies with the power of external factors to influence the internal to such an extent it becomes hard to reconcile the two into a workable harmonious form. It also feels important that the personal and unique history of each disabled person is not disregarded. It forms part of their life script and informs their responses to the disabling barriers they encounter. This is why disabled people are not a 'group' as society would have you believe. Diversity of culture, ethnic origin, religious belief, sexual orientation all form essential differences; although disability is to be found within and across this diversity and can be described as a common factor it does not unite or make 'the same as'. (Slack, 1999, p. 36)

For each 'group' described there will always be an individual who can tell their story in a different way.

These insights have important research implications. In particular, researchers have to resist pressures to homogenize the experiences and views of people they interview (their 'subjects' – a two-edged descriptor which exposes the tensions in the 'researcher-researched' relationship). We have to exchange one set of practices which smother individual voices and iron away differences between individuals in order to produce neat and manageable 'data', for a messier approach which is curious and reflective rather than being driven entirely by a narrative decided by the researcher. I have tried to address some of these issues in my own research, and in particular in my discussion in Chapter Three of the relationship between individual voices of people I listened to, and my own role as a kind of 'manager' of the research process and account writer. Nevertheless, the question of how to resist participating in a labelling culture as a researcher raises some difficult and uncomfortable questions which I have barely touched on.

Labelling plays an important role in the processes of boundary maintenance and social ordering which involve the placing of individuals and groups. The processes of identification and categorization used in the statementing procedures for learners perceived as experiencing difficulties in both the English and French education systems are examples of wider mechanisms of social ordering and regulation. The routine use of labels such as 'special educational needs', 'learning difficulties', 'disabled', 'single parent family', are examples of social responses to perceived difference from 'the norm' or deviance from the dominant values and behaviours in society. The use of labels both creates and confirms public identities and assumptions about people's abilities (Booth, 1987); labels assign particular places to individuals and groups on the basis of these same labels in a circular arrangement of naming and placing. Labelling is culturally produced and usually 'public' and therein lies its power.

The production of stereotypes allows 'the other' to be firmly fixed 'elsewhere', as 'them'; at the same time 'others' can be subjected to the controlling and civilizing actions of those who have been delegated to assume this task (e.g. warders, nurses, professionals of all kinds). Paradoxically there is a popular fascination with 'the other' which demands that deviance, while being shunned, is put on display. There is abundant evidence of this in literature and art. The film *The Elephant Man* portrays the prurient excitement of 'ordinary' citizens at the public exhibition of a man whose disfigurement was his only source of subsistence. The displaying of disturbing or 'deformed' people is a practice which has a long history. Writing in 1697, Daniel Defoe proposed:

> ... that a fool-house be erected, either by public authority, or by the City, or by an Act of Parliament, into which all that are naturals or born fools, without respect or distinction, should be admitted and maintained ... I make no question but that if such a hospital was erected within a mile or two of the City, one great circumstance would happen, viz., that the common sort of people, who are very much addicted to rambling in the fields, would make this house the customary walk, to divert themselves with the objects to be seen there, and make what they call sport with the calamity of others, as is now shamefully allowed in Bedlam, (Defoe, 1697, p. 105–9)

The modern version of the public display of disabled people – their tokenistic and sometimes demeaning representation in films, or fund raising publicity for charities, – achieves a kind of objectification and distancing from 'the audience' (Barnes *et.al.*, 1999, p. 42). 'Viewers' become 'gazers' as – far from allowing entry into the lives of disabled people – the representations in front of them present a series of stereotypes, divided by Shakespeare (1994) into three main categories of representation: 'the tragic but brave invalid', 'the sinister cripple' and 'the 'supercrip' who has triumphed over tragedy'. Such representations contribute to the formation of imagined geographies in which disabled people (or in other contexts black or gay people) assume limited and stereotypical identities and life styles.

There are a number of connections to be made between ideas relating to 'mythological landscapes' or 'imagined geographies' and the practices and attitudes surrounding the development of special education in France and England which will be discussed in Chapter Four. At this point it is enough to remark that the construction of imagined identities or stereotypes and their symbolic or literal removal from ordinary spheres (either in terms of artistic representation or in where children go to school) are part of the same sets of processes concerned with idealization and a 'heightened consciousness of difference' (Sibley, 1995, p. 18).

The repudiating gaze

The examples of people in Bedlam being 'exhibited like menagerie animals' (Gutherie, 1945, p. 249) or of the 'mad displaying the mad' at Bicêtre or of the putting on of plays at Charenton in which 'madmen sometimes played the role of actors, sometimes those of watched spectators' (Foucault, 1967, p. 69) all suggest a particular kind of excluding gaze which asserts the supremacy and unassailability of its own normality while exposing its object to public repudiation. Like the medical gaze described by Foucault (1976), the gaze cast by an orderly and conforming majority on a disorderly and deviant minority can be seen as part of the social processes by which society is ordered and 'human beings are made subjects' (Foucault, 1982, p. 208). The gaze is part of a wider discourse through which power is exerted over non-conforming others.

In this, the opening years of the twenty-first century in Europe, ordinary representations of disabled people are almost never seen. Unlike earlier periods – the late middle ages, for example – disabled people are never the subject of paintings or sculptures. In films disabled people are portrayed either as 'heroic' and extraordinary people, people who are different from the rest of us because they have 'special needs', or less frequently, they are demonized (e.g. in the film 'Waking Ned'). Images of disabled people are used dramatically in advertisements to raise money for charitable bodies such as The Children's Society; they are rarely presented as consumers of ordinary goods and services in daily life. Portrayals in the media represent disabled people as not requiring the same treatment as other members of the community or access to the same places, services and opportunities.

The portrayal of disability in the windows of specialist shops for 'the disabled' in

western consumer society suggests that commercial responses to disability involve
the marketing of technical solutions to deviance, just as the Victorians understood
sickness, impairment and insanity as requiring an incredible range of different
buildings and gadgets, each offering a particular solution to a particular category
of deviance (Taylor, 1991). Shop windows are a kind of display 'publicity' for
hegemonised social relationships and the fetishized body.

Berger argues that:

> Publicity is not merely an assembly of competing messages: it is a language
> in itself which is always being used to make the same general proposal ...
> that we transform ourselves, or our lives, by buying something more. (Berger,
> 1972, p. 131)

But 'publicity' is also about imposing order on the unruly and the undisciplined.
It is a type of power which exerts a kind of social quarantine (Foucault, 1977)
in separating deviance off from the mainstream. It is part of a set of wider social
processes and power relations whose hegemonic purpose is achieved in diverse
ways. As Kenway argues:

> The hegemonic effect ... is a consequence of the multiplicity of micro-powers
> – the 'proliferation of discourses' that produces consent. Each discourse has
> its effects in the construction of subjectivity and each exists in a complex
> matrix of intersection and connotation (Kenway, 1990, pp. 180–1)

The processes and mechanisms by which disabled people are spatially shifted
and placed outside the mainstream are multiple and complex, and deeply entrenched
in the social and psychological lives of all members of society. Lefebvre's concern
with the wider processes of spatialization within society and the multi-disciplinary
approach which he adopted, recognize both the externally visible evidence of
spatialization, and the 'subjectivity' which Kenway refers to in relation to the role
of discourse.

Space, schools and policy making

The multiple spaces in which social and ideological struggles take place include
the diverse arenas and discourses within which policies relating to education are
made. Apple has argued that:

> ... schools process both knowledge and people. In essence, the formal and
> informal knowledge is used as a complex filter to process people, often by
> class; and at the same time, different dispositions and values are taught
> to different school populations, again often by class (and sex and race).
> In effect ... schools latently recreate cultural and economic disparities ...
> (Apple, 1990 p. 34).

The selections, procedures and processes surrounding special education are part
of this filtering system in which spatialized education systems provide different
places for different learners. Children and young people are subject to a multitude
of tacit selection procedures relating to social status and geographical location

which often determine where they go to school. The identification of a 'special educational need' may be used as an overriding category which triggers placement outside mainstream education. Paradoxically, in some respects, special schools – from the point of view of social mix – may be more 'egalitarian' than other schools because of the pivotal role played by the category 'special need' – or, more often, the more specific categories of 'EBD', 'SLD' etc. – in deciding which school a child attends.

Policy, in this study, is not understood as something separate from the complex lives of people including LEA officers, teachers, pupils, parents, schools and local communities. It rejects a view of policy making as rational, and of change, reversals and contradictions as being *caused by* particular formal policies or a logical progression of visible events. Ball argues that:

> ... any decent theory of education policy must not be limited to a state control perspective. Policy is ... an 'economy of power', a set of technologies and practices which are realized and struggled over in local settings. Policy is both text and action, words and deeds, it is what is enacted as well as what is intended ... Policies are always incomplete insofar as they relate to or map on to the 'wild profusion' of local practice. Policies are crude and simple. Practice is sophisticated, contingent, complex and unstable. (Ball, 1994, p. 10–11)

The theorizing of policy as going on *everywhere, all the time*, is supported by the material gathered in my field work in which arguments, activity and tactics used to influence, dissuade and manipulate, are often on the edges or beyond what is commonly regarded as the mainstream arenas for policy making. In the English context I found the multiplicity (and duplicity) of policy making processes and venues disconcerting. In the French contexts, I did not have a similar opportunity of uncovering the many layers in which policy is made. My impression has been that in France there is greater central control over how choices and decisions are presented and made and this might mean that there is less room for overt and covert manipulation of the processes in policy making in different arenas. It is important to recognize the broad historical differences of the two national contexts. In France, there is a stated concern with citizenship and equality which has been apparent in the wording of legislation since the introduction of compulsory education in the nineteenth century and in the stated procedures which are intended to be applied uniformly. The procedures and choices about where disabled students should be educated appear to be more clearly laid out than in England, although there are enormous differences in the way in which policies are interpreted between regions and local authorities. However, there are some children in France who are not enrolled in schools at all, but attend therapeutic institutions or hospital-based settings. It is not possible, then, to justify simplistic generalizations about policies and practices in different cultures. Instead, I propose to make observations and raise questions which are intended to uncover the nature and processes of exclusion through spatial shifting, both at the physical level and at the levels of discourse and representation.

Educational systems create spaces which are reproductive of existing social relationships and dominant values in society but this does not mean that the transmission of these relationships and values is mechanical and not open to mediation and contest. The contested nature of curriculum, for example, is recognized by students and teachers in many schools and by their local communities; fundamental changes in emphasis and the development of creative pedagogies can bring about a shift of control over curricula and cultural spaces (see Sultana, 1989; Giroux, 1996). Such shifts of control are outcomes of struggles over policy (on the part of students, teachers, inspectors, parents ...) in particular 'arenas' (classrooms, meetings etc.) This notion, argues Fulcher:

> dissolves ... distinctions between theory, policy, practice – arguing against the top-down model of policy and the idea of implementation – and putting policy in a wider model of social life as social practice, in which we seek to achieve our objectives, deploying discourse as both tactic and theory about an aspect of the social world we want to influence, and engaging in *struggle*, in *political states of play* ... (Fulcher, 1993, p. 129).

Policy, then, creates and is made within and between spaces. Policy is about dislocation and struggle. This idea connects to Massey's argument that 'space is constituted through social relations and material social practices' and that relationships are formed through the 'defining of places through human experience, social practice and struggle' (Massey, 1994, p. 250).

CONCLUSION

I have identified a principle aim of this study as concerned with examining the significance of spatiality in shaping and ordering social relations through education policy making. An integral part of this discussion will be concerned with the ways in which discourses of space and place inform the processes and practices of policy making relating to the boundaries between 'the special' and 'the ordinary' in education. In thinking about a theoretical framework for my study, I have explored the possible connections which can be made between theories of space and place and theoretical understandings concerned with policy making.

Educational systems are concerned with social relations and the distribution of power. They are about confinement and struggles expressed through architecture, planning and distribution and about multiple sets of practices and beliefs. They are about history and ideology, and they connect to change and flux at local, national and global levels. This study is not about trying to find answers to the questions outlined in the introduction, but about exploring what these questions might mean and enhancing understanding of the implications of such an exploration for issues relating to equality and justice in education for all children and young people.

In the following chapter I critically discuss my attempts to develop a methodological framework for my research and explore some of the processes and difficulties which emerged.

CHAPTER 3

PROCESS, PRACTICE AND EMOTION:
RESEARCHING POLICY AND SPACE WITHIN
A CROSS-CULTURAL FRAMEWORK

INTRODUCTION

This chapter focuses on the context and methodological framework for the research which forms the basis for this book and the experience of carrying it out. It includes a discussion of the processes and ideas which led to its conceptualization as a distinctive project and the approaches adopted and the particular difficulties and issues which emerged. It endorses a view of social research as placing 'the researcher as positively present in empirical study' (Coffey 1999). This *presence* relates to the feelings, reflections and responses of the researcher to the unfolding research landscape as well as to her personal and professional history and its influence on the choice of research question, tools and analytical procedures. As Coffey remarks:

> Emotion is a real research experience and our intellectual autobiography is constructed and reconstructed through social research (Coffey, 1999, p. 11).

There is also a concern to recognize the '... potential of conventional research activity for reproducing, and even creating, disablement and oppression' (Moore, *et al.*, 1998, p. 36), and of the possibility that my research could have similar discriminatory effects; it does not follow that a piece of research is non-discriminatory because it breaks with particular conventions, such as an assumed objectivity.

My choice of research area has been influenced by my own educational and personal history such as my experience as a learner and as a teacher during many years. Others are harder to establish. To what extent has my experience as a non-disabled person living in a society which has routinely excluded disabled people, hidden them from view and represented them in ways which are patronizing and demeaning, been absorbed into the way I conceptualized the research? It would be difficult to measure the impact of the interaction between personal history and the wider social context in terms of the development of research questions and practices; but as Skeggs argues '... our social location, our situatedness in the world will influence how we speak, see, hear and know'. (Skeggs, 1994, p. 77).

BACKGROUND TO THE ENQUIRY

Much of the policy making which has a direct or indirect impact on education refers to domains outside what is formally thought of as 'education' , such as the design of buildings (e.g. Building Bulletin 91, DfEE, 1999a), town planning or government financial directives and budgetary decisions made at central and local government level. Financial interests have played an important role in debates which have taken place concerning the future of the staff and students of Freelands School. Frequently budgetary considerations and discourses relating to the 'efficient and effective use of resources' have taken centre stage, forcing issues relating to education or social justice onto the sidelines. All these processes have a sustained impact in terms of the power relations, the availability of opportunities and the marginalisation of some groups in society. At the centre of these issues is a concern with the social construction of differences between individuals and groups through practices relating to attitudes, the allocation of resources and categorization, partitioning and segregation in relation to particular groups and particular sites.

In 1993 I began to carry out research into education policy responses to disability in France. This has been an on-going project and has involved ethnographic work in some schools and institutions in or near Paris. In 1997 I began to investigate policy making concerning disabled children and their education in an English city. In both national contexts, which are discussed in Chapters Five to Eight, I have investigated the historical background to the emergence of special education and tried to make connections with current issues and practices.

The present study is situated within an ethnographic framework in which I have adopted practices which are intended to open up opportunities for different kinds of knowledge and diverse perspectives to emerge which would inform the on-going development of research questions and practices. Although I wanted to 'discover' issues and formulate questions as the research progressed, rather than determining what was important before starting the fieldwork, I started out with a broad focus on teachers' work lives and their perceptions about how policy is made. This broad focus was to change quite early on in the research process.

My research practices were formed in different ways as my enquiry changed in shape and focus as unexpected issues and questions surfaced. In the early stages of my fieldwork I began to interview teachers using a semi-structured schedule which asked them questions about policy making. But Potts has emphasized the complexity and the importance of 'understanding the relationship between events and experience and people's personal accounts'. She argues that:

> ... part of interviewing an individual or a group of people will be this
> exploration of the meanings assigned by the interviewees themselves to the
> events and feelings they describe. (Potts, 1992, p. 335)

The semi-structured interview schedules did not allow opportunities or space for such an exploration. Recognizing that this had implications both in terms of establishing a relationship of equality and mutual respect and in terms of fulfilling the goals of my enquiry, I was able to develop an alternative approach in which the interview became a shared project within which either interlocutor could introduce new topics, challenge what the other said, seek clarification, speak or remain silent. This opened up new opportunities and perspectives which, in turn, led to a shift in my research focus. It also involved re-negotiating my relationship with those I talked and listened to (rather than 'interviewed') and sharing responsibility more equitably. Here is an extract from my research diary:

> 17 April 1997
> ... I interviewed PG today using the schedule. We talked for nearly two hours, and we still didn't get through the schedule. It got quite tense. I felt I was chivvying her along, when in fact a lot of what she was saying was interesting and relevant. The schedule doesn't allow for anything really unexpected to crop up. PG started talking about her involvement with conductive education which – it became clear – has become an important issue surrounding the proposed closure of Freelands for parents and teachers. She was very insistent about pursuing this theme and then I could see why. In the end, I stopped using the schedule and PG took over!

Like Peters (1995), I '... quickly found that people were much more interested and articulate in talking about particular situations and their emotional responses to them' (Peters, 1995, p. 64). I also observed that out of these responses emerged historically and experientially situated knowledge which opened up new issues or provided alternative perspectives on questions. It was particularly interesting, for example, to listen to the historical accounts of teachers' own experiences, and the connections which they made between their own personal and professional lives and wider social contexts. Here is an extract from a discussion with G.B., a teacher at a special school, in which he weaves a story from his own autobiography and the educational values, structures and policies of the time, starting in the early 1960s when many disabled children were excluded from the education system in England and attended special residential institutions:

> My Dad was a quarryman, my granddad was a quarryman and I should have been a quarryman, but I passed the 11+ and went to grammar school. I intended going in for vetinary work – working with animals – and I only got two A levels so to save messing about – I was 18 and my mates were earning money – I decided to go to teacher training college instead, rather than stay on another year. This was 1961. So three years in training college and on my final teaching practice I was working with a small group of kids that were supposedly educationally subnormal and my tutor at the time suggested that I might be better in special education, and perhaps he was right because I wanted to be a vet and this is the same kind of work really ...
>
> So having got one job during the three months between college and September in a normal school somewhere in Lancashire – about ten days before I was to start I was offered another one in a residential special school. They were all educationally subnormal children and they were educationally subnormal because they had never been to school ...
>
> It was handy for me because I got home two weekends in three. It was

an old Victorian place in about 120 acres around it of woodland. I was paid
£120 a year special school's allowance and because I was boarding on the
premises, I had laundry done there, I had meals there. I was charged £120
a year to live on the premises so it just cancelled it out. One weekend in
three I was there from 4.00 o'clock on a Friday until 9.00 o'clock on a
Monday I was in total charge of the place, some 45 ESN lads aged 11–15.
with sometimes the gardener coming in to help and sometimes the caretaker.
This was when I was – oh, 21 until I was 23 when I left. After two years
I had just had enough of the place, living on the premises. I said I'd never
live on the job again.

So I applied for a job in B___. At the time I was living in T___. I
used to go over to B___, about 30 miles or so, travelling on a little motor
bike and it wasn't very good, so I stuck it for 12 months, then I moved to
an infant and junior Roman Catholic school, and then to a school the kids
called Bash Street School and after 12 months I moved again to a normal
secondary school where I taught Art and Science for 5 years, then I decided
to get married so I wanted the special school's allowance again – the extra
cash – it had gone up quite a bit in the meantime and I went to work in a
maladjusted school ...

It was this account, in particular, which finally persuaded me to abandon my
interview schedule (which this teacher had effectively demolished by talking over
it, anyway), and to start listening to the rich and varied stories, accounts and
arguments put forward.

In the previous chapter I described 'otherness' as being 'marked out or signalled
by spatial demarcations and social practices such as processes of identification
and categorization'. The construction of some groups as outsiders or 'others' is a
function of particular social practices in specific contexts which contribute to the
formation of stereotypes. Research practices are frequently themselves characterized
by the identification and categorization of groups and individuals within specific
contexts in which there is an imbalance of power between the researcher and the
'subjects'. In my fieldwork I have tried to renegotiate this relationship. One way of
doing this has been to respect the voices of individuals and to try to resist sorting
and categorizing material in ways which reflect and produce stereotypes. I tried
to avoid making observations which lump together groups of people according to
their professional or social role, so there are few general statements about 'teachers
in special schools', or 'parents of disabled children'. What has emerged, anyway,
is that groups and individuals adopt quite contradictory and complex positions in
the light of changing contexts.

I have tried to understand the historical and social contexts of the research
fields both in broad national terms, at the level of locality and neighbourhood
and at the level of the personal histories of individuals. The interviews I have
carried out, once I had abandoned my semi-structured schedules, are based on a
recognition that personal autobiography can elicit rich historical material, crucial
in understanding contemporary structures, values and processes and in bringing
about social transformation. As Potts argues:

> An auto/biographical approach to social enquiry is useful ... not because
> its conclusions are generalisable. Quite the reverse. Apart from making a
> positive difference to the lives of participants, it enables enquirers to develop
> an understanding whose worth is directly related to its transience. Valuable
> social knowledge is bound to change, as those who want to know, those who
> contribute to the knowing and the contexts in which questions are asked also
> change. (Potts, 1998, p. 23)

Any questions or statements I make concerning policy making and its effects
can only have meaning within an understanding of the social lives of people. Like
Potts:

> I do not expect to communicate research findings by means of generalisable
> true statements. I do expect to work towards contingently true statements.
> (Potts, op cit.)

Contingent because they belong to – and emerge out of – unique and specific social
contexts at particular historical moments. At the same time, while every 'event' is
individual and emerges out of unique and specific situations, these are of interest
in an historical and social study if they are illuminating in terms of other events.
It is the task of the researcher to use such instances to increase understanding of
a whole nexus of situations, events and contexts.

But, as Okely and Callaway observe:

> Monographs have too often been presented, then read as definitive and time-
> less, rather than selective and historically contingent. Ethnography requires
> a personal lens ... (Okely and Callaway, 1992, p. xii–xiii)

The idea of contingency is central to an understanding of the role of context and
self in the construction and interpretation of events and processes. In the example
given above in which a teacher, approaching retirement, describes his work life and
how he became a teacher in special schools, the development of his professional
life is contingent on events in his personal life and on broader historical conditions
and social and policy making responses to disability and difference.

RESEARCH PRACTICES IN DIFFERENT NATIONAL CONTEXTS

My enquiry has taken place in France and in England. In France, I was rarely able
to establish a relationship which broke through the boundaries of the 'researcher/
informant' paradigm, when examining policy making in the context of schools
and institutions. There were fleeting exceptions, in which I became a participant
observer in lessons and – on one occasion – a child intervened in an interview I
was engaged in with a head teacher and turned it into a discussion between the
three of us. In general, though, I observed, asked open-ended questions, listened
and recorded. One reason for this was the fact that my visits to France took place
over a number of short concentrated periods of a week or two weeks; this, and
the fact that I was very much a 'foreigner' as well as being a researcher from a
university, probably explains the relative formality and 'distance' which character-

ized my research relationships in the French context. However, the close working relationship which I have established with a group of French researchers has enabled me to understand the issues and arguments in greater depth. Furthermore, I have attended a number of meetings in which many of the contradictions and issues have emerged in a variety of settings – meetings of governors, public 'consultation' meetings, meetings of staff and so on. I have been able to listen, observe and record material in settings which are more natural than the interview setting. As in the English setting, I have managed to gather material from a range of sources and situations, although in France these have been more limited.

As my enquiry developed in England, I found myself becoming merged in the various sites of policy making surrounding the proposed closure of Freelands School in Greentown. Sometimes I have been positioned as a participant in some of the events unfolding around me; I have become one of 'the observed'. Usually this has occurred, not as a direct result of something I myself had initiated, but through solicitations from others involved as actors in the various arenas I was observing.

Okely describes the complex relationship between the participant observer, her field work and her informants:

> Participant observation does not mean mere observation, but often shared labour ... Fieldwork takes on its original meaning: work in fields. In both my major periods of research – among the Gypsies (Okely 1983) and among Normandy farmers (Okely 1991), participation in production brought a major breakthrough. I was perceived differently by the people and I learned through participation, however incompetent, in for example, potato picking, scrap metal dealing, harvesting and hand milking.
>
> When I asked to learn how to hand milk cows in a small Normandy farm, the woman who has done this for forty years left the stable for a few minutes. She returned with a flash camera and took several photos of me. The unsolicited act reversed the usual relationship between anthropologist and 'informant'. My attempts at manual labour, which continued for several months, undermined for peasant farmers the stereotype of the metropolitan *professeur*. It gave embodied knowledge of a daily practice and created a shared experience for ever-unfolding discussions between us. (Okely, 1992 pp. 16–17)

While I never experienced 'daily practice' or 'participation in production' in such an uncompromising form as Okely, I frequently found myself 'part of' a meeting or a discussion, rather than a mere observer looking in from the outside. The processes through which such a shift happened were often subtle and unplanned. Frequently an 'insider status' was conferred on me by those sitting near me who were anxious to exchange ideas. On one occasion I was asked to make the tea; quite frequently I found myself feeling a strong sense of belonging to one group and then another. I became (sometimes temporarily) won over by the 'reasonableness' of much of what was said by many – often opposing – sides in the struggles which I observed and became part of. At other times I felt profoundly at odds with positions put forward.

In gaining people's confidence there was, perhaps, an implicit assumption – felt, rather than articulated – that I would support their particular viewpoint and I was seen as a potentially powerful ally by some. This dilemma reflects some of the real tensions and struggles involved both at the level of policy making surrounding the proposed closure of the school and at the level of the research relationship and processes. In asking people to talk about their personal histories – sometimes an emotional and disturbing experience, as I was to discover – wasn't there an implicit promise of solidarity on my part? At the same time, I had no wish to be seen to support one group rather than another. I tried to resolve these issues by making it clear that I supported the rights of all children and young people to be treated equally and with dignity and respect. This inevitably drew me in to discussions about what this might mean in practice in the context of the situation concerning the proposed closure of Freelands.

In the French context, there appeared to be complete support for the principle of equality for all. In fact, in France issues relating to 'equality' and 'citizenship' were far more likely to be explicitly raised – or referred to in passing – than in England, in the context under discussion. However, as in England, the ways in which the notion of equality was interpreted were not necessarily opposed to segregation; many people I interviewed shared the view that highly specialized, segregated provision was the response which most clearly provided 'equality' for disabled children and that it would be unjust to expect them to follow 'the same' curriculum as other learners or put up with the vicissitudes of a large ordinary school. Sometimes they argued that the best way to combat social exclusion of disabled people in adult life was to provide highly specialized therapy and training so that they would be well prepared for the world 'outside' and even be able to contribute their labour in some form or another. The question of how principles of equality and human rights are applied or understood in practice within and across cultures is highly complex and we should be skeptical of attempts to lay down prescriptive universal criteria by which rights can be measured for a number of reasons:

> First, the ways in which 'rights' are conceptualized and understood in different cultures are diverse and not easily recognised by people living outside those cultures. Second, (this would represent) a number of assumptions about the particular structures and practices present in any society. Third, the act of creating such a list of criteria assumes some right to define the framework and language within which issues are to be discussed (Barton and Armstrong, 1999, p. 4)

This implies adopting a critical stance towards taken-for-granted assumptions within ones 'own' national setting. A cross-cultural approach helps to do this because it enables us to understand the relativity and contingency of conceptualizations such as 'human rights' and 'social justice' and 'equality'. This involves looking at processes and patterning, seeing structures and relationships as fluid, rather than fixed and static, and understanding the crucial importance of context in the construction and interpretation of events and the assigning of meanings. But this argument raises difficult questions concerning the problems of taking a relativist position in which 'no one framework is considered superior to another and we simply have to live with such value disagreements' (Scott, 1999). In fact, far from taking such a relativist position, I have clearly aligned myself with values which are profoundly different from those who support segregation. With Booth and Ainscow, I do not 'equally favour all directions for the development of practice, or value equally responses to difference' (Booth and Ainscow, 1998, p. 243). At the same time, I have to recognise that some of those who support the continuation of segregated schools believe this is the most effective way of protecting the rights and interests of disabled pupils to the kind of specialised provision they believe they need. On a different level, is the (ultimately discriminatory) argument put forward by some that the interests of children in mainstream schools could be damaged if special schools are closed. On a different level again, is the belief held by some 'proponents of a deficit view of education' that their view is 'not a perspective involving a value position but ... a scientific truth unconstructed by its context.' (op. cit. p 243). Increasingly, arguments based on principles of economic rationality and performativity have become treated as if they, too, represent a 'scientific truth'.

THE RESEARCH NOTEBOOKS

Much of my work in terms of ideas, reflections and observations – has been recorded in my research notebooks – or diary – which contain jottings, reflections, questions and quotations and drawings. The notebooks have been constant companions over the past eleven years (when I first started to 'do research') and they represent my ongoing 'intellectual production' (Wright Mills, 1959). The notebooks are the core of my collection of data and will be drawn on in different ways during this study. They contain comments, ideas, snippets of conversation, transcriptions of conversations and notes taken during meetings. The notebooks contain material relating to all my work carried out over this period and are not just concerned with material for this particular study. This has made it possible to cross-reference experiences and ideas, look back over things I was thinking about in the past and make connections with current issues. The notebooks also contain ideas for teaching which I have scribbled down and which relate directly to my field work. There are notes on practical information such as local bus time tables, telephone numbers and references to publications. The notebooks represent development at both the personal and the professional level. They enable me to connect and compare my present work and research to those of eight or nine years ago.

Some of the material I have drawn on in the development of my ideas has been unearthed from old research notebooks from a project (carried out with Tony Booth 1992–1993) which have been particularly useful in highlighting issues and inter-relationships concerning the social construction of space and the multiple processes of policy making. In that study we wanted to explore issues relating to the closure of a special school and its incorporation into an established comprehensive school in the North East of England (Armstrong and Booth, 1994; Booth, 1995).

I have read and re-read extracts such as the ones below as a means of enhancing my understanding of some of the ideas I have been grappling with in my present study.

Entries in research diary 1992

A___ September 1992
    I've been thinking about the way the physical organisation of buildings reflect underlying values and perceptions which may be at odds with 'what is being said'. The design and lay-out of any institution affects the degree to which those using it can circulate freely. This in turn affects the kinds of social relationships which can develop within it. The new Special Needs Department at S. High School is part of the main building and close to the office and dining hall. Geographically, it could be any other department in the school. It's central position should foster contact with the rest of the school. However, (as Tony Booth spotted straight away) the Department is separated from the rest of the school by some large double doors which were put in as part of the renovations. We were told they were put there to help to give the members of the Special Needs department a 'feeling of being in a secure base'!! It has also meant the pupils who use wheel chairs or have other mobility problems cannot go through those doors without assistance so they are effectively cut off from the rest of the school. Access to the rest of the school is also restricted to the ground floor for these pupils as there are no lifts to enable them to go up to the floors above. This means that they are not able to participate in classes or tutor groups which take place above the ground floor. What is being said is that the staff and students attached to the Special Needs Department are 'part of the school'. What is being done makes this impossible.

This extract from an old research notebook contains some observations which have a direct relationship to critical reflections on my current research, as well as to the research focus in the present study. First of all, it affirms the importance of looking at processes in terms of what is actually going on, rather than just relying on one version of events. Secondly, it shows how the use of discourse can be illuminating in revealing contradictions and sub-plots. For example, while the dominant, open version of the relationship between the 'Special Needs Department' is that it should be a part of the school, the sub-text is that it should 'provide a secure base'. Thirdly, it points out some of the different levels at which policy is taking place: at the level of discourse, architecture and the organization of the curriculum (i.e. the decision to teach some subjects in areas of the school which are out of reach of some students, effectively excludes them from ordinary participation in some aspects of learning and in the social life which surrounds lesson times). Fourthly, practices such as the above can have an impact on the way in which identities are created, as if, for example, it is 'natural' for some students to be excluded from full physical, social and academic access and participation in the life of the school.
    A further entry reads:

A___ September 1992

   At the beginning of the day a small group of mainstream pupils meet the
young people arriving at the Special Needs Department at S. School. They
help pupils in and out of vehicles when needed and accompany pupils in
wheel chairs to their classrooms. The entrance to the Special Needs Department is at the side of the building some distance from the main entrance to
the school, so pupils of the two communities arrive at the school at the same
time, but enter and leave through separate doors.

Again, disabled students are segregated in terms of their access to the school.
Instead of ordinary social exchanges which take place at the beginning and end of
the school day, a small group of 'mainstream' students 'help' disabled students,
positioning them as dependent others.

   This kind of material has been decisive in the formation of the ideas and questions underpinning the present study. These have been informed by discussions
which we had at that time, about the relationship between the social, the physical
and the political as they connect and confront each other in the use of space and
the organisation of schools. The material highlights physical, curricula, attitudinal
and resource-led barriers to inclusion, while at the same time suggesting the
possibilities which exist to overcome them. From a theoretical point of view, the
extracts above illustrate the overlapping processes involved in what Massey refers
to as the constitution of space '... through social relations and material social
practices' (Massey, 1994, p. 254). They point to the reciprocity between how space
is used and the formation of social relations. They also underline the importance
of looking at enacted policy (i.e. what is being done) and comparing it with stated
policy (what people say is happening).

   In re-reading my notebooks, I have become aware of the importance of keeping
alert for evidence of the formation of new spaces. Spaces such as 'resource bases',
'special needs departments', 'language units' may be newly created places with
their own boundaries which are used as containers for groups moved from other,
old-fashioned segregated settings such as special schools set up in the nineteen
fifties or sixties. They may appear to be 'part of' the ordinary school, but on
closer examination their physical organization, practices and procedures may be a
re-articulation of old segregative structures and cultures. In various arenas in which
I have been an observer during my research for the present study, questions such
as 'what sort of places should we create for these disabled students?' have been
raised as well as the question 'how do ordinary schools need to change?' This is not
to suggest some kind of plot to keep disabled students separated from their peers,
but simply to point out the real slippage which can occur between 'placement' and
'inclusion' at the levels of conceptualization and discourse.

   Researching 'spatiality' in policy making processes and discourses involves
investigating many areas and levels of social practice. It is not possible to engage
with all of these, but an important concern is to explore possible relationships
between some of these levels. I have focused on discourses and practices relating
to the use of space and issues of exclusion and inclusion, through an examina-

tion of policy documents, teachers' accounts of their work lives and some of the routine practices, perceptions and interpretations surrounding the use of space in schools. The selections I have made from the vast number of possible sources and arenas have been guided by the particular theoretical understanding of the nature of the social construction of space and place outlined in the previous chapter. These selections are concerned with both metaphorical spaces such as the notion of 'policy' or the principle of 'consultation', as realized through meetings, debates, reports and so on, and through space as it is realised through the creation of places with their unique attached and embedded particular histories, practices, discourses and associated memories. Places, as I have argued in the previous chapter, are constituted through social relations, shared experience and perceptions as well as being constituted in unique and particular ways by individuals.

MULTIPLE METHODOLOGIES AND POLICY RESEARCH

The different methodological approaches which I have adopted reflect the multi-faceted and multiply situated nature of policy making and spatializing processes. In the context of this study 'policy' is not understood as something separate from the complex lives of people including LEA officers, teachers, pupils, parents, schools and local communities. It rejects a view of policy making as rational and of change, reversals and contradictions, as being caused by particular formal policies or a logical progression of visible events. As Ball argues:

> ... we can see policies as representations which are encoded in different ways (via actors' interpretations and meanings in relation to their history, experiences, skills, resources and context). A policy is both contested and changing, always in a state of 'becoming', of 'was' and 'never was' and 'not quite' ... (Ball, 1994, p. 16)

In Chapter Two I outlined Fulcher's argument that policy is made at many levels and, not least, through 'practice' which, rather than being something separate and distinct from policy is itself enacted policy (Fulcher 1999). Thus, in the context of the earlier research carried out in North East England above, the placing of separating doors between the 'Special Needs Resource Base' and the rest of the school and the creation of separate entrances for different groups of pupils, are examples of enacted policy. That is to say, decisions about who is counted in and who is counted out are made through the planning and organization of the physical environment and the social practices established within it and are regulated through the discourses of school management processes.

I have described my research as 'ethnographic' and as drawing on 'case studies'. As a piece of qualitative research my enquiry has become a 'site of multiple methodologies and research practices' (Denzin and Lincoln, 1998) involving the:

> .... collection of a variety of empirical materials – case study, personal experience, introspective, life story, interviews, observational, historical, in-teractional, and visual texts – that describe routine and problematic moments and meanings in individuals' lives. (Denzin and Lincoln, 1998, p. 3)

The research has involved collecting the kinds of material mentioned by Denzin and Lincoln, drawing on different approaches and procedures.

My research has been concerned with examining policy as it emerges through social practices (or 'enacted policy') relating to structures, discourses, and procedures in all their many variations and locations. The use of multiple methods has been advocated by many researchers in different disciplines who have emphasized the need for gaining a range of perspectives or angles on a problem or set of problems (e.g. Malinowski, 1922; Lazerfeld, 1972; Denzin, 1970, 1978; Janesick, 1998). Burgess (1982) cites Gans (1962), for example, as explaining the use of diverse approaches in his study which enable the researcher to:

> .... cross-check between various forms of participant observation: where the researcher acted as an observer, where the researcher participated as a researcher and where the researcher acted as a participant. Similar cross-checks can be made between data obtained from participant observation and interviews. However, it is only when observational and interview data are integrated that the full potential of multiple field methods can be realised. (Burgess, 1982. p. 164)

Denzin (1970) argues for the use of 'different times, persons and situations in any study, so that researchers can obtain several different accounts of any single event' (Burgess, 1982, p. 166). My research has followed policy developments in 'real time' during three years and inevitably involved drawing on different persons and situations at different times.

'Bricolage', ethnography and case study

In the process of planning and carrying out my research I have drawn on a range of methods and approaches, but the term 'bricoleur', first used to refer to the researcher who draws on different research methods, tools and techniques (Lévi-Strauss, 1966), is only to some extent an appropriate one to apply to my research practice. Denzin and Lincoln describe the bricoleur as producing:

> ... a bricolage, that is, a pieced-together, close-knit set of practices that provide solutions to a problem in a concrete situation ... If new tools have to be invented, or pieced together, then the researcher will do this (Denzin and Lincoln, 1998, p. 3).

The focus of my research has been the *uncovering* of 'problems' (issues, questions and struggles) both in terms of the social field of my research and in the research process itself. It is concerned with revealing and understanding problems, rather than finding solutions to them. An example of what I mean may be found in the detailed analysis of the discourses deployed by various players as tactics in policy making to persuade others to a particular viewpoint or to close down options or reinforce stereotypes. My transcripts of meetings, sections of which are analysed and discussed in Chapters Seven and Eight, show how powerful such use of discourse can be in creating place-myths, maintaining segregation and generally 'bad-mouthing' those connected with special schools (Corbett, 1996).

The culture and processes of 'bad-mouthing' are exemplified in the discussion of a governors' meeting in Chapter 7. Counter-discourses which might have been adopted to oppose such tactics, were rarely heard in some of the meetings I attended, but were sometimes voiced after a meeting amongst trusted allies. This raises serious questions about democracy and how processes which are assumed to be protected areas in which fairness and balance will prevail, can be subverted in the interests of powerful groups. This is an example of a problem which has been uncovered during the research process itself. In Chapter 9 I will return to the relationship between 'discourse as policy' and the meaning of democracy.

Atkinson and Hammersley (1998) refer to ethnography as usually having a number of the following features:

> A strong emphasis on exploring the nature of particular social phenomena rather than setting out to test hypotheses about them.
>
> A tendency to work primarily with "unstructured" data, that is, data that have not been coded at the point of data collection in terms of a closed set of analytic categories.
>
> Investigation of a small number of cases, perhaps just one case, in detail.
>
> Analysis of data that involves explicit interpretation of the meanings and functions of human actions, the product of which mainly takes the form of verbal descriptions and explanations, with quantification and statistical analysis playing a subordinate role at most. (Atkinson and Hammersley, 1998, pp. 110–11)

In some respects, these characteristics could all be used to describe my research. However, while I have not started out with a clearly stated 'hypothesis' and my enquiry has been exploratory rather than concerned with testing or measuring, I did not approach it freed of all pre-suppositions or values. The belief that policy making occurs in complex ways at many different levels in social life, involving daily practices and discourse as fully as it involves policy documents or committee meetings, has informed the research right from the beginning. 'Planning' and 'policy making' are seen as being constantly fragmented, reinterpreted and reworked at different levels in response to changing contexts. The data has been 'unstructured' in that I have not adopted a 'closed set of analytical categories' at the point of data collection. However, once the focus on spatialization had emerged from the early stages of my enquiry and become established at its centre, subsequent material relating to space and policy making was highlighted as it was gathered. My notebooks show sections underlined and comments in the margins drawing attention to material which I regarded as particular 'relevant'. Thus, some informal coding mechanisms have taken place at the point of noting down the data.

In a sense, this investigation has focused on a 'small number of cases' in that it uses a number of different sites as key arenas for gathering material. But the 'case' I am examining is the case of educational policy making in relation to disabled children and young people. Policy making as a phenomenon is diffuse and contested, whereas a particular school has clear boundaries, a school gate and a perimeter and a more or less clearly defined locus within which a set of practices can be studied and various actors identified. Although the case of policy making lacks the boundedness and specificity normally associated with case study approaches (Denzin and Lincoln, 1998), and the edges between context and the case being studied are blurred, the identification of policy making as itself a set of social practices can justifiably be referred to as a case. In my study a small number of cases (relating to educational provision for disabled children) are used to enquire into the more general and diffuse phenomenon of policy making and this might be referred to as a *collective case study* (Stake, 1998).

Here, a small number of cases of schools and institutions have been used as sites in which to explore processes, values and procedures relating to a broader conceptual framework: the case of policy making and spatialization. There are problems with this description. For example, Adelman *et al.* (1980) saw the case as a bounded system selected as an instance of a class. There are other ways of describing my research which fit more harmoniously with traditional ideas of case study. For example, my research and analysis 'seek theory' through the study and application of particular instances in exploring the processes and relationships involved in policy making and spatiality. It is 'exploratory' in that it seeks to generate theory rather than 'explanatory' in seeking to test theory (Yin, 1993; Bassey, 1999).

The analysis of my data is explicitly interpretative. In telling the story of the research I am inevitably claiming the principle voice in the account. However, in drawing on the accounts of others who I interviewed or observed I have tried to make the story I tell reflect some of the contradictions and contrasts presented by different perspectives.

OVERVIEW OF METHODOLOGY

the English setting

In England I carried out an ethnographic case study of policy making surrounding the planned closure of Freelands, a special school in Greentown. I followed some of the processes involved in policy making through interviews with teachers, LEA officers, parents, a young disabled person and others concerned in the events surrounding the proposed closure of the school. I attended numerous meetings including meetings of governors, teaching and support staff, parents and LEA officers, and three public consultation meetings. I observed historical moments in the life of Freelands School in an attempt to understand the setting against which positions and actions are taken and perspectives formed by the various actors involved in my study. I wanted to become familiar with the daily life of the school community. More particularly, I hoped to uncover and observe the processes involved in policy making within the school context and through the lived experience of students, teachers, governors and support workers.

I have also examined documents, including policy documents from central government and the LEA concerned, minutes of council meetings, and documents associated with the life and history of Freelands School.

I recorded and transcribed the majority of the interviews I carried out and took copious notes in meetings and during my observation of school life. More informally, but of importance, has been the development of ideas and questions through discussion with colleagues, friends and during 'chance encounters'. Crucially, C.W., a young disabled man who left Freelands School in the early 1990s has played an important part in disturbing some of my own assumptions as well as introducing questions and insights I had never thought about. In the following section I have included an entry in my research diary as an example of the importance of gaining multiple perspectives, including – and especially – those of 'insiders'.

> *I went to talk to C.W. today. I asked him to tell me about his experience and his education. He typed everything onto the screen and I read it aloud back to him, sometimes asking him to explain or expand a particular point. I could see him getting more and more tired, but he insisted on carrying on. The entire interview took nearly two hours.*

I started my education at Freelands Special School in Greentown in the nursery. I went there because it was the best place for me at the time. In fact, it was the best place until the mid eighties and early nineties.

I was very happy there until nearly the end. I could foresee what was going to happen – it was happening already. Some of the older and brighter kids left and they were never replaced. At that time – some left because they reached their time. I mean, they died. Others transferred to normal school. That Christmas I wanted to leave and I felt so depressed. There was very little there that I enjoyed. The previous summer had seen all of my age group – and some tutors – leave as preparations were made for the Maynard move to our site. There was a huge amount of space but nobody was using it. I felt I was going backwards in everything – CDT, cookery, science. As I saw it, I was the only one there that really needed to get an education. I was the only person that needed something from school. The others had a different attitude because they knew that they were going to die because of their disability. They were only interested in car racing with their remote control cars – out on the playground or indoors.

I left just in time before the 1988 Education Act and the introduction of the National Curriculum became law for special schools. I did get a sneak preview because the teachers were discussing it with others. For Maths, it looked so easy in the National Curriculum (compared with what I had been doing). I left in 1993 and I was glad to leave. I kept wishing I could turn the clocks forward to September or back.

I could see a rapid decline in the school. Good equipment was being thrown away in the CDT department and in the Maths, English and Science areas. For the last few weeks I was at the school we were all busy moving things and throwing things in skips. That was the period of 'the Move' and the introduction of the National Curriculum. I'd watched the school gradually going down over a period of four years.

On the question of my education, I semi-agree with my Dad. I know that I wouldn't cope in a normal school because I would feel very, very frustrated at my level of ability to work and understand. I know for a fact, that I wouldn't have anyone to look up to (other disabled pupils) and perhaps no-one with whom I could communicate. There would be other disadvantages. For example, in my school I got to know what things were on the market for disability learning from my mates, both older and younger.

Another problem I might have had at a mainstream school is the attitudes of others and bullying. But I think that if people were educated by disabled people about disability issues, maybe then these problems could be overcome.

Are young disabled people ever asked what they think? Well, my parents have always discussed everything and wanted my opinion. But policy makers? Can cows fly?

In this extract C.W. raises a number of issues which were to become crucial and decisive in terms of my later analysis and writing. He traces the changes in the nature of the school and its composition as some students were moved out of the school into 'normal schools' (as a consequence of the 'integration' policies which became popular in many LEAs in the nineteen eighties). This illustrates one of the fundamental flaws with integration – that it is another form of selection which – as in all forms of selection (such as selection by 11+ examination, setting, selection by socio-economic location) – can result in extreme forms of segregation in grouping together students perceived, for example, as 'the least able' or 'the most disabled'. C.W. also refers to the fact that in special schools it is quite common for some students to die. This taboo subject, rarely mentioned by anybody else I spoke to, affects the composition of the school community because – C.W. seems to imply – those who are 'likely to die' are unlikely to be deemed suitable candidates for 'integration'. This raises questions about how this issue is treated in a situation in which plans are being made for Freelands to close down. Would all students move to an ordinary school, or would there still be a group who remained outside? I also began to ask myself more uncomfortable questions such as: if I were the parent of a child who was likely to die, what kind of education would I want for my child? What would my child want? Whose wishes should be paramount in making decisions? I do not know the answer but such questions cannot continue to be excluded from debates about inclusion and exclusion.

C.W. described some of the effects of the introduction of the National Curriculum from his perspective, raising issues about the difficulties of implementing the 1988 Education Act effectively in all settings. His comments about his own learning emphasize the importance of the social context in which learning takes place (e.g. the importance of having other disabled pupils as possible role models 'to look up to', and of sharing information about what was coming on the market to support disabled students). His assessment of his own 'level of ability to work and understand' suggests a mis-conception about the 'standards' expected in ordinary schools and his ability to reach those standards. Setting C.W.'s intellectual curiosity and analytical mind in the context of the enormous diversity of learners I have come across in schools during my teaching career, I feel shock that he should have had this negative view of his own abilities. His perception of mainstream schools as places where disabled people might be bullied and his stated belief that this could be overcome by disabled people 'educating' other people, demonstrate a keen awareness of the consequences of segregated education in terms of developing respectful relationships in the community, based on mutual understanding and an awareness of the political role that disabled people must, themselves, play in overcoming oppression. These and his comments about the failure of policy makers to ask young disabled people 'what they think' – all raise crucial questions concerning policy making, voice and the role and effects of segregated schooling. They also raise issues about possible barriers to inclusion and how some of these might be overcome. All these issues are connected in different ways to social processes involved in spatialization.

I will return to some of the ideas raised by C.W. in later chapters. I have included a brief analysis of parts of his account here as an example of the possibilities opened up by listening to multiple perspectives on issues. It is not a question of finding a methodology which would make it possible to establish which perspective is the right one, but of developing methodological approaches which reveal some of the complexity of the issues involved and the array of levels and arenas at which policy is made. It's about raising new questions and uncovering experience and knowledge which is often hidden or discounted.

The French setting

I was faced with a different situation and set of opportunities in terms of my work in France. My research had to be carried out in snatches, on a number of visits over the past five years. During this period I carried out fieldwork in six different settings. This has included interviewing, attending meetings in schools, examining policy documents and participating in discussions with professionals and other researchers. It has not been possible to study a particular policy development concerning change in relation to one particular site. The case study material relating to policy making in France has been built up in a more fragmented way. For the purposes of this study, I have focused on three settings in which disabled children and young people are placed according to policies relating to the categorization of impairment: a special school run by the Ministry for Health and Social Security, a Lycée run by the Ministry of Education in which 70% of students are disabled, and a hospital which has an education service funded by the Ministry of Education. In these settings I have sometimes been an observer-participant, and I have carried out interviews with teachers, psychologists and principles, although in the hospital setting I never actually saw any children. Some of the interviews I have carried out were audio recorded and transcribed and others were recorded in note form. In Chapter Eight I have also included discussion of other material which relates to processes of spatialization and segregation.

An important part of my work in France has been my participation in seminars, meetings and debates with colleagues at the University of Paris, the Institut Nationale de Recherche Pédagogique and at CNEFEI (Centre Nationale d'Education d'Enfants Inadaptés) as well as at international conferences. In addition, I have been able to meet and talk to a number of young disabled people during my visits, although this has always taken place during a lesson when the teacher is present. Interestingly only one of the settings I have studied is categorized as a school – the Lycée Bresson. One is an Externat Médico-Professionel; the other is the Institut National de Réadaptation – Hôpital de Sainte Thérèse. The names themselves suggest medical institutions with a medical orientation rather than 'schools'. Chapter Six will include case studies of all three settings in France and of Freelands School in England.

Developing strategies for critical enquiry

In planning, thinking and writing about my research I have tried to do a number of things, both in the process of carrying out my enquiry and in analysing the material I have gathered. I have tried to 'think reflectively, historically, and biographically', attempting to develop strategies of empirical enquiry that will allow me '...to make connections among lived experience, larger social and cultural structures, and the here and now' through the materials I have gathered (Denzin and Lincoln, 1998, p. xi).

Thinking 'reflectively' has involved critically engaging with my own experience, reading and knowledge and with the questions and insights and 'knowledge' generated by the research process itself. 'Thinking historically' has meant exploring the historical context for my study in both the French and English settings and relating this exploration to current issues in policy making and the social construction of space. In doing this I have drawn on archive material, some of the available literature and the historical accounts of teachers and others involved in the history of the different settings. 'Thinking biographically' has involved focusing upon people's lives and their own accounts of these. The historical, the reflective and the biographical aspects of my research are inseparable.

With this in mind, I invited teachers I interviewed at Freelands School to talk about the histories of their work lives. This material provided some important and unusual documentary evidence of the 'lived experience' of policy making in education (especially concerning special schools) reaching back in one case to the 1960s. Out of these personal historical accounts, a discussion of the 'larger social and cultural structures, and the here and now' developed quite naturally. I studied archive material in Greentown City Library relating to Freelands and the development of special education in the city and this has provided further historically contextualizing material for my study. Archive material of this kind is usually made up of the 'public face' of policy making and of the lives of schools and communities. It has been particularly illuminating to study such material along-side the insider historical accounts of teachers and to discover the connections between private lives and public records.

I later talked to a parent-governor of Freelands School, and his son (C.W.)

who had attended the school between the ages of 2–18. I recorded their historical perspectives of policy making concerning the school. This gave me three different perspectives which I have been able to draw on to examine 'public and private issues' and personal troubles that define the particular 'historical moment' in the English context under discussion in this study. It was at this stage, when I was in a position to look at teachers' historical accounts and those of a small group of parents and an ex-student, that the issues concerning the social construction of difference through spatializing processes and discourses began to emerge from the material so powerfully that I moved them to the centre of my enquiry. I have already briefly discussed some extracts from C.W.'s account earlier in this chapter and I will return to these later, along with material from other interviews with teachers and from notes taken in meetings.

In the French research context I have also adopted a multimethod approach but the perspectives I have drawn on have been concerned with a more general view of policy and educational responses to disabled children and young people, rather than those surrounding a specific policy making site at a particular historical moment (i.e. as in the case of Freelands).

FINDING A CROSS-CULTURAL PERSPECTIVE

This study is situated in the broad paradigm of comparative research, although I refer to it as 'cross-cultural' to distinguish the approach adopted from that of more traditional models of comparative research, which are commonly based on statistical analysis of particular 'features', for example, encompassing a belief that it is possible and reasonable to isolate particular features from their contexts in order to 'compare' them. In contrast to this approach, Poppleton argues that the importance of understanding different contexts is crucial in analysing data:

> The interpretation of findings in a cross-national study is much the most difficult part of the researcher's task. It assumes the possession of contemporary knowledge about how systems are constructed; historical knowledge of how they came to be what they are; anthropological knowledge of the mores and customs embodied in them; and sociological and psychological frameworks of reference in order both to contextualise the picture and to elaborate the finer details. (Poppleton, 1992, p. 215)

While it is most improbable that anyone other than an insider could gain such levels of broad and deep understanding of a particular country, in the present study the data collected is regarded as inseparable from the broader context. Booth and Ainscow argue that an implicit assumption commonly made in comparative research is that there is 'a single national perspective on inclusion or exclusion' and secondly that '… practice can be generalised across countries without attention to different contexts and meanings' (Booth and Ainscow, 1998, p. 4).

A second problem with many studies is that what is presented as a 'national perspective' is more often an official version of policy. Booth and Ainscow (1998) cite the example of the UK in which there are different education systems and legislative arrangements in Scotland, Northern Ireland, and England and Wales. It is also the case that in England there are enormous differences in the way in which formal policies are interpreted in different Local Education Authorities (LEAs) and that official 'national' versions of policy in England do not usually acknowledge this.

Research is itself a social practice, embedded in complex social and cultural contexts within which certain assumptions and 'ways of seeing' are important factors in determining research agendas, methodologies and analytical frameworks. However, researchers are not conditioned in some deterministic way by the social worlds they inhabit and research is itself an arena for struggle between values and ideologies which are fundamentally different. As Usher argues:

> ... if research is a social practice, a practice of producing certain types of knowledge that are socially validated, then as such it is a set of activities that constructs a world to be researched. When we delineate what we intend to study, when we adopt a particular theoretical position, when we ask certain questions rather than others, when we analyse and make sense of findings in one way rather than another, when we present our findings in a particular kind of text: all this is part of constructing a researchable world. In other words, research is not simply a matter of representing, reflecting or reporting the world but of 'creating' it through representation. (Usher, 1996, pp. 34–5)

These arguments have important implications for cross-cultural research in education and disability. For example, in my research I have inevitably created particular images, contrasts and similarities, and given prominence to particular kinds of questions and selections of issues as a result of my way of seeing the world. These issues are equally important in terms of research carried out in 'familiar' contexts in which stereotypical or essentializing representations may be deeply entrenched.

Different societies construct disability in culturally specific ways, expressing their particular dominant social norms and practices. Far from being 'scientific facts' based on universally understood definitions of difference, the categories and labels assigned to different groups in different societies are contingent, temporary and subjective.

A cross-cultural perspective attempts to take into account both the cultural and political legacies of historical change and the underlying processes and values within contemporary national contexts. Such an approach is powerful in terms of the possibilities it opens up of trying to understand different societies, their complexities and what we can learn from them. One outcome of cross-cultural research may be that assumptions concerning dominant values and practices and taken-for-granted power relationships in particular societies as universal, natural, rational or inevitable are challenged. This may strengthen the researcher's ability to look at the societies they themselves belong to from different angles and with greater critical awareness and sensitivity and may heighten understanding of the overt and covert processes and values relating to inclusion and exclusion. Finally, cross-cultural research encourages recognition of the subjectivity of the language used to describe and analyse, and acknowledges that what is 'seen' and selected for analysis is mediated by the researcher's own values and assumptions.

DISCOURSE, THE RESEARCHER AND THE FIELD

Some of the questions raised in the above sections relate to the need for the researcher to acknowledge their own responsibilities in the research process in relation to language and representation. As Heywood argues with reference to the role and responsibility of the researcher:

> One of the main practice consequences of a heightened awareness of language and modes of representation in general in the twentieth century has been to encourage a greater sensitivity to communication, not just to what is said overtly but to what is connoted or implied, not just to the content of representations but to their form and context. As well as focusing critically on the representations of others – in what has been referred to as a 'critique of representation' – this awareness also raises the question of the responsibility of each speaker for his or her own language. (Heywood, 1997, p. 85)

These arguments are as important in terms of my examination of the power relationships connected to the use of language by others in the research fields ('respondents', 'subjects' 'actors'), as they are in terms of critical reflection on my own use of language (or discourse). An important part of my enquiry and analysis is focused on the discourses deployed as tactics in policy struggles by different groups in arenas such as governors' or public consultation meetings.

The complexities, nuances and contradictions in policy making are often obscured by the language of official documents or the discourses used as common currency in educational settings and in the wider community. Documents from government such as the Green Paper 'Excellence for all children (DfEE, 1997) are littered with terms such as 'children with SEN', 'good practice', and 'support' for example, as if these terms were unproblematic and uncontested. Far from challenging existing barriers to inclusion, such discourses are ingrained in deeply rooted practices and values which sustain such barriers. Thus for example, the statement that 'District Health Authorities and NHS Trusts are under a duty to bring to the LEA's attention any child under five who they think has SEN' (DfEE, 1997, p. 13, my italics) implicitly promotes the medical model of disability and difference in situating difficulties as deficits belonging to individual children which need to be detected and administered. Thus, formal and written policy can be instruments of policy making in terms of what they hide or suggest rather than what they appear to 'lay down' in terms of principles and procedures. In contrast, the language used in the 'Index for Inclusion' (Booth *et al.*, 1999, 2002), a set of materials designed 'to support schools in a process of inclusive school development', represents issues of inclusion and exclusion in social terms. The Index takes as its starting point the need to develop 'inclusive school cultures, policies and practices' rather than focusing on 'how to include children with SEN'.

ISSUES AND DILEMMAS

At times I have become uncomfortably aware of the ambiguity of my relationship with many of the people who helped me by giving up time to meet me or to be interviewed, but who have also acted as gate-keepers and even tried to change the focus of my research. In addition, while I have introduced myself as someone 'trying to find something out', my position as a University Lecturer has assigned me a different role in the eyes of many people I have come across: that of the 'expert' . This has made it difficult to convince people that I really do want to learn from their perspectives, knowledge and experiences, that I don't already have answers to the questions I am asking. There have been times when I felt that once those I was interviewing – teachers, advisers or governors – have realized that I don't have any answers, but only questions or an alternative perspective, they experience feelings of surprise and possibly resentment. Although these moments have been difficult, they have usually opened up new possibilities for exploration and debate. It has been a relief to abandon the guise of the expert which can only hamper critical and open enquiry. I am reminded at this point, of the reaction of one teacher when I explained to her my research interests and the project I was involved in. She made no attempt to hide her sense of injustice that an outsider had been given the opportunity to do something she has been 'quietly doing' for many years but she hadn't been able to register for a higher degree because of time and financial constraints. Our personal biographies confronted each other and we fell silent. Later I came across the following extract included in Sanjek's book 'Field notes: The Making of Anthropology' (1990, p. 39):

> 'Mirth and horror' seized Ethel Albert when in 1956 her Rwandan field assistant Muntu failed to appear one morning,
>
> *and I went to the kitchen to get my coffee for myself. He was there, leaning against his work-table, notebook and pencil in hand. He was talking to one of my informants and appeared to be taking notes. I asked what he was doing. 'Anthropological research, like you. But I know the language so my research will be better than yours.' I asked if he meant to turn the notes over to me. He did not. This was his research. Happily the professional rivalry did not last long.* (Albert, 1960, p. 369).

This passage may not incite 'mirth and horror' but it is a stinging reminder of the power relationships involved in research processes. I wondered how the issues of 'professional rivalry' were resolved? Not, I suspect, by changing roles or re-negotiating shared ownership of the research process and outcomes, (and neither was I able to do this).

Unexpected critical events

There were a number of twists and turns in events which I could not have foreseen and which dramatically altered the course of my research in the English setting. When I started planning my research in the mid 1990s, I assumed that I would see the consultation process and the closure of Freelands school through until the students and staff had all become 'members of ordinary schools' which was expected to be in September 1998 or 1999. This would have made a neat story about policy making and inclusion with a beginning, a middle and an end. This idea disregarded the messiness of real life and of the research process; it denied the power of the unexpected and the complexity of the social and political relations and tensions involved in policy making. It underestimated the deeply held beliefs, passions and interests of many of those involved in the consultation process as well as their fallibility and weaknesses.

My field work in the school was delayed by the unexpected intervention of some critical events entailing major policy changes at local authority level. These events included: the resignation of the head teacher of the special school; the departure of the officer responsible for guiding and implementing policy relating to special education in the LEA, and their replacement by an adviser who had been working in another authority; a 'shake-up' of personnel in the LEA education department; the decision not to proceed with transfer arrangements to the comprehensive school which had been designated to receive the secondary aged pupils; the opening of negotiations with a second comprehensive school, thus delaying the closing down of the special school; the emergence of a powerful voice from an organization which claimed to represent parents of 'children with cerebral palsy'.

I had seen myself as being 'in at the beginning' of a process of policy making and change in relation to a particular school. In reality, of course, my chosen 'research field' – or the situation I became immersed in – had grown out of the social history surrounding education policy making in England, and the lives of people in Greentown. It continued to change before my eyes. I arrived on the scene at a particular moment in the history of policy making and it is important that my account reflects all the raggedness at the edges, stops and starts, mistakes and confusions which have been integral to the policy making processes and to the research process itself.

There were also a number of issues which arose in relation to my research in the French settings which disturbed my plans but enriched my understanding in the process. One example will give a flavour of the kind of tangled webs I struggled with. Once I had decided that my research would look at policy making in two countries, I started to look for two 'matching' schools, one in England and one in France, so that I could 'compare' policy making processes relating to them. I discussed my research and my requirements with my colleagues in France. One looked bemused and said that there were no schools in France like Freelands School in Greentown and anyway, most children with complex physical disabilities would receive their education in medically based settings outside the education system. Another colleague said that she knew of a school which would 'match' with Freelands school very well. When I visited it, I found that the children and young people who attended it had been placed there because of psychological or behavioural problems and experienced 'associated learning difficulties', while a few had some physical or sensory impairments. This school was also not part of the education system and there was a strong emphasis on psycho-therapy and counselling. This led to some critical reflection about the social construction of categories of disability and the usefulness of using such categories uncritically as a basis for making comparisons between policy making in different countries.

I also had to face up to important issues relating to working in what is to me a 'foreign' language, even though I speak French and lived and worked in France for several years. Not only is terminology relating to disability and difference constructed and used in different ways in France and England, but I had to recognize that I was not always using, or interpreting the language used by my French colleagues, in ways which reflected important nuances. Thus, for example, I became conscious that the word 'politique' in French can be used to mean 'political' or 'policy'. In English the common usage of the word 'policy' often wrongly suggests a kind of a-political, neutral process connected with decision making and governance. Of course, policy making is always political in that it involves struggles and decisions over values, interests and ideologies. This was one area which required considerable discussion. My French colleagues thought – at the beginning – that 'politics should be left out of the debate' and that we should focus primarily on 'good practice in special and ordinary schools'. In the process of negotiating the scope and purpose of our discussions, we learnt a great deal about the importance of discussing language issues and not making assumptions about common interpretations about terminology. We also increased our mutual understanding of the interrelation between policy and practice and how the two concepts are inseparable.

The question of voice

Another set of questions which I have encountered during the process of developing and carrying out my research relate to representation of the research process, my 'findings', and the voices and lives of other people who I have interviewed. There are two major issues which have particularly puzzled me. One concerns finding a way to draw upon and use the voices of others in writing about my research. Much of the material discussed in the study is taken from interviews with teachers, parents, governors and LEA officer (in England) and teachers, other professionals and researchers (in France). At the time of the interviews, I was not sure where they were going to lead or how I would use the material. Those who agreed to talk to me did so generously and with apparent confidence that I would be respectful of their words, feelings and opinions. But, however convinced I am of the need to question and disrupt my own assumptions and beliefs in order to explain how inequalities are produced, it would be impossible to present an account which did not reflect my own choices and concerns in terms of the selections I make from the material I have gathered. In making selections, I have taken control of the voices of others and used them in ways which reflect my interests and concerns first and foremost rather than theirs. At the same time, as I have explained earlier in this chapter, the issues, questions and perspectives of the people I interviewed in the early stages of my enquiry had a crucial impact in terms of reconceptualizing the focus and main emphasis of my research. In this sense, the voices of others have informed my research. Their accounts have also strengthened the contextualization of the study in that the historical accounts of their own work lives include discussion of the impact of changing social contexts and policies on educational structures and practices as well as on their own personal and professional lives. One teacher started teaching in the 1960s and was on the point of retiring when I interviewed him. His historical and personal account of his work life, and the accounts of other teachers in France and in England, have been invaluable to me in locating and anchoring my thinking to real lives and in making connections between 'major public and private issues and personal troubles' and how they define 'a particular historical moment.' I have already discussed the crucial importance and impact on my thinking of C.W.'s account and analysis of his education. However, In drawing selectively on the voices of others and building a text around them, I am not assuming any authority to speak for the participants being studied (Emihovich, 1995), and I acknowledge the risks involved in quoting from what they have said to support my arguments or to build theories in ways which were not necessarily meant by the speakers.

CONCLUSION

In this chapter I have attempted to outline some of the methodological and ethical issues which have arisen during the research process and the kinds of questions they have thrown up. In particular I have emphasised the role of subjectivity and the importance of exploring contexts in as much depth and breadth as possible in order to begin to analyse and interpret surface features of education systems and the accounts put forward by insiders.

Chapter Four, discusses the problems and challenges which arise in attempting to construct historical accounts. 'Historical background' is routinely included as 'context' in the presentation of many pieces of research and, early in the writing process I set out to write about 'the history' of special education in France and in England. As I drew on what others had written and tried to put things together in a smooth, and unproblematic chronology, I began to feel this was a rather empty exercise. Firstly, because this 'history' seemed to be taking on a life of its own, quite separate from the lives of real people. In excluding people in general, and disabled people in particular, I was contributing to their exclusion and ignoring their experience as if it did not count as knowledge. Secondly, there is an assumption in much of the literature that the history of special education is an unproblematic arrangement of (arte)facts such as government documents, legislation and statistical indicators which is unsatisfying

The chapter critically discusses some traditional accounts of the development of special education in England and France and challenges the idea that the passing of time is synonymous with 'progress' or improvement in the human condition.

CHAPTER 4

THE HISTORY OF SPECIAL EDUCATION: HUMANITARIAN RATIONALITY OR 'WILD PROFUSION OF ENTANGLED EVENTS'?

INTRODUCTION

> ...the implied cultural-utilitarian formula does not explain, assuming the importance primitive peoples must have ascribed to strength, stamina and sensory acuity, archeological and anthropological evidences of protection and inclusion of members with physical and sensory impairments (...). Nor is the idea of inexorable progress in treatment of people with disabilities or of children entirely valid. The broad "eras" often identified do not represent discrete periods or stages through which human society has passed, abandoning practices of one era as the next is born. Vestiges of older beliefs remain, even today. No one would assert that humanity has left behind cruelty, apathy, ignorance, and fear, and that is surely true of attitudes towards persons with disabilities. (Safford and Safford, 1996, p. 3)

This chapter critically discusses the historical development of special education in England and France. Through an interpretation of Foucault's distinction between 'traditional' history and 'effective' history (Foucault, 1971), it questions the idea that the passing of time is synonymous with 'progress' or improvement in the human condition. It also engages with the epistemological question of how historical knowledge concerning disability and special education is created and suggests alternative (or additional) historical sources.

The quotation used to open the chapter is a reminder that attitudes and practices relating to difference are culture-specific. Rather than being *determined* by the need to be socially useful or productive, even in periods when the fight for physical survival was a routine fact of life, other values and concerns have played their part. It underlines the importance of drawing on evidence wherever it may be found and from different disciplines in an attempt to develop greater understanding of historically and culturally situated practice. Finally, the quotation underlines the unevenness of historical development and challenges assumptions that societies follow a developmental pathway, away from superstition, prejudice and cruelty, and in the direction of greater enlightenment and humanity. This scrambles the hegemony of 'historical periods' in which beliefs and practices of entire societies across an arbitrarily defined period of time (or 'slice of history') are reduced to crude generalizations.

WRITING HISTORY

The task of writing history is inseparable from the writer's own understanding about how knowledge is constituted and existing accounts interpreted. How are we to interpret, for example, the absence of 'actors' themselves in the majority of history texts and the almost total absence of the voices and perspectives of disabled people in dominant accounts of the history of disability and education? What historical sources are relevant and important, and to what extent are the absences and silences in routine historical accounts themselves worthy of examination? What do we make of the silences around where disabled children were and how they lived in the past? The glimpses of the ordinary lives of disabled children – fleetingly, as sick and dying in Dickens' *Nicholas Nickleby*, with revulsion in Charlotte Bronte's *Villette* – are rare in the broader fields of literature too. There are passing references to disabled people in the literature relating to other domains such as the history of the workhouse or the architecture of asylums. This is one reason why the exploration of the history of social life in general, and of education in particular, calls for a multi-disciplinary approach.

Potts (1995) has critically explored the possible contribution of history to enhancing (or changing) understanding of the development of special education in England. She argues against a view 'which separates history from contemporary life', and insists that, 'Histories can only be of use if we put ourselves into the historical picture, allowing history to affect our lives and our lives to affect history' (p. 410). It is the many actors whose (partial) accounts contribute to the material who are drafted into 'the historical picture' and it is their lives, and those of researchers and writers, which affect the different historical and social landscapes we paint. Slee (1999) provides an example of a reflexive account in which personal history joins with a particular moment in the history of special education in Australia to create a kind of knowledge which is located spatially, temporally, culturally and autobiographically:

> My own biography produces shameful memories. I recollect the way that my friends and I would break into a run as we passed Mullaratarong (many special centres were given Aboriginal names, but not I think as a sign of solidarity). It was necessary to run in order to avoid ending up like the kids inside. The mythology, en epistemic etching, exerted such powers over us. Parents disabused us of the fear of contagion and adjusted our emotions to an attitude of pity. Thinking back, it now occurs to me that I never saw any of the kids behind their purpose built high fences. The point was, we didn't need to, we had knowledge about them revolving around loose conceptions of illness, deformity and above all else 'abnormality'. (Slee, 1999, p. 124)

Slee's (1999) personal account of his fearful race past a special school with its 'mythology' and 'epistemic etching' and the 'knowledge' about 'the kids inside' is drafted into *his* 'historical picture' of the social, emotional and symbolic implications of special education. These approaches emphasize the importance of acknowledging the embededness of subjectivity in terms of mapping personal experience and values onto the bigger picture as part of historical interpretation.

In their edited book *Silences and Images: The Social History of the Classroom*, Grosvenor, Lawn and Rousmaniere (1999) address the '… great "silences" in the history of education' across a range of cultures about 'the practice, meaning and cultures of classrooms in the past'. The chapters explore curricula, pedagogy and the 'lived reality of the teachers' work and students' lives with the purpose of beginning to 'reconstruct the culture of such common social spaces in schools and to ask questions about how historians can begin to piece together the silent history of education' (p. 1). This present chapter is also concerned with exploring historical silences and with the methodological issues about how such explorations can be undertaken.

Foucault's distinction between 'traditional history' and 'effective history' is helpful in exploring the disjuncture between formal histories of special education as a 'humanitarian project' and other possible sources of knowledge. These might include, for example, historical accounts of the workhouse in England, the design and organisation of buildings, themes and images in paintings or literature. A study of these alternative sources reveals multiple possible histories of special education waiting to be created. For example, in exploring the history of the workhouse, drawing on a variety of material from contemporary sources, there is much evidence to suggest that the workhouse in many instances provided formal education and training for children and young people, including those who were disabled, pre-dating the period when mass education was formally introduced. The traditional history of special education has rarely recognized or explored the contribution made by the early nineteenth century workhouse to the development of the institutionalization of disabled children.

EDUCATION AND THE WORKHOUSE

Markus (1993) identifies 'the seeds of many educational practices' as being sown in the eighteenth century workhouse, based on the twin projects of ensuring 'order and work'. Production and education had been connected in the emergence of schools dedicated to particular trades in the late seventeenth century and, with religion, were characteristics of the seventeenth century Charity schools. The early industrial schools were later replaced by the far larger workhouses with their immediate on-site supply of labour and by reformatory industrial schools. As Tomlinson has argued:

> education systems and their parts do not develop spontaneously, or in an evolutionary manner, and they do not develop out of purely humanitarian motives. They develop because it is in the interests of particular groups in a society that they should develop and that they should develop in particular ways … what actually becomes 'education' is seldom the realisation of some ideal form of instruction. (Tomlinson, 1982, p. 27)

There was a close link between education, poor relief and incarceration and there were many examples of large institutions which provided a kind of productive ecosystem, incorporating factory, school, chapel and workhouse. Children who lived in workhouses were taught reading and writing, religious instruction and sometimes arithmetic – although girls were sometimes excluded from this basic education – and were trained only in production processes such as weaving or spinning (Markus, 1993).

Scull (1979) links the development of industrial capitalism and modes of production to the growth of workhouses and asylums as part of the changing social and economic landscape. Schooling and training in manufacturing skills were an integral part of this relationship. Disabled people, children in particular, made up part of the workhouse community. When the St Marylebone workhouse moved to new premises the 1774 Enabling Act specified that it was:

> ... to admit the poor, both healthy and sick, diseased and infirm; the profligate and idle who were to be corrected; and infant poor to be educated 'in habits of industry, religion and honesty', the profits from their labour to be used for their own upkeep as well as for the parish. (Markus, 1993, p. 43)

Workhouses were complex institutions characterized by the imposition of care, control, discipline, training, religion and productivity. They represented a particular kind of rationality which embraced all aspects of the lives of inmates. Like Bentham's Panopticon, this rationality worked *through* the design of the buildings themselves which were vehicles for the spatial organization and control of people and the expression of particular values:

> In Bishopsgate Street there were 129 children (increased to 400 by the early nineteenth century) ... in two 150-foot long workshops. The boys' lodgings were located above these workrooms, the girls' over the chapel which separated the workhouse from the prison. Boys had reading and writing lessons; for the girls sewing and knitting replaced writing. The children worked eighty spinning wheels. In other houses they often shared in the adults' oakum picking, weaving or shoemaking. (Markus, 1993, p. 43)

This 'rationality' in which social usefulness, discipline, productivity and moral rectitude were part of the core values expressed through the buildings themselves and through the daily regime, can be traced as a thread running through the development of special education in France and in England. It is also one which has underpinned the practices in some ordinary schools in England during particular periods. (When I started working at a Church of England maintained school in Oxford in the mid 1970s, a large area of the school buildings was made up of workshops for training boys for the assembly lines in the nearby car factory at Cowley which they could see in the distance from the workshop windows.)

In France, some special institutions still train young people in gardening, laundry work, cooking, cleaning and home maintenance as an important part of the curriculum (Armstrong, F., 1995) and particular areas of the building and sites are designated for these purposes. The current return to an insistence on the importance of technical and vocational skills as a key part of the curriculum in schools for some pupils, harnessed to the moral agenda of 'citizenship' and 'family values' are a reinterpretation of earlier rationalities linked to social usefulness and economic productivity.

These arguments challenge assumptions about the progressive unfolding of an even and rational 'history of education' in which policy documents, acts of parliament, dates and 'big events' are seen as providing an adequate framework for interpretation. How helpful is Foucault's distinction between 'traditional history' and 'effective history' in providing an alternative, more powerful approach, to the understanding of the development of special education?

'TRADITIONAL HISTORY' AND 'EFFECTIVE HISTORY'

Foucault argues that in 'traditional history':

> An entire historical tradition (theological or rationalistic) aims at dissolving the singular event into an ideal continuity – as a teleological movement or natural process. 'Effective' history, however, deals with events in terms of their unique characteristics, their most acute manifestations ...
> ... The world we know is not (an) ultimately simple configuration where events are reduced to accentuate their essential traits, their final meaning, or their initial and final value. On the contrary, it is a profusion of entangled events. (Foucault and Rabinow, 1994, pp 88–89)

This chapter is particularly concerned with exploring some of the 'profusion of entangled events' which have a bearing on the political struggles surrounding issues of disability and exclusion in education. In this context, the reductionist 'traditional' humanitarian account of the growth of special education as concerned with 'doing good' *to* disabled children and young people is contested through the examination of material which suggests – not a rational, benevolent, progressive continuity – but a set of contradictory processes, events and values in which 'the past' is complex and discontinuous and the future unpredictable.

Historical accounts which trace the development of special education only through formal policy making and its documents leave out the messiness, variety and unpredictability of policies as they are enacted through social practice. Social practices are socially and culturally rooted within particular political, temporal and spatial contexts. Importantly, what is going on where, who is involved and in what historical period are all crucial elements in the unraveling of social practice.

An example, which supports this approach, can be found in terms of the effects of war on the social and economic relations within communities. Drawing on the work of other researchers, Safford and Safford comment:

> ... for persons with disabilities, war has had paradoxical benefits ... For deaf persons, war had demographic consequences that furthered cultural identification, for 'undraftable deaf men found themselves in great demand. A peculiar consequence ... was the creation of a large deaf community in Akron, Ohio, drawn by the rubber industry (Van Cleve and Crouch, 1989,

> p. 163). In both world wars and the Korean conflict, psychological evaluation
> of recruits heightened awareness of retardation, often a basis for rejection
> ... Nonetheless, many with retardation did in fact serve, while World War II
> brought unprecedented employment opportunity to many of those rejected
> – though after the war most were, as Doll (1962) had predicted 'quickly shuf-
> fled back to poverty and dependency'. (Safford and Safford, 1996, p. 211)

Paradoxically, wars – which, as well as causing massive numbers of fatalities, 'create' hundreds of thousands, or millions, of disabled people – have provided opportunities for ordinary employment to disabled people. Although disabled women are not mentioned in the quotation above, women also had unprecedented 'opportunities' opened up to them in wartime. In England, in both the First and Second World Wars, women played a vital part in the labour force, both on the land and in the factories, as well as playing key roles in the armed forces and in the nursing profession. During the Second World War young disabled people were also drawn into the workforce in England and were able to leave school early so that they could take their place in employment. Wars, then, may play a curiously progressive role in allowing greater freedom and opportunity to oppressed groups such as women and disabled people in terms of the adjustment of rules so that they may participate in social arenas and activities not usually available to them. In general, these freedoms and opportunities are taken back when the groups concerned are no longer 'useful'. Nevertheless, it is probable that the 'old' rules are never fully re-instated and that the image of such groups is modified in the common gaze to incorporate new and different perceptions about their capabilities and 'place' in society.

In later sections of this chapter the histories of special education in France and England are discussed through a critique of traditional approaches. There is no suggestion, of course, that all those who have written about the history of special education speak with one voice. Traditional history does allow for differences in analysis and interpretation, but is characterized by having a clear and traceable pathway and coherence, and by remaining within certain disciplinary boundaries. Events are rationalized, explained and constructed as logical. 'Effective' history, on the other hand:

> ...differs from traditional history in being without constants...The traditional
> devices for constructing a comprehensive view of history and for retracing
> the past as a patient and continuous development must be systematically
> dismantled. (Chartier, 1994, p. 171)

The 'natural' assumptions made about the traditional history of education such as, for example, that modern systems of education emerged from earlier forms, need to be challenged. As Hamilton argues:

> Such assumptions ... are immediately constraining. They give preferential
> attention to continuity over change. They highlight the evolution rather than
> the genesis of social institutions. (Hamilton, 2001, p. 188)

The distinction between traditional history and effective history is best understood in the context of Foucault's notions of power and discourse. Power is everywhere, permeating all social relations and embedded in discourse. Power, argued Foucault (1972), is an 'open-ended, more or less coordinated cluster of relations' and he discounted any attempt to pin the notion of power to a definition or single principle, arguing that 'nothing is fundamental' (see Foucault, 1980). Power is embedded in forms of knowledge which are hegemonicallly constructed, reconstructed and reinterpreted through discourses which produce meanings, rules and practices. Power and knowledge are inseparable; they cohabit and are expressed within each other.

Thus the growth of 'experts' and 'expertise' in medicine, the identification, measuring and recording of differences between groups and individuals and the imposition of notions of normality, the typological obsession with identification, categorisation, labelling and ordering – all contributed to the emergence of sets of power relations based on the privileging of certain forms of knowledge over others. The power embedded in professional knowledge and practices has been, and continues to be, the bedrock of special education and the processes and procedures surrounding identification, categorisation, labelling and treatment. Foucault's notion of bio-power is useful in describing the 'shift in the nature of power' in which 'the pastoral' becomes merged with 'the disciplinary' as part of a technology of care and control:

> The point of bio-power is that it represents a shift in the very nature of government and in the very nature of power. Bio-power works through the dual, but necessarily combined, forces of pastoral-discipline – and its end point is the production of self-disciplinary, self-regulatory citizenry overlaid with an array of attributes. (Peim, 2001, p. 177)

In terms of the history and effects of special education one example of 'bio-power' is the role of labelling in the creation of deviant and marginalised identities as a mechanism for the management (i.e. care and control) of disturbing others.

HISTORY, EDUCATION AND DISABILITY IN ENGLAND AND FRANCE

England

Historically, formal educational structures in England are grounded in systems, structures, processes and curricula based upon the division, assessment and categorization of learners. These divisions have taken place according to formal and informal measures relating to place, class, gender, race, perceived ability and disability, academic performance and assumptions about learners. Education also has some of its roots in charitable and philanthropic projects which developed separately from state controlled educational provision. Churches and religious groups, firms and industries, trade unions and workers' organizations – have also made important contributions to the complexity and character of what is referred to as 'the education system' in England (Armytage, 1965). Other less commonly cited contributors to the growth of the education system in England were the nineteenth century workhouses (discussed above) set up to contain, control and render productive poor and destitute people, in which children, in addition to being put to work and to pray, were often taught basic arithmetic, reading and writing.

While mass elementary education was introduced in England through the education acts of 1870, 1876 and 1880, as Peim argues:

> The school did not emerge fully formed out of the 1870 Education Act. The process of its definition seems to have been concerned with the developing conception of a number of key elements. Of particular significance was the architectural organisation of the social spaces of the school – along with the clarification of their symbolic social functioning...the 'new' school represents an array of spaces, techniques and occasions for the transformation of populations. (Peim, 2001, pp. 178–179)

This argument is particularly apposite in relation to the growth of special education which constituted literal and symbolic sets of spaces and practices relating to the removal of disabled children. There are many accounts of earlier experiments in training or teaching children who experienced learning difficulties or those who were deaf or blind in schools, 'idiot asylums' or other institutions, but it was not until the end of the nineteenth century that state provision for disabled children was introduced with the opening of a special class for deaf children by the London School Board in 1874, followed by the 1893 Elementary Education (Blind and Deaf Children) Act. This opened the way for a period of massive expansion of the special education system with the accompanying proliferation of categories of handicap and specialists, schools and institutions to accommodate them.

Tomlinson argued (1982) that dominant accounts of the rise of special education in England as being the result of 'altruism and disinterested humanitarianism' fail to take account of the influence and constraints of 'prevailing cultural values and social interests':

> ... the history of special education must be viewed in terms of the benefits it brought for a developing industrial society, the benefits for the normal mass education system of a 'special' sub-system of education, and the benefits that medical, psychological, educational and other personnel derived from encouraging new areas of professional expertise.(Tomlinson, 1982, p. 29)

This argument relates to the notion of power-knowledge discussed in the previous section. In contrast, Cole (1989) observed that Tomlinson's arguments '... seem to rest upon the selective view of the late nineteenth and twentieth centuries' and that compassion and humanitarianism 'played a very major part':

> Furthermore, social control arguments have little relevance to the deaf, the blind, the physically handicapped, the delicate, the epileptic and other categories who clearly posed no threat to teachers in ordinary schools or society at large. (Cole, 1989, p. 170)

Cole's understanding of 'social control' is based on an assumption that the idea of 'control' is necessarily associated with a response to 'anti-social' or 'destructive' behaviour. But the idea that special education is concerned with social control rests on the argument that '... those categorized as "in need" of special education can be regarded as deviating from behaviour required in ordinary education'. (Tomlinson, 1982, p. 19)

Furthermore, in Cole's litany of non-threatening others – *the* deaf, *the* blind, *the* physically handicapped, *the* delicate, *the* epileptic – whole groups of people are positioned as submissive, as occupying a deficit and dependency role (Barton, 1996) and incapable of exercising any behaviour which might undermine the stability of the established social order. They are declared *hors jeu* and hence, for Cole, the argument that such groups are placed in segregated institutions because of a perceived need to control them, is invalid.

Cole's analysis contrasts sharply with the view, put forward by, for example, Foucault and Scull, that the rise of special institutions and the confinement of disabled children were part of a wider, profound social movement in Europe which introduced and refined the identification and removal from ordinary public spaces of those were regarded as deviant. Cole appears to see the 'humanitarian' account as different and distinctive from the 'social control' account. An alternative approach is the recognition of the deployment of particular humanitarian discourses to usher in and embellish policies of removal and confinement as part and parcel of the special education project.

The development of special education in the late nineteenth and early twentieth centuries was linked to a number of complex factors, not least of which was the emergent and sometimes competing professionalism of teachers and doctors and psychologists (Armstrong, D., 1995) and a growth of official interest in the health of school children. The early attempts to make some kind of social provision for 'defective' children in 'special' classes or schools (the word special began to be used towards the end of the 19th century) were, argues Hall, based on a desire to relieve their distress rather than offer them an education (Hall, 1997). Furthermore:

> ... there remained a hierarchy of perceived rights with the greatest opportunities being accorded to those with sensory impairments while children with significant learning difficulties trailed along behind in (an) ... 'impairment pecking order'. (Hall, 1997, p. 19)

In general, 'education' was not the first concern of special schools and institutions. On the contrary, historical accounts of the dehumanizing experience of life in special schools and institutions in the first half of the twentieth century and beyond emphasize the restrictive, harsh and unstimulating regimes in special schools, in which remediation, care and control provided an organizing framework for the daily lives of those within.

As in the growth in asylums during the nineteenth century in which insane people were confined in a highly bureaucratic state-run asylum system which '... isolated them both physically and symbolically from the larger society.' (Scull, 1979, p. 14) the number and size of special schools grew dramatically between the end of the 19th century and the 1960s. The early part of the twentieth century, under the influence of the eugenics movement and the burgeoning medical professions was characterized by a particular concern with 'care' and 'control', especially in relation to children deemed to be 'feeble-minded' and 'defective' and the development of 'mental testing' (Tomlinson, 1982, p. 45–46). In this climate, there was an important increase in segregated residential institutions and schools of all sorts.

The development of special education is a social process and, contrary to some accounts, has not followed an orderly and progressive pathway or been planned according to rational principles. Pritchard (1963) offers a particular example of the haphazard patterning of social and educational structures and processes in his account of some of the unplanned and unexpected effects of the Second World War on educational provision for disabled children in England. The air-raids on big cities, particularly London, and the evacuation of children to the country led to the disorganization of schools, the closing down of some special schools in the cities and the opening up of some residential special schools in the reception areas. Many disabled children remained behind in the cities because it was hard to find a family to receive them, and attended one of the ordinary schools which remained open. When evacuees returned to the cities, many disabled children found themselves placed in ordinary schools as numbers of residential schools had been closed:

> ... Because of the reduction of boarding places available, there existed for the first time in many years a shortage of accommodation for handicapped children and consequently the number of children attending special schools fell sharply. In addition, the demand for labour induced some authorities to allow children to leave special schools at fourteen. At the same time fewer children were being ascertained as in need of special education, partly because of the shortage of accommodation, partly because of the general disorganization of the education services, and partly because medical officers were pre-occupied with extra duties connected with evacuation and Civil Defence. It is therefore understandable that in 1941 the number of London, mentally and physically handicapped children attending special schools had decreased by fifty per cent. Other cities reported a similar decline. (Pritchard, 1963, p. 208)

Pritchard's account underlines the unpredictability of the outcomes of the relationship between historical events and social structures, and the fluidity of change in human society. It demonstrates that 'planning' and 'policy making' should be seen as being constantly fragmented, reinterpreted and reworked at different levels in response to changing contexts. It also emphasizes the crucial role of spatiality and of movement of different groups between places in different historical periods, which are constructed within particular socio-economic and political contexts. Finally, Pritchard's examples highlight the relationship between social identity and historical context: young disabled people formerly segregated from the rest of society by removal to a special school, are transformed into young, active, economically productive and necessary members of society. Disabled, useless outsiders are socially reconstructed as contributing insiders.

After the Second World War, there were some changes in attitudes towards disabled children and young people for a number of reasons. The fact that disabled people contributed to productivity and were more visible during wartime, and possibly that 'disability' had become more 'normal' as a result of war-inflicted maiming and impairment, as well as the apparent national wish for some levelling out of differences between people as part of national reconstruction, may all be factors which contributed to the drawing up of recommendations that special schools should be brought into the wider education framework. The 1944 Education Act, as well as introducing a system of mass primary and secondary education, made LEAs responsible for the education of children 'in accordance with their ages, aptitudes and abilities'. Children who were labelled 'ineducable' were excluded from this legislation and remained outside the education system until the passing of the 1970 Education (Handicapped Children) Act.

Ministry of Education regulations following the 1944 Education Act replaced the existing four categories of handicap, with eleven – preparing the way for a further proliferation in bureaucratic procedures relating to identification and labelling and the burgeoning of new professional identities and careers. The expanded array of categories represented new refinements in the decanting of children:

> Partially sighted and partially hearing children were separated from blind and deaf, delicate, diabetic, epileptic and physically handicapped formed four separate categories, educable defective children became educationally subnormal, and two new categories, speech defect and maladjusted, were created. (Tomlinson, 1982, p. 50)

In this way, there was a realignment of the procedural exercise of power through developing fields of professional activity (and the production of 'knowledge') based on the reconfiguration of 'the normal'. The relationship between power and knowledge hinged on discourses of categorisation and the expertise of professionals as they expanded and re-ordered the territory. The numbers of children labelled and placed in special schools increased in spite of processes linked to widening access through the development of a system of compulsory primary and secondary education. The examination (in the form of tests and psychological and medical as-sessments) – remains the key micro-technology of power, at the same time coercive and arbiter of 'truth', through which the naming, sorting and placing of pupils takes place. This re-ordering of the territory by professionals and the construction through labelling of new identities and forms of deviance (e.g. 'ADHD' - attention deficit hyperactivity disorder, 'EBD' – emotional and behavioural difficulties, 'Asperger's Syndrome' etc) continues to play a key role in education systems and the special education project, through the sifting and sorting of children and young people on the basis of perceived differences between them.

This brief discussion of the growth of special education in England reveals some of the complexities and contradictions which need to be considered in constructing histories of special education. Questions are raised, too, about accounts which challenge familiar and comfortable narratives about the gradual, uninterrupted hu-manitarian 'march of progress'. Traditional histories tend to iron out unevenness, discontinuities and contradictions. Effective history, in contrast, seeks to *render more complex*, eschewing generalities and simplifications.

France

In France the principles of 'liberty, equality and fraternity' which emerged during the French Revolution found expression in all aspects of civil life, including the education system (Armstrong, 1996), supported by the highly centralized and powerful state apparatus first established under Napoleon. The education system was governed by statutory national curriculum and government directives on pedagogy, assessment and the structure and management of local, regional and national education systems.

Historically, provision for disabled children and young people developed outside the state education system and has not traditionally been included in its frame of reference. The structures and institutions which developed separately from the state education apparatus adopted therapeutic, social or medical goals rather than educational. In addition, although state schools are ostensibly 'for everybody', it is only relatively recently that the question of how the needs of individual pupils in ordinary schools can be met, has become the focus of national debate in education (Cohen and Hugon, 1995). It is still generally assumed that some young people will continue to be excluded from ordinary schools, and the education system.

Mass, compulsory primary education was introduced in France in 1882 and later extended to the secondary stage. One of the founding principles of state education was its secularism, still vehemently defended today. Prior to the introduction of compulsory state education, primary schools had generally been under the control of the Catholic Church. Underlying this principle was another still more fundamental one – that of the common right to social inclusion. No child should be excluded on the grounds of religion, gender or nationality, but exclusion on the grounds of disability or learning difficulty has never been part of that general principle. This contradiction might be critically examined through an 'effective history' approach as one of the great and many paradoxes contained implicitly in 'traditional' histories of special education which rest on an assumption that the special education project is concerned with 'doing good' to disabled children, rather than with their 'rights'.

Responses to disability, difference and deviance have, historically, included the systematic segregation of groups of people from the rest of society. In 1793 Philippe Pinel was granted permission from the Commune of Paris to release eighty-nine 'lunatics' from their shackles, marking a move away from a purely custodial model towards a medical model of care and treatment. This opened the way to the practice of diagnosing and categorizing conditions and disabilities and using these categories as a basis for the matching of impairment to institution or therapy. Today in France placements of children in particular institutions designated for particular conditions or impairments may still require a medical prescription. (Similarly, in England, medical assessments frequently still play a major part in procedures relating to assessment and educational placements.)

A second development in the history of special education in France was the opening of schools for deaf children and blind children in the eighteenth century (Rée, 1999). These were often run by religious institutions; the Abbé de l'Epée set up a school for 'the deaf-mute' and Valentin Haüy opened an institution for blind children during this period. Other similar institutions followed. There is little evidence in formal accounts that there was provision for physically disabled children or those who experience learning difficulties during this period. As in England at the time, education was not compulsory and the state did not, therefore, have to provide any schools for the population as a whole.

In the late nineteenth and early part of the twentieth century a number of large medically orientated institutions were created for disabled children and those with a range of medical conditions whose purpose was 'rehabilitation' or 'retraining'. These were usually on the coast, built almost on the beach overlooking sand dunes, in areas outside seaside towns. Stiker (1999) argues that with the growth of the asylum in the nineteenth century, spatial and bureaucratic separation occurred between those who were psychiatrically ill and physically sick and disabled people. But with the arrival of the vast, segregated medical institutions, the asylum was in a sense recreated:

> ... from an epistemological point of view, are retraining centers that different from the asylums? The large establishment of Berck-Plage, for example, founded for the treatment of tuberculoses patients, did it not recreate the space of the asylum? All those designated and selected by medical expertise were collected as if in a zoo and left to wander in a universe of illness. There was neither school nor culture nor contact with the world of the healthy. (Stiker, 1999, p. 139)

This comment is eerily illustrated by the painting *Sad Inheritance* by Joaquín Sorolla y Bastida (1899) which depicts a large group of disabled children, naked, exposed to the elements, standing or crouching aimlessly on the beach under the stern and powerful gaze of a towering priest clad in black. Some of these institutions still exist and large groups of sick or disabled children can sometimes be seen in the distance on the beaches beyond the throng of holidaymakers at French seaside resorts. As in other parts of Europe and in England, there have been institutions which shared some characteristics with such establishments as Berck-Plage: the 'open-air schools' (Wilmot, and Saul, 1998) and the hospital schools of the twentieth century for example. Such establishments both removed sick and disabled children and constructed their identities as 'other'.

In 1909 a law was passed in France enabling the setting up through local initiatives of 'improvement classes' (*classes de perfectionnement*) attached to ordinary elementary schools for children identified as having learning difficulties (*les enfants handicapés mentaux*). They received children between the ages of 6–14. In reality such classes contained a broad diversity of pupils including those with physical and sensory disabilities, those with learning difficulties and others with emotional and behavioural difficulties. The reason for this was not because there were accepted policies concerning integration or access for all but because there were no easily accessible alternatives for pupils with a wide range of difficulties (Lantier, *et al.*, 1994).

During the period between 1950–70 a large network of 'médico-educatif' establishments began to grow up outside the education system in response to pressure from parents (organized in *Associations*) and in a favourable economic climate which allowed the government to assist with the funding of such expansion. By 1975 it had become widely recognized that such a system effectively segregated many young people from the rest of the community. In response to this change in attitude the *Loi d'Orientation en Faveur des Personnes Handicapées* was passed in June 1975. This law asserted the right of access to social integration of all children, young people and adults with physical, sensory or mental disabilities. In addition it laid down the right to education, training, work and financial support and outlined the structural and procedural changes which would enable and facilitate increased participation of children and young people in ordinary schools. The law stated that children should where possible be admitted to ordinary schools 'in spite of their handicap'. This was followed by government circulars (e.g. 1983, 1985) with guidelines on the mechanisms through which integration should take place. In spite of the legislation and a common acceptance of the principles which underlay it, the continued existence of a large and complex network of special schools and institutions and the selective and regulatory nature of the curriculum and assessment in ordinary schools has acted as a break on the inclusion of disabled pupils and those who experience learning difficulties in mainstream state education. Policy, therefore, needs to be placed in the wider context of existing policies and conditions against which 'new' initiatives are realized through practice.

In France, the separate development of education and the structures and practices relating to health and impairment which have grown up over the past two hundred years pose one of the main challenges to a fully inclusive system of education for all learners. According to an information report from the Social Affairs Commission on policy relating to compensation and disability (rapport d'information de la Commission des affaires socials sur la 'politique de compensation du handicap') which was presented to parliament (24 July 2002), a quarter of children and young people who have a physical impairment and 8% of those who have a sensory impairment are not 'scolarisés' – which means that they do not attend school. The same report deplores the lack of access to public transport, buildings, ordinary workplaces, and schools (*Liberation*, 25.7.02, p 2).

In England and in France, an important social practice underpinning the development of what is routinely referred to as 'special education' is the categorization of children and young people and their allocation to different settings on the basis of these categories. Categorization is a discourse of power which has its roots deeply entrenched within the complex apparatuses of the state education, health and welfare systems, and is used as a mechanism for spatializing procedures which sort and place people in different sites. Special education is conceptualized, observes Linda Ware, 'as a place rather than a service' (Ware, 2000). This observation points to tensions surrounding the relationship between the processes and procedures which maintain and control the borders between the central reproductive education project and the (equally reproductive) spatialized outer sites of particular institutions. An awareness of the complexity of the educational landscape made up of so many fractured and contradictory policies, ideologies and practices needs to be informed by sources and voices other than those of 'traditional history'.

A CRITIQUE OF 'TRADITIONAL HISTORY'

The traditional history of special education, usually begins with a brief statement about the barbaric treatment of disabled new-born babies in 'ancient times' and the negative attitudes which then prevailed based on fear and superstition and the spurious 'surplus population thesis' (Oliver and Barnes, 1998). The account moves swiftly on, by-passing the centuries, to the 'birth' of special education with its roots in eighteenth century Europe, beginning with the education of deaf children.

Mass compulsory education, an 'essential precondition for both a policy and any systematic provision of special education', (Sutherland, 1981, p. 95) was introduced in England in 1880. Under conditions which resemble the current performance led values of today's education system, teachers were paid according to students' achievement in public examinations organized in a series of 'Standards' through which children were supposed to move each year. Such a system quickly exposed children who were experiencing difficulties and:

> The difficulties of trying to teach undernourished, sick and handicapped children were dramatized at a very early stage because the school curriculum embodies what was simultaneously a very crude and a very elaborate notion of normality. (Sutherland, 1981, p. 95)

It was against this background that an organized and structured system of special education – designed to 'relieve' ordinary schools of difficult pupils as well as being intended to 'meet their needs' – emerged.

We have seen how special education expanded as a 'system', with a proliferation of categories of impairment and corresponding specialist institutions in the late nineteenth and the twentieth century. As scientific knowledge increased and official humanitarian and medical discourses took a firmer hold in a period of economic growth (1950s–1970s), special education and paramedical services achieved a formidable and seemingly unassailable position, embracing the multiple roles of supplying care, medical aid, remediation, education and training, protection and control. Then the scene shifted. In the wake of the period of radicalization of the 1960s and the slide in the economy in the 1970s competing demands relating to equality and – in England and Wales – the question of cost, came to the fore. In the 1980s the debate about integration rumbled on, following the publication of the Warnock Report (DES, 1978) and the 1981 Education Act in England and the 1975 Loi d'Orientation in France. In England there was a progressive reduction in the number of special schools in some areas, although only a gradual reduction in the number of children placed in segregated schools. In France, where many disabled children attend settings outside the education system, the 1989 Loi Jospin declared the right of all children to attend an ordinary school 'as far as possible'.

Implicit in this account is the construction of the history of social attitudes as becoming more enlightened, tolerant and 'caring' and of an emerging general acceptance that disabled children and young people should be included in ordinary education. Such accounts represent an amalgam of histories, a potted version of the big story of special education and the exclusion of the voices of disabled people. Also implicit in dominant accounts is the suggestion that policies are rational, made from above by central government and passed down in a logical and even way through the processes of local government and the management of schools, budgets and curriculum. Knight *et al.* (1990) denounce conceptualizations of official state policies in terms which harmonize with Foucault's critique of 'traditional' historical accounts:

> Such policies attempt to represent the world in factual terms so that certain kinds of practices flow 'naturally' from them. They appropriate scientific methodologies and social science theory in order to create a reality which is rational, objective, seamless, and which taps into the sensibilities of national popular consciousness. In doing so, such policies tell stories which, once interpreted by audiences, are emptied of meaning and filled with available social myths (Barthes, 1973). Competing stories are thus available as resources for decoding and recoding and otherwise clashing or collaborating with official policy. (Knight *et al.*, 1990, p. 133)

This statement is particularly fitting when applied to the role of identification, categorization and labelling of certain groups of learners as *having* 'special educational needs' and the elision which occurs between the label and the myth that these learners have characteristics and 'needs' which require different treatment and often removal from ordinary education sites and practices. An example of the construction of a 'social myth' is the belief in the 19th and early 20th century that disability was caused by syphilis – or, at least, sins committed by parents or forefathers. The paintings *Sad Inheritance* painted by Joaquín Sorolla y Bastida and *Inheritance* painted by Edvard Munch between 1903–1905, both exhibited in the Paris 'Exposition Universelle' in 1900, both depicting disabled children, suggest by their titles that disabilities are 'handed down' from parents or through generations and are manifestations of 'the sins of the forefathers'.

Traditional accounts of the nature and development of special education such as the one presented above are exemplified in, for example, the work of Cole (1989), Wedell (1990), O'Hanlon (1993, 1995), Ballarin (1994). Much of this work supports dominant accounts of the uninterrupted progressive development of special education and its humanitarian purpose. In doing so, there is a silence imposed on conflictual or contesting voices and perspectives. This silence constitutes 'a set of values that on the one hand deny social divisions and on the other celebrate them as being natural and inevitable' (Knight *et al.*, 1990, p. 146).

In contrast to the traditional accounts referred to, the critical work of Fulcher on policy making (1999) and Tomlinson's historical and sociological work on the role and development of special education (Tomlinson, 1982), Booth's work on categorization and the history of integration (Booth, 1981) and Barton and Slee's work (1998, 1999) on the nature and effects of the market on education, all challenge traditional accounts.

Copeland's critical appraisal of the work of historians in the field of special education (Copeland, 1999) relates to the *selectivity* of the material considered and the *inadequacy of the analyses* put forward to explain the emergence of special education. In his discussion of the work of Foucault, Copeland develops a critique of traditional historical accounts which is exemplified in his enquiry into the construction of 'the backward pupil' during the period 1870–1914 through an exploration of contemporary documents and commentaries. Copeland's study provides a challenge to simplistic versions of the historical development of education systems and traditional accounts of the development of special education as rational and humanitarian.

Hurt's study of the growth of special education (Hurt, 1988) which links the history of the workhouse as a site of care and control of the frail and dispossessed with the growth of special education, argues that 'pioneers of education' were motivated by a desire for social order and cost effectiveness – 'keeping beggars off the street and the indigent out of the workhouse – as well as a 'genuine concern for the socially, physically and mentally disadvantaged'.

Some historical accounts, while being couched within apparently traditional frameworks and terms of reference, are informed by possible alternative narratives. Of particular interest is Pritchard's rich and detailed study 'Education and the Handicapped 1760–1960' (Pritchard, 1963) which, as well as extending historical and analytical understanding, also provides insights into contemporary 'progressive' assumptions and thinking surrounding special education. In the preface Pritchard explains:

> During the nineteenth century and part of the twentieth the children now known as physically handicapped and educationally sub-normal were termed physically defective and mentally defective; the schools that they and the blind and the deaf attended were frequently called institutions; the education they received bore the name of instruction. In the interest of historical accuracy the nineteenth century terms have therefore been used when dealing with that period, and reference is made to the change of nomenclature when it occurs. Indeed it is the story of the advance in opinion and outlook from 1760 to 1960, which brought about the change from instruction to education, from institution to school, and from mentally defective to educationally sub-normal, that the book sets out to tell. (Pritchard, 1963, vii–viii)

Would 'effective' history tell a different story to the one outlined by Pritchard? He draws attention to the importance of terminology and its embeddedness in particular social-historical contexts; in spite of the statement made on the book's dust cover that 'The integration of the handicapped into, and their acceptance by, society is one of the fundamental aims of workers on their behalf', Pritchard's own use of terminology would today be regarded as oppressive and demeaning. It is interesting to reflect on the possible constructions in future periods of the contemporary language of 'special needs' and labels such as 'severe', or 'moderate', 'learning difficulties', 'EBD' and 'autistic' in England or *'handicapé' leger, moyen* or *profond* in France. A further point of interest is the assumption of an 'advance in opinion and outlook' towards disabled people in England since 1760, a view which subscribes to the model of uninterrupted progress across the 'eras'. But as Safford and Safford comment:

> Successive eras of extermination, ridicule, asylum, and education are usually identified, but ... extermination, ridicule, and asylum have not disappeared. The horrors of systematic extermination under the nazi regime continue to be revealed and infanticide, considered a sin in the Middle Ages, continues, even in industrialized nations ... as when surgical correction of gastrointestinal complications, otherwise routinely provided, has been withheld from newborns with Downs syndrome. Although denial of medical treatment constitutes unlawful discrimination, debate continues over ... issues of 'who shall survive'. (Safford and Safford, 1996, p. 3)

These observations raise issues surrounding the deadly paradox of the co-existence of official policies apparently endorsing 'inclusion' in ordinary schools while at the same time medical intervention to save lives may be refused.

There appears to be little historical work in the area of disability and special education which draws on the lives and voices of disabled people themselves. One exception is the book 'Out of sight: childhood and disability 1900–1950' by Humphries and Gordon which traces the history of policy making and institutional practices through insider accounts of childhood experience by disabled people. The book offers a rare insight into the terribly harsh daily lives of children in special schools and institutions during the period. Disabled children were frequently classed as ineducable:

> ... children with physical disabilities ... swelled the numbers who were locked up in asylums and mental handicap hospitals at this time. The numbers of asylums increased from four hundred in the mid-nineteenth century to around 2,000 by 1914. This increase was fuelled by a fear – strongly influenced by the new science of Eugenics – that the mentally disabled were undermining the health and strength of the British nation. They were closely associated in much official thinking with crime, poverty, physical degeneration and sexual immorality. The favoured solution was to segregate them from the rest of society to avoid further contamination. (Humphries and Gordon, 1992, p. 88)

The assumption that physical disability denotes intellectual impairment (and possibly social deviance) is common, and the belief that disabled children belong in segregated settings even more so. These attitudes are often embedded in arguments and discourses surrounding the presumed special and particular 'needs' of disabled children, 'fairness' to other children and economic viability; underpinning these 'concerns' are attitudes based on fear and distrust. As Safford and Safford

(1996) observe, 'vestiges of older beliefs remain', and inform policy making in different arenas.

The quotation above from Humphries and Gordon disrupts the assumption made in many accounts that formal categories of disability and difference and the sites officially designated for these can be taken to represent the actual dispersal and placement of people in different institutions. Examples of physically disabled children being placed in settings for children identified as 'having learning difficulties' or in asylums or hospitals (Humphries and Gordon, 1992), show the apparent arbitrariness of practices involved in processes of sorting, labelling and placing of groups and individuals on the basis of difference.

This 'arbitrariness', however, is only superficial; the processes which underpin the labelling and repartitioning of people across institutions derive from power relations and values in society. They are made possible by the investing of professionals such as doctors, psychologists, 'specialists' of all kinds, with power derived from their disciplines which are accepted or privileged as 'regimes of truth' in which legitimacy and knowledge are joined.

IDENTITY CREATION AND THE POWER OF LABELLING

A different and more powerful critique of processes and practices surrounding labelling concerns not only the technicist argument that they are arbitrary and inefficient, but that they have consequences for both the labellers and the labelled concerning identity, power relations, and social role. Labelling is central to the processes involved in social categorization and stratification. At its core is the belief in the idea of a 'normal human being'. Labels are used both to signal deviance and as organizational mechanisms for managing deviant groups. An extreme example of labelling was the obligatory wearing of the Star of David badge by Jews in Nazi Germany and occupied parts of Europe. Jews were to be 'known' by the sign they wore, and the subject of 'special treatment' which not only segregated them from the rest of the community but removed them definitively through extermination. Labels frequently entail a kind of literal removal or separation and are thus part of spatializing processes of exclusion. At the same time they also name certain individuals and groups as 'other' while conferring on the labellers (frequently 'professionals' such as doctors, psychologists, therapists) the power to name. Finally, labelling achieves a hegemonic consensus – reassuring to the majority – of what it means to be 'a normal human being'. Becker rightly argued that deviance is socially created, not in the sense that 'social factors' are the *cause* of deviant action but that:

> social groups create deviance by making the rules whose infraction constitutes deviance, and by applying those rules to particular people and labeling them as outsiders. From this point of view, deviance is *not* a quality of the act the person commits, but rather a consequence of the application by others of rules and sanctions to an 'offender'. The deviant is one to whom that label has been successfully applied; deviant behaviour is behaviour that people so label. (Becker, 1963, p. 9)

In contrast with traditional humanitarian accounts, the history of special education in France and in England may be seen as the history of the categorization of differences and their transformation into deviance by powerful professionals and institutions. The use of predominantly medical and psychological deficit labels such as 'subnormal', 'severely subnormal' 'language disordered' reinforced:

> ... the perceived inadequacies and pathology of the individual child' (Apple, 1990), psychological notions of intelligence and intelligence testing, and the construction of definitions of 'ability' and 'need', confirmed the disabled pupil's demeaned status. (Barnes *et al.*, 1999, p. 105)

Thus, the humanitarian explanation of special education as being concerned with doing good is intricately bound up with the creation of deviants and their social exclusion through labelling mechanisms.

CONCLUSION

The examples given in this chapter of the way in which historical events and processes affect perceptions and opportunities concerning marginalized groups, support the argument that the complexity and paradoxes of social life cannot be expressed through a recitation of legislation, government reports and public records, the setting up or closing down of institutions, the development of formal assessment procedures and the introduction of training programmes. Nevertheless, this material – the formal, public facade of historical development – is important in providing *one* set of frameworks for understanding social change. But this framework needs to be tested out through the study of other material from a variety of sources – the history of town planning and the design of buildings, representations in novels and films of disabled people, the study of paintings and other historically situated material, and – most of all – the lives of people themselves as they are expressed through their own accounts. It is the connections and discontinuities between these different levels and arenas and the 'received wisdom' of traditional accounts which open up new questions and issues concerning hegemonic assumptions about the 'humanitarian' role of special education and the positioning and experience of disabled people through institutional practices. The growing interest in researching the positioning and exclusion of disabled people through, for example, representations in films and the media, and the built environment, the effects of legislation and embedded social practices, are part of a wider concern to understand and challenge existing dominant accounts and interpretations of social ordering. These concerns are inseparable from historical enquiry and reflexivity about how historical knowledge is constituted and evaluated.

CHAPTER 5

SPACE, PLACE AND EXCLUSION:
CONSTRUCTING ALTERNATIVE HISTORIES

In Chapter 4 some arguments were put forward about the need to challenge 'available social myths' as well as to evaluate, contest or expand on traditional interpretations of the history of special education by drawing on different materials and disciplines. Some of the material discussed in this chapter relates to processes which are closely associated with what Imrie describes as 'the delineation of oppressive spaces' (Imrie, 1996, p. 12). It explores the struggles which arise over representation of difference and the claiming of identity. The discussion involves beginning to sketch out some possible frameworks and angles from which to explore issues of space, place and identity. It seeks, tentatively, to open up questions through examples of different kinds of struggles over representation and identity. The chapter also considers some possible interpretations of paintings from different historical periods from the perspective of contemporary issues around the representation of marginalised others.

THE SPACE OF SOCIAL REPRODUCTION

In thinking about some of the ideas in the previous chapters, a number of critical questions have emerged such as: what is it about the organization of space in a particular school which constitutes Lefebvre's (1972) 'space of social reproduction'? And what are 'the spatial relations of the body with ideology and social practice,'? How are these realised through housing, urbanization and 'public' space, architecture and art? What response can be made to Lefebvre's call for:

> ... a new kind of spatial imagination capable of confronting the past in a new way and reading its less tangible secrets off the template of its spatial structures – body, cosmos, city ... (Jameson, 1991, pp. 364–5)

This endeavour, linked to the need to deconstruct texts such as paintings and architecture, is how I understand the task of discovering alternative (or at least *more detailed*) landscapes and the task of constructing 'effective' history. I do not expect to answer the questions raised in the previous paragraphs but they will serve as a prompt in exploring briefly the possible contributions of architecture, planning and painting in the construction of a different kind of historical understanding and in making connections with contemporary social relations, events and processes. Such an exploration is intended to illuminate and inform an analysis and understanding of the spatial dimensions in the ordering and production of difference through special education institutions and practices.

In examining the *history* of special education in France and in England and the different sources I have drawn on, I have been conscious of the multiple *possible* 'histories', and of those already produced – historical texts, images, buildings or accounts already available for consideration. Importantly, all of these are uniquely and socially constructed through an infinite number of possible relationships, media, metaphor and interpretations.

The task of presenting a historical context for this study, is inseparable from my own understanding about how knowledge is constituted, an important part of which is linked to my positionality in relation to the particular sources and experiences I am drawing on. During the course of my research I have encountered many 'gaps', contradictions and silences. How am I to interpret, for example, the almost total absence of the perspectives of disabled people in 'the literature' in which dominant accounts of the history of disability and education have been canonized?

The absence of disabled children from both formal historical accounts and artistic representation confirm their historical physical exclusion and repudiation by society, in many eras and many cultural settings. The dominant history of the development of special education in France and England closes round that absence and that silence, becoming embedded in collective understanding of 'who disabled people are'.

In raising these issues, I am thinking particularly about the Foucauldian notion of discourse (Foucault, 1974, 1982) and the many texts through which discourses make themselves known in a multitude of ways. The idea of text and texts and the ways in which these are fragmented through the experiences and representations of different people (as actors, authors, artists and commentators of all sorts) inform my own understanding of what has happened and how things are as they are. The related notion of deconstruction as dismantling and displacing 'solid' and familiar structures (or texts) to reveal their 'manifold significations' (Soltan, 1996) is an integral part of exploring the multiple levels and arenas through which social relations are configured.

The task of deconstructing architecture, buildings and the organization of towns and landscapes of all kinds is complex. Derrida describes his struggle with the idea that architecture was much more than mere representation:

> ... when I first met, I won't say 'Deconstructive architecture' but the De-constructive discourse on architecture, I was rather puzzled and suspicious. I thought at first that this was an analogy, a displaced discourse, and something more analogical than rigorous. And then ... I realised that on the contrary, the most efficient way of putting Deconstruction to work was by going through art and architecture. As you know, Deconstruction is not simply a matter of discourse or a matter of displacing the semantic content of the discourse, its conceptual structure or whatever. Deconstruction *goes through* certain social and political structures, meeting with resistance and displacing institutions as it does so. I think that in these forms of art, and in any architecture,

> to deconstruct traditional sanctions – theoretical, philosophical, cultural
> – effectively, you have to displace ... I would say 'solid' structures, not
> only in the sense of material structures, but 'solid' in the sense of cultural,
> pedagogical, political, economic structures. (Derrida, 1989, p. 8)

In the context of this study these ideas can be interpreted, for example, as meaning that special schools, asylums and workhouses do not merely *stand for* or represent a particular set of social relations, values, beliefs and practices, (because if this were the case there would be no 'resistance', no struggle), but as playing an active and crucial role in their construction. Special institutions are material places, solid structures which actively contain and control people. They fulfill both a physical, bureaucratic and spatializing role and a social and ideological role in producing and reproducing ideas, values, cultures and economies which, far from being ephemeral, are fundamentally implicated in the ordering and management of social relations. Perhaps the fear of the workhouse in the 19th century (the idea of which was still an oppressive reality in the first half of twentieth century in England) related to the breakdown in ordinary, familiar social relations, the crossing over into the realm of the excluded other as much as to the material, solid structures which housed, contained and regulated social relations and coercive production.

The use of the term 'deconstruction' relates to the complexity of meanings and different levels of interpretation associated with 'works' such as buildings or paintings. It relates to their embodiment of power relations and social organization and how they produce, reproduce, intervene and are present in social and political processes, as well as their symbolic or metaphorical value. It refers also to the struggles and dichotomies which work their way through the physical, spatial and social organization of – say – an institution such as a modern prison ('rehabilitation through exclusion', 'protection by punishment') or special school ('care and segregation', 'identification and labelling'). These struggles and contradictions challenge the traditionally sanctioned image of the world as rational, developmental, progressive.

Space, place and claiming struggles around identity

The histories of buildings and town planning open up the possibility of constructing alternative historical accounts to traditional social history; sometimes these accounts harmonize, sometimes they seem to be contradictory. One reason for this is that they are particularly and literally concerned with spatialization. In considering buildings and their social political role in processes of inclusion and exclusion, I have focused – not on the dominant spaces used by the general throng (or 'the mainstream'), but on '... the margins and the marginal use of space by those who have, in various ways, been located on the fringes of society.' (Hetherington, 1997, p. 4 and see Shields, 1991). It is these 'outer sites', which are removed from the common gaze, which may provide new perspectives on dominant historical accounts and understandings. As Harvey suggests, such explorations:

... should help to clarify the thorny problem of 'otherness' and 'difference' because territorial place-based identity ... is one of the most pervasive bases for both progressive political mobilizations...as well as for reactionary exclusionary politics. (Harvey, 1996, p. 209).

The idea that spaces of exclusion can form arenas for radical political movements is exciting and challenges traditional assumptions about how power is distributed and exercised. In 1991 sections of the population of the Blackbird Leys Estate in Oxford – at the time, one of the most stigmatized estates in England – became involved (some as performers, the majority as on-lookers) in 'hotting' events in which young people performed stunts in stolen cars. From the outside, there was a sense of pride and community-identity being asserted and this came over clearly in a television programme made by a local resident in which he denounced the lack of facilities for young people living on the estate and questioned the role of the police in their treatment of members of the Blackbird Leys Community. Other examples of sustained progressive movements which emerged from situations of exclusion and oppression can be found in the anti-apartheid movement and the mobilization against internment of asylum seekers such as those at Campsfield in Oxfordshire, or the movement of 'sans papiers' in France.

Shakespeare (1993) has argued that there has been a great deal of academic work which has focused on 'identifying' disabled people which takes '... disability to refer to medically assessable impairment and functional limitation' in contrast to,

> ... identity in a political sense: with identifying as part of an oppressed group, with part of a cultural minority.
>
> This process of identification seems the reverse of ... 'blaming the victim' because it is about converting private woes into public wrongs. It is about 'the victim' refusing the label, and instead focusing attention on the structural causes of victimization. It is about the subversion of stigma: taking a negative appellation and converting it into a badge of pride. (Shakespeare, 1993, p. 253).

The claiming of identity, then, is a political act, a celebration of the self, a show of power. For this reason, people who openly identify themselves with, or as members of, oppressed groups are deeply threatening. An extraordinary example of this paradoxical show of strength by identification with negative or deviant images and life styles is that of the guerrilla artists of New York City of the 1970s and 1980s. The apparently sudden appearance in the city of graffiti, in which car and subway murals were created as new and challenging texts, overlaying the 'legitimate' ones of consumerism, transport systems and capital, represented a political, cultural and creative movement. This movement was regarded by those in power as an 'attack on society' (Miller, 1993) and they launched a campaign to eradicate the art work and arrest the artists. At the heart of the murals and graffiti was a claim to identities commonly denigrated or marginalized by mainstream north American society – African-American, Puerto Rican, Latino and white youth gathered in culturally mixed groups to transform public spaces and put their image on them. In doing so, they created an art movement which celebrated the power of the individual and of cultural diversity. Crucial to this creativity was the impact of images and voices moving between and within spaces to which they did not 'belong' and publicly owning identities which were regarded as inferior or discordant. As one graffiti artist, Phase 2, commented:

> We're not living in an atmosphere that tells us to love our brother, and harmonise with everybody, or teaches us how to deal with somebody that speaks Spanish or Arabic or something or another, because where I come from, you judge people's personalities depending on where they come from. You don't judge them as people. You say, 'Well, what do you expect from a (so and so), he's this colour, or from that part of town ...'. Yet this culture brings all of the cultures here together as one. Maybe if this art was not from a 'ghetto', there would be a different approach to the art from our society. If it wasn't just a bunch of kids who weren't expected to make anything with their lives anyway. All this art came up from the gutter. This art brings the masses together. (Phase 2, quoted in Miller, 1993, p. 30)

The artists themselves often had to overcome prejudices within their own families toward members of other communities. But this movement which 'brought all cultures together' was deeply threatening to those governing the city because it brought onto the streets and into people's daily lives a challenge to prejudices and stereotypes and existing distributions of power and it presented a transgressing, semi-organized show of resistance which defiled private property and brought 'the ghetto' into new spaces.

Groups who are ascribed one identity in public consciousness because of perceptions about a shared characteristic (and one which is commonly regarded as 'undesirable' such as deafness) may be regarded with fear and hysteria by other 'ordinary folk'. Take, for example, the case of 58 deaf people who were evicted from their holiday chalets at a Butlin's camp in North Wales in 1998. After a disturbance in a night-club and complaints from 'other holiday makers', all the deaf people staying at the holiday camp were evicted, although there was no evidence that they had anything to do with the alleged disturbance. Security guards evicted deaf holiday makers, including families, with the words 'Out! Out! Out! All Deaf out!' Claiming aggressive behaviour and sexual harassment of 'other holiday makers' by 'a group of male and female deaf people from different parts of the country', Butlin's agreed that not all the deaf people were involved and that they had made 'separate bookings' but defended their actions in evicting all 58 deaf people on the grounds that, 'It was clear during their stay that they constituted one large group who had planned to meet at the centre' (*The Independent,* 25.9.98).

The common 'identity' of deafness ascribed to 58 people who were constructed as an organized, disruptive group of undesirable others by 'other holiday makers' and Butlin's 'management' and their eviction from the holiday centre, can be explained in terms of the fears and panic aroused when boundaries are transgressed by those who are assigned identities and to places 'elsewhere' on the grounds of their perceived difference. The two examples – of the eviction of 58 deaf people on holiday and of the oppressive responses to the invasion of spaces by youths who were deemed to belong elsewhere, support the argument that identities are socially homogenized and spatialized. In both examples the construction of identity and the challenge to those constructions are pivotal factors in the struggles which took place. Shakespeare (1993) stresses the crucial role in political struggle of oppressed groups 'doing it for themselves'. He links the action taken by disabled people in demonstrating about inaccessible public transport to other forms of segregation such as the targeting of segregated buses by the civil rights movement.

In Chapter 7 I shall explore some situations in which the same kinds of attitudes and processes played a crucial role in struggles over the exclusion of disabled children and young people from an ordinary school in England.

The power of buildings

Ware's (2000) observation that 'special education is a place' rather than 'a service' is both seductive and provocative. After all, the traditional history says that special education has been for disabled children and young people; it's purpose has been to 'help' or 'provide' *for* them. As soon as this view is challenged by the statement that 'special education is a place' a number of questions are raised about the embodi- ment of relationships through processes of spatialization and the constructions of particular sites for particular purposes. These sites are often buildings, placed in specific relationships to communities and associated with particular social practices, identities and power relations.

During my field work in England the question of the use of space in school and perceptions about and struggles over particular spaces emerged very frequently. For example, teachers and parents at Freelands consistently raised the issue of the erosion of the space available for students to circulate. At Hillbank School, teachers and governors insisted that the creation of a special unit for disabled students would encroach on space which was used by 'their' children. This opened up unexpected questions and angles on the embededness and reproduction of social relations and identities through the identification and use of spaces for particular purposes by particular people. It was when issues surrounding the reduction of social and educational exclusion of disabled students were raised in meetings or interviews that the struggles over space emerged most urgently. These issues raise questions about the values which underpin and work themselves through the design and organization of buildings. Thus, buildings which are not physically accessible to all disabled people actually bar them from entry on the grounds of difference just as powerfully as systems of apartheid have debarred entry and participation on the basis of race and skin colour.

Imrie points out that while the built environment is generally inaccessible to people with a range of impairments, the national accessibility standards which local authorities have statutory responsibilities to enforce, are limited, only requiring:

... developers to provide 'reasonable' access for wheelchair users and for

> people with vision impairments and loss of hearing. In addition, local
> authorities often use a range of informal, non-statutory and/or voluntary
> mechanisms, to try and persuade developers to sensitize buildings to disabled
> people's needs. Their use will often depend on local political support, and
> officers' willingness to step beyond the boundaries of statutory regulations
> and guide-lines. (Imrie, 2000, p. 9)

The degree of accessibility of the built environment, therefore, depends on attitudes, values and practices of those involved in policy making at different levels. The discourse deployed relating to 'reasonableness' is itself a mode of policy making, in that it implicitly attempts to persuade and intimidate by suggesting that some demands – including, for example, that children attend their local schools as a right – are 'unreasonable'. Chapter Seven examines a number of examples of discourse used as weaponry in struggles over space and resources.

In many instances, while buildings may be apparently physically accessible, once inside other modes of segregation and oppression kick in. In one school we visited during the research in the North East of England mentioned earlier (Armstrong and Booth, 1994; Booth 1995), some of the disabled young people who were 'being integrated' into an ordinary school could not attend lessons and activities above the ground floor because there were no lifts. They had to stay indoors in 'their' resource base during break times because the playground supervisors didn't feel able to 'look after' them; students using wheel chairs had to have their lunch before the rest of the school in order that they 'didn't cause a safety hazard in the dining hall', and those who had assistance with eating and drinking were not allowed into the dining room as it 'wouldn't be very nice for the other students'. Disabled students were unable to circulate freely around the school because of the presence of large doors which separated the resource base from the rest of the school and which could not be opened mechanically.

In many buildings 'disabled toilets' are separate from 'normal' toilets for 'normal' Men and Women. Disabled people have to share a 'disabled' public lavatory, regardless of gender, sustaining stereotypes by treating disabled people as undifferentiated, asexual 'others'. This practice constructs the 'otherness' of disabled people at the same time as appearing to provide for their specific 'needs' (Armstrong, 1999b). Lavatories in schools designated for use by disabled students and teachers often open out onto communal spaces, including classrooms, denying users ordinary levels of privacy. The DfEE (1996) School Premises Regulations, Circular number 10/96 specifies that schools should have separate washrooms for male and female pupils of 8 years and older, but that 'exceptions may be made for facilities for disabled users' (DfEE, 1996). The ordinary requirements of personal dignity, privacy and a degree of comfort are dispensed with in the interests of the efficient use of space and resources, constructing oppressive social relations and identities (Armstrong, 1999b).

Buildings, internally and externally, and their situatedness in the environment in relation to other spaces and places create social divisions and identities through spatialization. Just as some people are labelled as 'deviant' or different, places take on deviant or 'outside' identities. Shields argues that the classification of people 'by the places they come from' has misleadingly been studied as 'pathologically irrational forms of behaviour' when, in fact, such classifications are a form of 'everyday knowledge ... (which) betrays a systematic disposition towards the world ... coded into the framework of common sense'(Shields, 1991, p. 11).

PLACE, IDENTITY AND POWER

People are categorized, not only by where they come from, but also where they go to, or are placed by more powerful others. Disabled children do not *come from* special schools; they are sent there by professionals and politicians. The existence of special buildings and sites removed from the ordinary life of the community has sustained the social myth that disabled people belong elsewhere and are other.

Slee's account of his own biography as it intermeshes with a particular historical and cultural context (quoted in Chapter Four) exemplifies the argument that places, sites, buildings 'on the margins' are powerful in focusing the imagination on mythical others. Buildings, such as special schools, asylums and factories are more than a set of metaphors *for* social processes, identities and power relations. On the contrary, they are organically part of their production and reproduction. Buildings provide precious historical material through which we can try to understand the past from a number of fresh angles by allowing us to get beneath the brickwork and explore social organization. Far from being neutral and functional in a purely material sense, buildings play an essential role as 'spaces of social reproduction' and in regulating social and bodily relationships. These insights open up further possibilities for exploring (or confronting) the past in ways which disturb the traditional history of disability, 'provision' and the humanitarian 'march of progress'. A particular opening is suggested in terms of the connections which can be made between the organization and control of people (in the context of this study, particularly disabled people) through buildings in different social and historical contexts. Planning and architecture create landscapes which both manage and represent people and social relationships. Parallels can be drawn between the role played by the curriculum in schools in managing and differentiating students and the transmission of cultural values and practices and the built environment which plays an integral part in social ordering and governance. The existence of separate physical places for the housing of elderly people, for example, both allows for and legitimates segregated collective management as well as fixing the notion and the image of the 'old people's home' in the collective consciousness.

While buildings both create particular representations and mythologies associated with their occupants, as well as exerting physical control over them, pictures, on the other hand, have a more purely symbolic role in terms of representation and meaning. The following section discusses the role of pictures in representing identities and informing and raising questions about the past and throwing light on the present.

Picturing difference

References to, or images of, impairment or difference were rare in twentieth century western societies, except in contexts in which impairment was 'what was being advertised'. In this sense, images of disability are located in 'places on the margin' which both participate in the process of exclusion and represent disabled people as deviant others. Paradoxically, the positioning of disabled people as outsiders through the media, is frequently accompanied by a discourse of social cohesion and acceptance of the 'he's just like us really' or 'isn't she brave and don't we all admire her' variety.

From the point of view of the traditional story of special education in which responses to impairment have become more 'humane', it is surely a contradiction that disabled people are almost certainly 'less visible' in ordinary life and in the media (except as 'disabled people', often played by non disabled actors) than in previous historical periods.

Drawing on Scull (1979) Oliver and Barnes observe that:

> Until the seventeenth century, despite the harshness of living conditions, most people were included in their village communities even if they were subjected to controlling measures such as the pillar and the stocks and even ridicule. Exclusion from the community was unusual and those people rejected by their families without resources relied on the haphazard and often ineffectual tradition of Christian charity for subsistence. People with 'severe' impairments were usually herded together in one of the very small hospitals in which were gathered 'the poor, the sick and the bedridden'. The ethos of these establishments was ecclesiastical rather than medical. (Oliver and Barnes, 1998, p. 27–8)

Following the Poor Law Act of 1601 each parish was made responsible for maintaining its paupers which included the old and the sick as well as 'able-bodied' people for whom work was to be provided. Thus the care of 'the senile, the incurably ill, the blind, the cripples, and the maimed' became primarily 'a secular rather than a religious responsibility' (Scull, 1979, p. 22). This laid the basis for the establishment of the role of the state in terms of the designation, segregation and control of people deemed incapable of looking after themselves, or the provision of 'support' to their families (Mencher, 1967; Scull, 1979).

On a trip to the Louvre Museum in Paris in 1999, I found myself looking out for images relating to the spacing and placing of disabled people in different historical periods. Starting with the beginning of the sixteenth century, I came across the famous painting *The Ship of Fools* painted by Hieronymus Bosch (circa 1500) and referred to by Foucault in *Madness and Civilization*. Indeed, the painting is vividly present in Foucault's description of:

> ... a strange 'drunken boat' that glides along the calm rivers of the Rhineland and the Flemish canals.
> ... for they *did* exist, these boats that conveyed their insane cargo from town to town. Madmen (in the middle ages) then led an easy wondering

existence. The town drove them outside their limits; they were allowed to wander in the open countryside, when not entrusted to a group of merchants or pilgrims ... Frequently they were handed over to boatmen ... Often the cities of Europe must have seen these 'ships of fools' approaching their harbors. (Foucault, 1971, p. 7–8)

Bearing in mind that the medically based categorization of disabled people did not begin to be significantly developed until the late eighteenth century and that prior to that period people with impairments of all kinds were part of the much broader collective category of 'unfortunates' (Safford and Safford, 1996), it is very probable that some of those 'handed over to boatmen' would have been disabled or would today have been among those people categorized as 'having learning difficulties'.

The picture depicts, not misery and oppression, but a scene of festive disorder and merry-making. Nevertheless, the practice of removing 'deviant' people from ordinary social life to places 'elsewhere' is resonant of practices which are embedded in social and political responses to difference and this is still the case at the beginning of the twenty-first century. The examples of the 'bussing' of black students to white areas during the 1960s in the United States, the continued ferrying of disabled children in taxis and special buses between their homes and segregated special schools, and the removal and dispersal of groups of asylum seekers from urban areas in the UK, are evidence that the removal of people on the grounds of difference is a deeply embedded social practice.

Another picture in the Louvre *The Beggars* painted by Pieter Bruegal, the Elder at around 1568, presents a group of physically impaired people, grouped together in the foreground. They are disabled and appear to be supporting themselves on sticks or simple crutches and have what look like feathers attached to their clothes (possibly a sign to warn others that they are lepers or to show that they have been granted the right to beg). Two have part of their faces covered; others are crying out (possibly asking for alms). In the background on either side of the picture are the large walls which either enclose or exclude the group (are they being contained or put outside?). In the distance is an open gateway which suggests that the beggars will not try to cross this boundary; they are in their 'proper place' to which they acquiesce. Moving quietly away behind the group is a figure carrying an empty metal dish, probably a woman – possibly a nun. The picture expresses anguish and tumult. There is horror, but not in the representation of the beggars themselves, but at their positioning as excluded others. The clamour of their voices and the clacking of their sticks on the ground contrast shockingly with the quiet movement of the figure in the background whose form suggests both that of the carer and that of the keeper. Is the dish she is carrying for food or for collecting up coins received from passers by? This painting depicts a particular social response to impairment (possibly as a result of leprosy) in mediaeval Europe, although it is not clear if the group are inside a leper house or if they are begging outside the city gates. Without intending to ascribe particular intentions to the artist (which would be meaningless), my reading of the picture challenges the charity, medical and personal tragedy models of disability, urging an alternative social and political significance. Again the picture reminds me of the work of David Hevey (e.g. in Hevey, 1992) in which disabled people claim their individuality and dignity, contesting stereotypical imagery evoking fear, pity and prejudice and, most of all, claiming their space. Through his work, Hevey has mounted a powerful assault on traditional lines of demarcation which place disabled people beyond the periphery of the normal. He describes charity advertising – which uses dramatic or pathetic pictures of disabled people (or other oppressed groups such as homeless people) – as ' ... the calling card of an inaccessible society which systematically segregates disabled people' (Hevey, 1992, p. 24). 'Charities promote a brand not to buy, but to buy your distance from' (Hevey, 1992, p. 35).

Hevey's work challenges traditional paradigms in which the subjects are 'posed' in positions which make them look attractive, powerful or cute. In keeping with his revulsion at the stereotyping of disabled people (and people in general) and regarding the individual life histories of his subjects as crucial in constructing their portraits, he encourages people to talk about themselves and their experiences. This is part of the task of constructing an individual and meaningful image. He sees his work as a ' ... journey of representation in which the cross-identity between myself and the people whom I have photographed has been the paramount connection' (Hevey, 1992, p. 93), acknowledging the importance of construction as a collaborative project. Hevey reverses the ordinary relationship between portrait and viewer, in that the gaze of the person depicted, such as his portrait of Ian, challenges and draws in the regard of the viewer, juxtaposing the expected distribution of power in ways which are both exhilarating and disturbing.

Inheriting 'the sins of the fathers...'
Hung in the exhibition '1900: Art at the Crossroads' at the Royal Academy, London (January 2000) two paintings (mentioned in Chapter Four), *Sad Inheritance* painted by Joaquín Sorolla y Bastida in 1899 and *Inheritance* painted by Edvard Munch between 1903–1905 were of particular significance in the context of this discussion. In different ways, they provide revealing and unique insights into the historical period in which they were painted as well as suggesting important connections with the struggles and contradictions of the present period.

At first sight, the subject matter of *Sad Inheritance* and *The Beggars* appears remarkably similar and both paintings suggest a concern with social realism, although separated by nearly three and a half centuries. This observation is of interest for a number of reasons. Firstly, because it contests the traditional view of society as becoming progressively more humane and of social attitudes and social structures becoming increasingly concerned with issues of social equality. Secondly, because the figures in both pictures are positioned as outsiders, existing on the margins. Thirdly, there is a clearly discernible carer, or 'minder', in both images (but these are represented very differently). Fourthly, the pictures share an unusual feature: they include images of disabled people.

The contrasts between the two pictures are even more striking. In *The Beggars*, the group of disabled people are foregrounded and represented as a cohesive and powerful force. In the later picture the figures of disabled boys are naked, weak and elicit pity. There appears to be a malodorous concern, too, on the artist's part, that as many impairments as possible should be represented in this chilling scene. Most striking of all are the cold hand of the priest as he grips the arm of the abject figure bent in front of him and the contrast between the power and authority invested in his height and dress and the naked submission of the staggering bodies of the naked boys under his care and control. In contrast, in *The Beggars* it is the group of disabled people who appear powerful and unbowed, in spite of their apparent exclusion/confinement; the carer is an ambiguous, more humble looking figure in the background.

The picture, *Inheritance* by Munch, depicts a woman loosely holding on her lap, but positioned away from her, a baby who, we are to suppose from the splashes of red on the body and the blurred brush strokes which could be taken for stunted or deformed limbs, is sickly and tainted. The face of the woman is bitter, disappointed and hostile; her clothes, face and whole body are shadowed in dark colours. In contrast, the baby has an open, expectant bright face with sparkling eyes; the child is painted as lying in a pool of light, suggesting innocence and purity. The title of the picture, and the one by Bastida, suggest that sickness, deformity, impairment are handed down through generations as punishment for the sins of the parents or of earlier generations. In the Spanish picture, the presence of the priest suggests 'God's will'. In the painting by Munch, the image is altogether less idealized: it suggests the social consequences of (probably), syphilis and – by extension – a moral agenda. Both pictures connect with current images and concerns. *Sad Inheritance* has its counterpart in much of the advertising of the contemporary charity industry in which children are presented as being weak and in need of care from competent others as a result of failed families, poverty or disability. The other picture, *Inheritance*, presages current debate and stigmatizing practices associated with 'HIV babies' although in England pictures in the media are more likely to represent 'foreign' babies and children who are 'HIV positive', rarely 'English' ones.

One issue which has struck me forcibly in writing this section is the recognition that the 'same' subject matter can disappear from one medium, such as painting, only to re-emerge, located in different media – such as publicity posters – in a later period.

Paintings, like other landscapes, are mediated through the experiences and values of the beholder; they do not have meaning without an audience. This audience will interpret them in different ways, each individual bringing to bear their own particular history and perspective and set of values. However, Jonathon Rée, drawing on Merlau-Ponty, writes:

> a successful painting will not be an account of how the mountain happens to look to us subjectively; nor will it be how the mountain is in itself objectively. The painting will discuss how the mountain manages to be as it looks to us, and how it manages to look to us as it is in itself. It will investigate, in other words, how it is constituted as a reality in our experience. The painting

puts questions to the mountain: as Maurice Merlau-Ponty said, it 'asks to
reveal the means ... by which it comes to be a mountain before our eyes'
(Merleau-Ponty, 1964, p. 28–9)

The painting reveals a truth, but not the kind of truth that we contribute to
the solution of a scientific problem. (Rée, 1999, p. 363)

Practice, representation and knowledge

Buildings, towns, landscapes of all kinds, are all forms of text or discourse. They
are constructions which reveal truths in the sense that they show a part of social life
(either 'in action', or as a testimony of social life in the past, often both) or many
layers of social life at the same time. A busy street or a classroom, a dole queue
or a disused mine, a nineteenth century warehouse converted to luxury 'river-side'
flats ('canal-side' is less marketable), a government document on 'inclusion' – these
are all discourses which are socially constructed out of time, place, community
and practice set against a wider framework of economic and cultural conditions.
As Stiker argues:

> ... social constructions are as important as effective practices in representing
> society. Even more: these representations of a phenomenon are just as much
> part of reality as 'what happens' and ... discourse is just as important for so-
> cial reality. Moreover, discourse often differs from the praxis of the moment,
> but at one time or another informs it even more than earlier praxis. There is
> a false opposition between discourse and the real. The realism of common
> sense is not so real as one thinks. Discourse is nowhere else than in the real.
> Is praxis itself anything but part of the discursive? (Stiker, 1999, p. 73)

The relationship between praxis and discourse provides a key focus for Chapter
Seven which considers this relationship from a number of different angles. It is a
powerful reason for wanting to try and understand processes and struggles from the
perspective of different people, rather than accepting a particular set of accounts
which are neatly fitted together. There is ambivalence. There is contradiction and
hesitation. There is incompleteness and contingency, and the blurring of all these
does create a kind of truth.

The paintings and buildings discussed here have been presented under my gaze
and through my interpretative framework. In this sense, the same argument put
forward in Chapter Three concerning the role of the researcher in constructing the
world she is researching and in interpreting her findings through her own history,
experience and values, may also be related to responses to paintings, buildings,
novels, films, shop windows or whatever. To quote Skeggs (1994) again, '... our
social location, our situatedness in the world will influence how we speak, see, hear
and know'. Or, the interpretation of the creativity of others – as Okely observed
in relation to ethnography – '... involves so much of the self that it is impossible
to reflect upon it fully by extracting the self' (Okely, 1992, p. 8).

How much is the 'self' invested with dominant values and constructions in any
particular context? To what extent does the 'knowledge' created by representations

in the media, and by the organisation of difference in terms of dominant social structures and relations, infect the 'self'? Valentine (2001) explains in his study of the representations of deafness in the Japanese media, how the portrayal of particular examples of otherness can become fashionable at particular moments, creating a market for particular 'others'. Particular forms of difference become commodified:

> Thus in the early 1990s there was a 'gay boom' in Japan, in which film, television and popular magazines showed considerable interest in the supposed lives of gay men (Valentine, 1997). By the mid-1990s this boom had faded, to be replaced by a fashion for representing certain kinds of disability, particularly learning disabilities and deafness. (Valentine, 2001, p. 707)

Valentine explores the construction of deafness by, usually, hearing actors and directors for, primarily, hearing audiences:

> ...the deaf character is conceived as dramatically vulnerable ... through the ubiquitous assumption that speech and voice are absent: this avoids the problem of hearing actors impersonating deaf speech, and constructs the character as doubly disabled in a hearing society. Not only is the character contrived to be unable to sense danger, but also unable to communicate it readily to others – the hearing characters who are endowed with the ability to help. The exaggerated silence of the deaf character contributes to what is regarded as their disabled communication – a disability within them that is seen as trapping them in themselves and from which their struggle affords much of the dramatic impulse of the narrative. The deaf character at times of crisis is shown frantically trying to communicate with the hearing, to the extent of dramatically breaking out of the constructed world of silence through sounds that never otherwise escape. The enactment of strained sounds of distress conveys the tremendous barrier that has been crossed, and the practical and emotional extremity of the situation. Climactic voicing confirms the normal silence of the deaf character as primarily indicative of an intrinsic quality of character, which can be breached in extreme situations. (Valentine, 2001, p. 721)

In this example, a constructed 'deaf character' is manipulated and harnessed to the demands for ever-more sensation and emotion and the voracious appetite of the box office. The fact that such characterizations are bogus remains largely unchallenged because they confirm the 'knowledge' of deafness shared by the hearing audience, although Valentine also warns against constructing 'deaf people as victims not only in the dramas, but of the dramas' on the grounds that some visibility may be preferable to none at all. But, as Shakespeare argues:

> ... there is a need for broader debate about disabling representations. While the common problems of stereotypes have been identified, there is less consensus about what constitutes a 'positive image' (Shakespeae, 1999, p. 172).

The question remains: what is the relationship between dominant representations, the 'self' and the act of interpretation? In making judgments about representations in film and the media, or in assessing particular policies and their presumed effects, we need to take into account our own subjective relationship to dominant values and assumptions, rather than assuming that 'we' are immune from them.

CONCLUSION

A key argument in the chapter is that there are other histories and representations to be discovered through an exploration of a range of materials and sources beyond the kinds of traditional accounts discussed in Chapter Four. I have argued that traditional histories could be explored or challenged through other historically situated material or used to extend existing knowledge. In thinking about a conclusion, however, I am confronted by the numbers of questions that have surfaced through an enquiry focusing on buildings and paintings rather than policy documents. I don't know, at this stage, if I have succeeded in challenging or dislodging 'traditional' historical accounts or dominant representations. However, the histories and the lives of disabled people and social responses to difference lie elsewhere, and are not to be found in histories and representations which present a seamless view of uninterrupted development, pegged to formal policy documents and legislation. This view has been confirmed by insights gained from other vantage points, uncovered in my field work. The next chapter will explore this theme from a different perspective through case studies of four settings based on accounts of different people involved in, or affected by, different levels of policy making.

At this stage I want to recall what I wrote about the relationship of the researcher, and her presence, within the research experience. I wrote:

> This *presence* is concerned as much with the feelings, reflections and responses of the researcher to the unfolding research landscape as it is with the personal and professional histories of the researcher and their influence on her choice of research questions, tools and analytical procedures. As Coffey remarks, 'Emotion is a real research experience and our intellectual autobiography is constructed and reconstructed through social research' (Coffey, 1999, p. 11).

In examining and exploring materials from sources outside the traditional history paradigm the truth of Coffey's statement is highlighted and has raised a number of further questions. To what extent can the history of the architecture of the asylum, the factory and the workhouse in the 18th and 19th centuries be seen as representing a struggle between the rational and the emotional? How is the relationship between the control and administrations by powerful people of disabled people expressed through painting and architecture? How useful has this discussion relating to representation been in exploring issues relating to space, place and social exclusion?

In this chapter, I wanted to try and gain a different handle on my subject, or even shift the boundaries of the subject altogether. I have not 'matched' the material in the chapter with the 'French' story or the 'English' story in Chapter Four. In fact not one French or English painting is mentioned. My purpose, though, was to raise questions about traditional history as a practice, and its 'truthfulness' and limitations, rather than trying to focus just on two national contexts.

In the next chapter the case studies will be used to provide a background to a presentation and discussion of some of the material which I have gathered during my research. They, and the discussion in later chapters, will also be used to continue the task of contesting traditional accounts through people's experiences of policy making and the way they intertwine with 'the sense of place and the politics of space' (Hayden, 1996).

CHAPTER 6

FOUR SETTINGS: DIVIDING SPACES

INTRODUCTION

In Chapter Three I outlined the work I had carried out in four different settings – one English and three French. I am using the term 'setting' to refer to sites with their unique histories, populations, practices and discourses. Only the English setting and one of the French settings are called 'schools'; the others are medically based institutions which incorporate medical treatment, therapy and 'care' as part of the curriculum. All of the French settings had a strong medical presence but the uses and discourses associated with this medical presence differed radically.

My work in the English setting allowed me to attend numerous meetings and to interview many people who were – or had been – connected with the school and its background over a period of three years. In the French contexts, my opportunities were more limited. In the first French setting – an educational 'resource base' in a large hospital, I only had access to the director, M.M. who spoke to me for several hours and showed me around the classroom base and therapy rooms. I spent a mere two days in the second setting, a Lycée, where I observed lessons and interviewed the director, M.L., teachers and medical staff and chatted with some of the students. I made several visits to the third setting described in this chapter, the Externat Médico-Professionel (EMPRO), during which I was able to interview teachers and children and observe lessons. I was accompanied by P.C., the director of the establishment who spent hours talking to me about the life of the institution, its goals and the outcomes for the young people concerned. In Chapter Eight I have also drawn on material gathered in other research situations in France, beyond the three main sites discussed in the present chapter. This additional material is used to make links between different aspects of exclusion and marginalization within the French education system. Needless to say, the material and discussion included in these chapters offers a limited view of the structures, systems and values at work. Most of the material relating to the particular visits to settings in France was gathered between 1996–1999, although I made my first visit to the EMPRO in 1994.

In trying to present the four settings I have encountered various dilemmas. How, for example, do I describe and tell the story of a particular setting without smoothing away all the rough edges, contradictions and gaps into a homogenized and seamless account? How do I include the voices of those who contributed to my material and their unique individual perspectives and concerns? To what extent do I allow room in my writing for the insights and questions raised by those who spoke to me, and how far can I avoid super-imposing my own voice over those? Shouldn't I as 'the writer' focus on achieving clarity and coherence for the reader, even if that means the silencing of other voices and the cleaning up all the messiness involved in the research process?

I stated in earlier chapters that I want to challenge 'traditional accounts' by drawing on individual accounts of policy making. With this in mind, I initially decided that by using personal accounts and 'insider' voices to describe the different settings involved in the study, I would achieve an alternative kind of analysis to a standard case study which would be richer, more textured and 'more true'. Although this is the approach I have tried to adopt in this and in the following chapters, two important issues have arisen which have made the task more complex – or even, at times, impossible. First, while many of the people I interviewed in England settled quite naturally into an autobiographical approach in discussing, for example, the development of policy and the changes in the role of special schools, in France most people I interviewed revealed little about their experience and history in relation to changes in policy or the circumstances which led them to work in a particular setting.

Some of the English teachers told me about their work histories with relish. Their accounts have provided invaluable and unexpected material in which personal histories have interwoven with discussions of national and local policy making and social change. In contrast, the majority of those interviewed in France kept a clear focus on what they perceived as the job in hand which was to give a factual account of their professional role and work setting. In doing so, they used language which was less personal and they were more likely to cite legislation and to use official statements and explanations for particular procedures than their English counterparts. They sometimes appeared mildly surprised to be asked about their own work lives or reasons for coming to work in a particular place, as if their experiences could hardly be seen as relevant to research into policy making.

The differences between the kinds of accounts given in response to my questions has inevitably led to the accumulation of rather different bodies of material to draw on. The more 'objective' and official tone adopted by most of those interviewed in France, in which 'factual' information was offered rather than 'experiential', sits more comfortably with a view of policy making as formal and legislative, rather than as made through practice and interpretation. It is possible that this difference reflects the position of teachers in France as civil servants whose tasks and responsibilities are laid down in government documents, and who are assigned to posts by the Ministry for Education. This is rather different from the case of English teachers who can apply for posts advertised in the press and – in spite of increasing state control of all aspects of education – are not employed by central government.

Another issue which makes the task of constructing case studies based on insider accounts difficult is closely related to the first and concerns homogeneity. The autobiographical approach adopted by most of those interviewed in England, encouraged a more reflective and critical analysis on the part of individuals than was generally the case in France. Information concerning, for example, criteria and procedures for admission or post-sixteen opportunities was sometimes difficult to identify in the 'stream of consciousness' approach adopted by some English participants, and accounts were sometimes contradictory. An outcome of this is that the 'English' material is less homogeneous, more unruly and more difficult to categorize than the French material. One reason for this is that a far wider range of people relating to the single context in England were interviewed, than those interviewed in France. I have also wondered if those in France attempted to simplify their accounts in order to assist me in making sense of the material in a second language and in another national context. Again, my impression is that the kind of qualitative approaches which I used, such as the open ended interview, are less usual in France than in England and it is possible that the more structured and contained responses in the French context reflect attempts to get the interview under control, but these observations remain at the level of conjectures on my part.

A major difference between the English setting and the French ones was the fact that the English school had been undergoing a process of change over a number of years and that it faced closure at some time in the near future. The French settings appeared to be 'static', part of, and firmly rooted in, a wider system. The recent changes experienced by those involved with the English school and preparations for its possible absorption into other structures, provoked questions and concerns, and position-taking on the part of those interviewed. The changes were both internal (the head teacher left shortly after I began my enquiry, to be replaced by the deputy head in an 'acting head' capacity), and external as central government and the local education authority moved towards a stated policy of greater participation in ordinary schools by disabled children and young people.

The accounts in this chapter are part of an interpretative analysis of my data and have entailed selecting and organizing material in a particular way to create a particular set of meanings. In constructing these 'cameos' I am inevitably 'claiming the principle voice' by the choices I make and structures of meaning which I develop. Although the material is based largely on chunks of discourse taken from the accounts of individuals, and hence 'includes' the voices of those interviewed, the overriding voice is my own as I select from, manipulate and knit what has been said into some kind of story.

The remainder of this chapter presents four distinct landscapes of particular sites. Issues relating to policies and processes of spatialization and the othering of certain groups, are inseparable from the accounts set out here, but these will be explicitly discussed in relation to a closer examination of the material in the following two chapters.

THE ENGLISH RESEARCH SETTING

Freelands School, Greentown, England

Freelands School opened in the nineteen sixties. It is a special school designated for students described as having complex physical and associated learning difficulties. There are 50 students aged between 3–16 on the role who attend the school on a full-time basis. There is a support service based at the school which has 'a large caseload of disabled children' who attend mainstream schools. At one time there were as many as 180 pupils at Freelands School. The deputy head teacher explained:

> the children that we have all have additional learning difficulties or visual difficulties or hearing difficulties or communication difficulties or behaviour difficulties. We don't have any ordinary children in wheelchairs.

This statement was echoed in a different context later on in my field work when parents, teachers and governors of a mainstream primary school expressed opposition to the proposed inclusion of Freelands children in 'their' school on the grounds that they were 'not like our children'. Some examples of this positioning of the children at Freelands as 'other' are discussed in the following chapter. The children at Freelands were regarded as 'not ordinary' because they experienced 'additional difficulties' which go beyond 'being in a wheel chair'. On a semantic level, the great divide between those who can be admitted into the ranks of the mainstream and those who can't, is the category of 'ordinariness' and disabled children 'in wheelchairs' may be welcomed provided they have no additional impairments. Another teacher described the history of Freelands School:

> This was a residential school for children with cerebral palsy – not just for the local authority but for other authorities and it cost more than Eton or Harrow. In the late 70s, when the money dried up we amalgamated with the school for spina bifada kids and we became a day school. So we became a school for disabled pupils but not for those with learning difficulties. Some were bright kids. We had over 150 kids. But our numbers have gone down because of integration – because integration – or inclusion – is the in-thing.
>
> The children who are here now are the ones no-one knows what to do with. Take that kid earlier – the one I got feeling leaves in Science. He is losing his sight very quickly. He shouldn't be here, but they've shut all the special schools because of integration so there's nowhere for partially sighted and totally blind children to go. There are more kids with learning difficulties now. All the more capable and mobile ones have been integrated.

This account raises questions about the supposed rationality and humanitarian concerns of special education. In Chapter Four I drew on examples from the work of Humphries and Gordon (1992) which revealed the arbitrariness of the processes involved in the creation of populations and cultures of special schools and institutions in the earlier part of the twentieth century. Among other examples of situations and contexts in which disabled people have been 're-invented' as ordinary and converted from being socially useless and unproductive others into being an essential part of the labour force, I cited Safford and Safford's (1996) account of how disabled people were re-categorized during the First and Second World Wars to allow them to work. I linked Pritchard's (1963) discussion of the evacuation and the closure of many special schools in the cities in England during the Second World War and the effect on the composition of ordinary schools, to the argument that categorizations and exclusions are irrational in the sense that while pretending to be based on the perceived deficiencies of groups and individuals, they are contingent upon other socially and historical factors such as the economy, war and levels of social cohesion. The population of Freelands was transformed from being one selected according to narrow medical categories, into one in which selections are made on a kind of 'hold-all' principle of 'children who no-one knows what to do with'. This provides a further example of the irrational and unprincipled nature of the processes by which children are selected in and out of particular settings. All the examples reveal the powerful impact of change in one area (e.g. the evacuation of children from cities in wartime, the closure or amalgamation of some special schools, and the adoption of 'integration' policies for some groups of children and not others) on other areas such as the composition of remaining special schools and perceptions about children who go to them. One of the unanticipated – or at least, unplanned for – effects of the falling role at Freelands became critically apparent when the introduction of the national curriculum for special schools was introduced.

The out-going head-teacher explained:

> Because our numbers have dropped and dropped, we only have one full-time teacher for the secondary aged pupils and four part-time. This is to cover all the NC (National Curriculum) subjects. I don't see how we can provide 22 secondary aged students with varying disabilities the right sort of curriculum and all the right sort of leisure activities that they need.

The falling role at the school which accompanied the increasing numbers 'being integrated' during the nineteen eighties and nineties, resulted in a reduction of teachers at the school and those left were unable to cover all the national curriculum subjects at secondary level. This emerged as one of the major arguments put forward by the LEA in favour of closing Freelands School altogether. In Chapter Three, C.W.'s account of the effects of the introduction of 'integration policies' and the national curriculum exposed some of the usually obscured consequences of top-down policy making (which is focused on the dominant landscape of the 'ordinary') on those who are spatially and culturally positioned 'on the margins' in hidden landscapes. The introduction of the National Curriculum and the advent of league tables coincided with – and accelerated – a strengthening of the local education authority's policies on integration. While these factors were cited most frequently by teachers as the background to the proposed closure of Freelands school, one teacher felt that these changes were not in the interests of the pupils and were responsible for the demise of the school. In articulating this view, he drew a clear boundary between 'disabled kids' who, he believed, had particular learning needs, and other children:

> We shouldn't be in the league tables. We've been zero since the league tables started and morale in the school has just gone down. The legal requirement now is morally wrong, we shouldn't be doing it. We should be preparing these kids in social skills, life skills for when they leave school. If something says they've got a record of achievement for being able to tow a little truck

around at the back of an electric wheelchair or something – that's no good to them, is it?

Interestingly, though, the views expressed by this particular teacher are in contrast to C.W.'s insistence that he 'needed an education'.

There was also a belief expressed by teachers, parents and governors that the school was to be closed for 'economic reasons' which disregarded the 'real' interests of disabled pupils. As one teacher commented:

> This LEA seems to push for integration all the time but somebody said the other day that it costs four times more to keep a child in special school than it does in mainstream. So I feel it is run on an economic standard rather than an educational standard – personally.

Challenging the proposed closure of the school were the attitudes of some Freelands parents and teachers, professionals and members of particular pressure groups, who emphasize the *specialness* and *difference* of particular groups of children and young people and of the teachers and professionals who work with them. The framework within which these views are presented are couched in terms of the 'rights' of disabled students to an appropriate education and level of support. Interestingly, in the process of the research, teachers, parents and governors in ordinary schools sometimes expressed similar views, but in the material put forward in Chapter Seven these arguments about the 'difference' and 'specialness' of the special school community are set in a framework of their possible disruptiveness and negative effects on the mainstream school community. Both sets of views focus upon the 'difference' between students in special schools and those in ordinary schools, but they are set in opposing positions in which, implicitly, the 'rights' of different groups of students are seen as potentially conflictual. Surrounding such attitudes are particular discourses which sustain and support practices of selection and segregation and these are pervasive in both 'special' and 'mainstream' contexts, although they take different forms. Examples of discourses deployed in different contexts are discussed in the following chapter.

Teachers at Freelands school varied widely in the way they spoke about their own professional roles. One teacher, taking early retirement, saw himself as both protecting the pupils in his care and saving ordinary schools from what he saw as the inevitable trouble of having to accommodate them. Another teacher in mid-career thought her role was essentially educational and that she should support the move away from segregated provision so that disabled children and young people would have enhanced educational opportunities.

Although teachers at the school did not all share the same perceptions concerning their roles and the education and rights of the pupils at the school, their statements and arguments were all based on the assumption that their pupils were *different* from pupils in ordinary schools and that this difference should be one of the organizing principles around which policies are formulated. Some saw the pupils' disabilities as being a fundamental part of their identities as 'other', necessarily implying a segregated school life. As one teacher explained:

> I think specials should be treated as specials. Have a comprehensive and
> then a special on the same campus. I mean they could have their own
> special garden and say – you know – that's yours and then be able to walk
> across – or go across – and dip in as needs be but still have the cosy family
> atmosphere.

This quotation illustrates the profoundly spatialized characterization of disabled
students as both 'different' (i.e. 'special', not 'ordinary'), requiring 'cosiness'
(i.e. 'protection') and as belonging to segregated spaces whose boundaries are
embedded in the whole conceptualization of the relationship between 'special' and
'ordinary'. Much of the material I have gathered is unusual in that it encompasses
the particular gaze of those working in segregated settings on 'the mainstream'.
In the quotation above there is a sensation of seeing the world through the 'wrong
end' of a telescope with the intimate details of a familiar landscape coming into
sharp relief against the more general blur of a distant one.

Another teacher saw the potential for positive benefits for Freelands pupils
attending an on-site resource base because of its possible therapeutic benefits:

> We could maybe put really nice groups together, drawing on children there
> and giving our children better models. There are all sorts of possibilities.
> So you don't quite know whether it is going to be an advantage or a dis-
> advantage yet.

Both views are based on a professional gaze which focuses on children's
impairments or disabilities rather than on what all children and young people
have in common and on their right to be full members of the community. Such
impairment-led thinking and attitudes are a constant leitmotif underpinning the
views expressed and positions taken by the vast majority of actors in the different
arenas in which I carried out my field work.

Policy making contradictions

Greentown Local Education Authority (LEA) states that it supports the goal of
'inclusive education' and has declared that it is 'moving towards schools for all'
entailing the gradual closing down of special schools in the authority. Oddly, one
reason given for the closing down of one special school was the expansion of
another. On an adjoining site was Maynard School which is designated for children and young people with 'severe learning difficulties' and 'complex behaviour
problems'. The population of this school had been expanding and becoming more
diverse over the past few years and this, paradoxically, was one consequence of the
LEA's 'integration' policies. 'Integration', as opposed to inclusive education within
which ordinary schools and colleges are for all members of the community as a
matter of right, inevitably leads to the continuing entrenchment of segregated special
schools for those for whom, professionals argue, 'there will always be a need'. As
special schools of different kinds closed in Greentown, and as increasing numbers
of children were 'integrated' into ordinary schools from schools such as Freelands,
processes of identification and selection intensified around the apparent dilemma

of who was 'suitable' for integration and who wasn't. Those who were deemed not suitable, either remained in their special school – or – if it had been closed down or its purpose had been altered, were moved to one of the remaining special schools. There was even some movement of students from Freelands to Maynard School in preparation for its long expected closure. One example of the causes of this kind of redistribution of students can be found in the arbitrary bench-mark for integration adopted by the LEA. The deputy head teacher suggested that:

> When we move, it will be to a specially built wing in an ordinary school; it would be very much part of the school. But I think it's been said that all pupils that come with us, must be able to have some form of integration. They must be able to benefit from at least 30% of integration or they won't come with us. There are some borderline children who would go to the severe learning difficulties school probably. (Teacher, Freelands School)

Thus, far from being a project concerned with social justice and equal access for all to common educational settings, 'integration' (sometimes re-articulated in some contexts as 'inclusion') rests on processes of selection and exclusion. Many teachers talked of children 'being included' to refer to situations in which they were 'visitors' to ordinary schools and whose main school was a segregated special school, revealing the slippage which can occur in language which masks what is happening. 'Inclusion' – while being a powerful political concept – has also become the language of 'spin' surrounding 'new' policies and is to some extent fashionable. At the same time, the shifting meanings ascribed to 'inclusion' also express the complexities of the processes of displacement and movement involved in widening participation in ordinary settings. These issues will be returned to in the concluding chapter.

Unlike the issues and struggles which are overtly present in the discussion surrounding the English setting, the material gathered in France does not immediately present visible signs of struggles between actors about the values and principles underpinning the social and selective organization of education and how these relate to disabled children and young people. I have already explained the differences in terms of the research methodology and how those interviewed responded to my enquiry in the different sites. I did not gain any real insight into personal views and values of individuals, and the accounts presented in this section are descriptive rather than analytical or critical. At the same time they are highly political in that they describe aspects of whole sets of social relations and organization in which some groups of children and young people are systematically assessed, labelled and excluded from the life of ordinary communities on the grounds of disability and impairment.

FRANCE

L'Institut National de Réadaption – Hôpital Sainte Thérèse

The material in this section is based entirely on an extended interview with the director, M.M., and on my impressions after being shown round the hospital-based educational provision which he manages. Where quotation marks are used, these are the words used by him, translated into English, unless otherwise stated.

Hôpital Sainte Thérèse is a vast hospital complex surrounded by high walls, situated in a quiet suburb on the outskirts of Paris. It is made up of a number of large red brick buildings linked by a network of tree lined roads and pathways. As I passed through the gates I had the impression of entering a small, fortified, silent and sparsely populated town. The National Institute for Re-adaptation (Institut National de Réadaptation) is one of the hospital 'Centres'. M.M. is responsible for the education of children and young people who are admitted to the hospital. The reason why I have included this setting in the study is because some of the young people who receive their education there might, in England, attend a school such as Freelands School. M.M. explained the relationship of the provision at the Hôpital Sainte Thérèse to the wider system of education in France, and its internal organization.

In France there are a number of structures for 'handicapped young people and children' only some of which are under the control of the Ministry for Education. This provision in made up of specialist education classes (SES) which are integrated into, or attached to, ordinary schools and the RAS – 'réseaux d'aide spécialisés' (special education networks) – which are staffed by psychologists, teachers and *rééducateurs*. *Rééducateurs* work in ordinary and special schools and are trained in psychology and are concerned with the social and emotional development of pupils. The role of the SES and the RAS is to prevent – or find solutions to – the occurrence of difficulties in learning among pupils, and this may include in-class support for students in ordinary schools. Students are placed in an SES setting as a result of the deliberations of a 'commission', a body which makes decisions about where a child should be placed and the kind of support they should receive. The support of the RAS, on the other hand, is something negotiated between the staff of the RAS, the school and the family. In France schools have 'educators' ('éducateurs') as well as teachers (enseignants). The difference between their roles varies according to the setting. At the Centre the *éducateurs* are responsible for the children who are not attending classes or are only attending part-time for some reason. In addition, they take all the children outside school hours for various activities such as games and outings and this concerns particularly those children (50% of the total number) who are interns and do not go home at the end of the day. The structures described here are provided by the Ministry of Education. Beyond this provision, are a whole range of structures 'for children who are more seriously handicapped'.

The Hôpital Sainte Thérèse was opened in the 1960s and a school was established there immediately. The 1975 law – described in Chapter Four – had a considerable impact on the type of provision, especially concerning children with cerebral palsy. In the past, M.M. explained, children who had cerebral palsy usually lived in institutions often at a great distance from their families and cut off from ordinary society. These days, however, stays in hospital are much shorter and children do not stay in hospital 'indefinitely' as might have been the case in the past. A therapeutic and educational programme 'tailored to fit the child' is put in place and the aim is to 'integrate' the children into schools or institutions near their homes where possible so that they can be part of their local community.

In France, the decision of a commission is never obligatorily imposed on parents. However, M.M. emphasized that:

> decisions are made only after very careful and reflective work, which includes working with the family in order to reach a decision which is the most appropriate. But if the family rejects the decision, it is they who would win the case in law. The Ministry for Education does have the right, however, to remove from the school ('déscolariser') the child or to refuse the parents' choice if there is a danger either to the child or if the child is a danger to others.

There is clearly a tension here between the 'right' of parents to choose the school they want for their child and the overriding right of a school to exclude a child on the familiar grounds that they are deemed 'dangerous'.

There is a major sector outside the national education system which is made up of specialist institutions which are no longer, strictly speaking, under the control of the Ministry of Education. These institutions provide for children under four broad headings: therapy, 're-education', education and school. These four elements are not always present in any one institution. Outside the education system, institutions are managed by different associations which may be national, or purely local. The Ministry for Education may or may not have an involvement in such institutions. Some institutions don't have a school as such, and no educational provision, but then the Ministry for Education intervenes to assure 'some education' for the children. This could mean one or two teachers being provided on a full or part-time basis who are assigned to the institution to ensure the children receive some education. The level of this intervention varies.

There are a number of hospitals in France which provide education for patients of school age. Again, the form that this takes varies. All the children who attend the centre at the Hôpital Sainte Thérèse have been admitted to the hospital for medical treatment. Those who are well enough or old enough are enrolled in educational programmes. The National Institute for Re-adaptation (Institut National de Réadaptation) has three distinct sections, A, B and C.

Service A is for children who have 'suffered some kind of brain injury as a result of accident or a stroke or after an operation for a tumour'. The orthopaedic service – Service B – is designated for children who have all kinds of problems to do with their bones which may be post-operative or caused by 'congenital orthopaedic pathologies requiring a programme of re-education with a great deal of physiotherapy which can only take place in a hospital. The children may be on traction, lying flat for long periods of time'. Sector C is 'for children who have suffered neurological problems from birth, such as cerebral palsy' or 'other congenital neurological problems which are hereditary in origin.' M.M. described these children are 'usually very seriously handicapped – often paraplegic, or tetraplegic, without speech and with very restricted motor control.'

The school provides education for children from all three services. Approximately 160–170 children and young people are patients at the National Institute for Re-adaptation and about 140 of those are on the role in the school or attend the kindergarten. The others are not deemed well enough to receive education.

In the past, the period of care at the centre could be anything up to twelve or thirteen years. For those in Sector A the length of stay is now between a minimum of 6 weeks and a maximum of 2 years. In Sector B the children can stay for periods between 4 weeks and 1 year while in Sector C the minimum stay is about 1 year extending to anything up to 4 years or more.

Children and young people in Sector B usually return to their original school, provided it is physically accessible because 'they don't necessarily have any particular learning difficulties associated with their pathology'. However, in general most of the young people in Sector A, 'do not regain the educational skills and abilities which they had before the accident'. For many, M.M. explained, 'even if they can regain their earlier performance levels, they will be unable to learn new concepts and skills easily'. Some are able to return to their original school, but many are placed in a specialist class under the control of the Ministry for Education. Young people who have serious brain damage are moved to another kind of establishment outside the Ministry for Education.

For children in Sector C. the overarching concern is to put together an intensive package of therapy, re-education and schooling and to explore possible pathways to try and establish the best kind of programme for the individual child. Children from Sector C usually progress to an establishment under the control of the Local (or 'departmental') Commission for Special Education (Commission Departmental de L'Education Specialisée (CDES) which includes 'both treatment and education'. Some go on to institutions in which, M.M. explained, there is:

> no teaching as such because it has been decided that there is no point. The child needs a comprehensive programme of care and treatment and therapy and it is considered that schooling is not beneficial.
>
> This is often difficult for the parents to accept. School represents 'a kind of normality' (even if it is in a special institution) and to abandon schooling is often experienced by the parents as 'a kind of failure' or at least the end of a vision that the family had for their child.

M.M. sees the role of the centre as being primarily educational and, while differences between students are taken into account including the effects of any impairment, the curriculum and teaching are based on what goes on in ordinary state schools (in contrast to the third French setting discussed in this chapter). The teacher-pupil ratio is high with approximately one teacher to six students. The teachers are, between them, able to cover all areas of the national curriculum at primary age, to a much lesser extent at the secondary stage. There are approximately twice as many pre-school and primary aged children as secondary at the centre.

Teaching staff at the centre are fully qualified teachers and have additional specialist training. Other staff working there are also highly specialized:

... we have twelve physiotherapists working full time. Each of the three sectors I've described has its own team of professionals including speech therapists, physios, ergo therapists, psycho-motricians and psychologists. You see, the psychological difficulties of the children in the different sectors are very different. A child who has had a brain injury or stroke, for example, has very specialized psychological needs which are different from those of a child who has broken a leg. There are whole bodies of knowledge and professional expertise which are associated with the different kinds of difficulty.

This highlights the close relationship between places and categories and professional 'knowledge'. One of the issues I will examine in Chapter Eight is the use of professional discourses as a means of placing and fixing identities in the context of the highly differentiated and compartmentalized system of medically-based provision for groups of children and young people in France. In Chapter Seven I discuss some of the discourses of normality, needs and protection deployed in the English context. I appear to be setting up a contrast between what might be seen as 'socially' impaired identities (England) versus 'medically' impaired identities (France), but of course, 'the medical' is part of 'the social', not something separate from it. My intention is not to set up a simplistic model based on a reductionist and false dichotomy between the values and systems in the two countries.

The Lycée Bresson

The Lycée Bresson lies on the outskirts of a quiet town which is twenty minutes by train outside Paris. I spent two days at the school, and was able to sit in on classes, talk informally to students and teachers and observe lessons. The only formal interview which I carried out was with the director.

In 1958 a professor of medicine asked the Ministry of Education to open a school within the large hospital complex where he worked, arguing that children and young people in long-stay hospitals required an education and should be seen as students as well as patients. The school was planned by the students themselves, their parents, their teachers and medical staff. Emerging from this unusual history, a large school complex was constructed at Bresson in 1980 which included an elementary school, a middle school and a secondary school. Later a centre for technical studies for school leavers was added. An important medical centre which could support disabled students in terms of treatment and technology was a central part of the complex. This section focuses only on the Lycée which is for students aged 15–19.

At the time of my visit (1998) there were 250 students at the Lycée, over two thirds of whom were disabled. Forty percent of the students had impairments associated with cerebral palsy: other impairments were related to paralysis, brain injury, genetic factors, and a range of other conditions. (My judgment is that if these young people lived in Greentown, many of them would attend Freelands School, but those with less complex difficulties would be able to attend ordinary schools provided access arrangements and technical, personal and learning support were available and adequate).

The school extends over a very large area, incorporating a number of low two story purpose-built buildings in a neighbourhood which is clearly middle class with many green spaces and an impeccably maintained golf course. On entering the building there is an impression of space and light. The school throbs with life and activity. I noticed that in the recreation area outside young people were talking, listening to music on their headphones, playing basket-ball, chasing after each other. Many students were using wheel chairs to get around; others were using technology to communicate with other students. The outside recreation area and the inside circulation areas seemed to be part of the same space. This is because of a system of massive sliding glass walls which link 'outside' to 'inside'. The director, M.F., explained this:

> We have brought 'outside' into the building. We didn't want a situation in which everybody is crowded together unable to circulate. That's bad for everybody but there are particular problems when you have large numbers of people using wheel chairs who are trying to get to lessons or go and meet their friends. So as you see, there are no corridors – we've got these large common spaces – like avenues or freeways. As you see, we get a lot of speeding!

The 'avenues' thronged with people talking, laughing, moving in groups deep in conversation – some walking, others in wheel chairs. A girl was sitting on the knee of a young man, her arms around his neck as he steered his wheel chair at speed through the crowd. At the side there were low coffee tables and comfortable chairs. Staff and students were sitting at these, eating snacks, reading magazines, talking. The space and its activity reminded me of the busy and varied Ramblas in Barcelona which runs down from the centre of the city to the port and provides both a thoroughfare and meeting place. I was struck forcibly once again with the idea that the use of space constructs and defines social relationships and that values and power relations are expressed through these constructions.

The director opened our first conversation:

> This is a school like any other. Disability is a secondary issue. In special schools all the teachers are specialised in terms of learning difficulty or specific impairment. Here, the teachers are ordinary, highly qualified teachers. There is an important 'centre de soins' (medical centre) here which is the responsibility of the Ministry for Health and Social Affairs. Teachers come here because they say they want to work here. They are not 'special' teachers and don't have any specific training. The principle is that all the young people here are students, without exception. The fact that many are disabled is not the point. They do have to have the intellectual capacity to follow the curriculum and that's the same for all students going to a Lycée with an academic curriculum.

The director is here suggesting a relationship between the 'ordinariness' of the teachers (exemplified by their lack of impairment-based 'specific training') and the primacy given to students' academic interests (rather than their 'disability'). The equation 'specific training of teachers' equals 'impairment led paradigm' is an interesting and unexpected one in the context of a school in which the majority of students have impairments.

In addition to all the teaching staff, there are whole teams of medical and therapeutic specialists who work in conjunction with the teachers and the young people themselves. The students follow an ordinary curriculum – the same as in any other Lycée – and the medical centre functions quite separately from the school. The director explained:

> At the same time, the teachers and educators here are in a research situation. We are all trying to work together to find ways of counterbalancing the effects of the physical impairments experienced by many of our students so that they have full access to the curriculum. There are whole teams of professional and medical staff of all sorts here, but the idea is that we work collaboratively with students so that they have the possible scenario for participation in all aspects of the life of the school. It is not a question of the students going off for therapy or medical treatments as an activity which is separate from teaching and learning (although there are occasions when this will happen). No ... we are a multi-disciplinary team and we try to complement each other and learn from each other. This is one of the principles on which all our work is founded and in that sense we are all involved in research activity all the time.

The idea that the medical and therapeutic staff work in conjunction with the teachers and the young people themselves and that all are engaged in 'research activity all the time' could almost be described as revolutionary in challenging the deficit-driven medical model in which professionals and management make decisions about the lives and opportunities of disabled children and young people based on power residing in their 'expertise' or position in the management hierarchy.

The school is highly selective in a number of ways. First because the majority of students 'must have a disability' and be able to follow an academic pathway which is the same as at any other Lycée in France. The majority of the 30% of non-disabled students are from the local community and from families who 'have chosen the school because of its high academic standards and who are actively supportive of the mix of disabled and non-disabled students and staff who make up the school community'. But, the director explained:

> Among the 30% is a special group of students who are exceptional golf players. It was my idea that as well as having diversity in terms of disabled and non-disabled students being part of the same school community, we should also have a group of students who are exceptional because of their sporting prowess. They are on a special golf training programme in addition to the ordinary academic curriculum. So while some students receive specialist support in terms of medical treatment and physiotherapy or whatever, others get specialist support to make them more effective golf players.
>
> There's a lot of sport here for everybody, though. We've got an internationally known mixed basketball team here. The teams here are made up of pupils of all ages – and of course, boys and girls. The differences between what the players can do physically are so great that there is little point in

having teams grouped by age. This means that students are entirely used to
being in mixed age and gender groups and working together co-operatively
as well as competitively. The life of the whole school is about working co-
operatively and collaboratively, each one being valued for what they have to
offer. Everybody does sport. We have an Olympic size swimming pool which
is used for sport and therapy – in fact the two overlap of course – and rock
climbing. It's terrific to see a disabled youngster climbing up our artificial
rock face. Those students who are able to climb, do so in teams supported by
other people on the ground who, perhaps, are not able to climb themselves.
And then there's golf, which everyone can play – not just the group of
golfers.

The emphasis on sport and 'physical prowess' challenges the stereotype of disability as signifying weakness and helplessness. I watched a game of volley ball
in which the teams were made up of a mix of ages, gender and levels and means
of mobility, including the use of wheel chairs. The game was fast and complex,
involving collaboration and differentiation of skills between the players, with none
of the self-consciousness frequently imposed by the media on disabled people who
'do' sport.

The naturalness about the sporting activities was also a feature of other aspects
of the life of the school. Much is made of supposed 'toileting problems' in many
English settings (which could be removed by changing the physical and cultural
environment) – and frequently cited as one justification for segregation. The director
at the Lycée Bresson disturbed a number of English 'lavatory icons' concerned with
segregation – of the sexes, of children from adults, of teachers from pupils, and of
disabled people from non-disabled people – at one fell swoop.

> Over here are one of our 'points urinoire' ('toilet stops'). There are always two
> people there – one male and one female – to help anyone with their personal
> needs (a young man in a wheel chair speeds into the area and screeches to a
> halt). You can see there is plenty of space and privacy. The areas are uni-sex.
> Everyone uses them, regardless of gender, age or whether they are disabled or
> not. One thing I've done is insist that all the toilet areas have contraceptive
> machines which are accessible to all students – so they have to be at wheel
> chair level. You can see how important that message is.

There are a number of other messages here too: using the lavatory is a routine
part of life and having assistance to do so is ordinary; community lavatories break
down mystiques surrounding gender, disability and segregation; community lavatories say that the dignity and authority of teachers are not undermined by sharing
toilet areas with students.

Another unusual feature of the Lycée is the presence of disabled teachers. I had
a conversation with a Maths teacher who is a wheel-chair user. She explained:

> It's important to have disabled adults teaching in a school like this. Of course,
> I could teach in an ordinary school but frequently there are access problems
> in terms of getting into the building and moving around.

Lack of access to ordinary schools for disabled people is routine in England and
France. Such issues are usually discussed in relation to 'integration' or 'inclusion'

of individual children or of small groups, thus locating 'the problem' with them, rather than as seeing the issues as concerning rights and the physical and cultural transformation of the environment. This obscures a situation in which inaccessible environments affect parents, teachers and members of the wider community who may be debarred from their local school on the grounds of disability. The Maths teacher outlined the conditions which make the Lycée Bresson 'accessible' in holistic terms:

> There are some very disabled young people here, many of whom would usu-
> ally attend a specialist institution outside the education system. This means
> that they are shut off from the ordinary community and don't have the same
> opportunities as everybody else. Some need a lot of medical input of various
> kinds, and that's available here. This means that the students have everything
> they need on one site. This is the reverse of the usual situation in which you
> have a kind of medical institution with classes attached. The emphasis here is
> on the education not the medical side. But without the medical centre, some of
> the students couldn't come here. Also, here, being disabled, requiring medical
> care sometimes or some kind of therapy or medication, is just accepted as
> 'everyday'. It's not a big deal and is certainly not used as a reason for treating
> students differently in terms of their education and social life.

The culture, organization and practices at the Lycée Bresson allow all students, whatever they require, to gain access to an ordinary education and social life. This includes medical and therapeutic support for many students but this support is provided as part of a wider framework in which education and social relations are the prime considerations. Sport is part of that wider framework, not as something 'therapeutic', but as an ordinary activity for young people at school. Far from 'denying' the importance of impairments and their possible effects on the students' lives, medical and therapeutic support are provided as a matter of course – not instead of education, but in support of it. The principle that disability should not be used as a reason 'for treating students differently' underpins the culture and practices of the school.

The Lycée Bresson sets out to challenge the routine medicalization of physical impairment through the values and practices it has developed. The time I spent there was very limited and there were many questions and issues which I was not able to pursue. However, my visit to this school gave me a new focus on the importance of spatial organization in the creation of relationships. The spatial seemed to be a dimension of social life which was consciously recognized and considered. An example of this was the design of the buildings in which, the director said, the 'outside' had been brought 'inside'. There were no special places for disabled students and other places for non-disabled students. The ethos was one of collaboration rather than 'care' and this means bringing people together rather than separating them up into groups for special treatment. The Lycée had no special units or classes for people identified as having particular 'syndromes' or 'disorders'. Staff and students work collaboratively to ensure that all students are able to participate in all aspects of the life of the school. There is a determination to challenge stereotypes and the othering of disabled students. Teachers, medical staff and students see themselves engaged in a research project to overcome exclusion and to make full participation possible. In my notebook I wrote:

> Why can't all students attend this school regardless of attainment or perceptions about academic ability? Couldn't students who experience difficulties in learning become part of this collaboration?

I put this question to the director who explained that this wouldn't be possible because this was a Lycée and in France only students who are 'intellectually able' can attend the Lycée. This reminded me of the embededness and complexity of the structures, processes and sets of values within which categorization, labelling and exclusions take place.

L'Externat Médico-Professionel

My third French setting is l'Externat Médico-Professionel (literally translated this becomes 'non-residential medical training school or centre') situated in a town about 40 kilometres to the west of Paris which over the past thirty years has become part of the conglomeration of the Paris suburbs. In an earlier period the setting provided a peaceful, 'healthy' and non urban environment for children who were 'delicate' or disabled. Not far from the Externat is an 'Open Air school', built in the 1930s which only closed its (sliding glass) doors in the 1990s.

L'Externat Médico-Professionel is a small non residential special school with places for 50 young people aged from 14–20, who have been assessed and categorized as having difficulties in learning or 'medical conditions'. At the time of my visits to the school (during the period 1994–1998) , there were also some students who were there because they were considered 'delicate' and had missed a lot of school in the past, or who were considered too vulnerable in some way to withstand the life and regime of an ordinary school. The majority of the students had attended special schools, often outside the education system, during their primary years but some had attended their local primary school and were transferred out of the mainstream education system when the processes of selection intensified in secondary phase of education at the age of thirteen or fourteen. (Armstrong, 1995). The school provides a range of specialist medical services, including physiotherapy.

I have included the Externat in my study because there are a small number of young people at Freelands who have similar difficulties to some of those at the Externat where, although only a few have visible physical disabilities, some have, for example, a heart condition or asthma. Sometimes young people are absent for long periods because they are receiving treatment in hospital.

The prospectus for the institution explained that the Externat Médico-Professionel (EMPRO) opened in 1957 for young people who are 'intellectually deficient' and require specialist provision. Its purpose was to allow 'such young people to overcome their difficulties and to benefit from a form of training which will allow them access to an active working life' and 'to facilitate the social integration of these young people and to allow them dignity and full citizenship in the life of the community.'

The students were divided into 8 different classes, five of which were designated for students aged 14 to 18 organized into levels according to perceived ability, measured by the administration of psychological tests. The remaining three classes were for 'training older students for employment and preparing them for life in the community'. Students in the classes arranged in levels 1–5 spent either the morning or the afternoon in formal school lessons (based on the national curriculum used in ordinary primary schools) and half the day engaged in practical activities in workshops or sport, swimming or other 'recreational activities'. The aim, P.C. explained, was to help young people learn independence and confidence and acquire skills which would help them achieve these:

> Learning to write a letter, manage a weekly budget and keep their homes clean and tidy could make the difference to many of these young people between living independently and being dependent.

There was also a major emphasis, she said, on helping the students feel that they are 'part of the community' and that what they have to offer is valued. There was an ethos of collaboration, friendship and mutual respect in the school which informed relationships across all its activities.

P.C. talked to me about the school:

> In this institution we are free to decide what we do, but we do try to follow the same programmes as in ordinary schools but of course we can only do what is possible with the young people here. Level 1 is the weakest class, for example, and the teacher decides on the programme to follow. The young people who are aged between 14–17 have 12 hours of lessons a week in the mornings and attend workshops in the afternoon.

P.C. pointed out that the 12 hours of teaching were not obligatory and there was no legislation laying down numbers of hours of teaching in an institution such as the EMPRO. There are still no statutory regulations concerning the employment of teachers or the pupil-teacher ratio.

Once a young person has been referred by a Special Education Commission to the EMPRO they visit the institution with their family and then attend on a trial basis for a week. A report is prepared which goes to the CDES (Departmental Special Education Commission) and then, when an agreement has been reached, the documents are sent to the Department for Social Security and Health which funds the placement.

P.C. explained that if parents don't want their child to be removed from an ordinary school:

> the commissions tends to be sensitive to the views of the parents, and the child would stay where they are. This could cause problems, of course.
>
> If the teachers are able to provide evidence that there is a danger for the child themselves or to other children, then that would be a deciding factor. But there has to be the notion of danger for a child to be removed.

The notion of 'danger' as being linked to disability or learning difficulty and the requirement that 'evidence' is to be produced if a child is to be 'removed' on the grounds that they are 'a danger to themselves or to other children' are central to the maintenance of boundaries in the French and in the English education systems. The bureaucratically sanctioned practice of compiling 'evidence' of deviance by special education commissions or by multi-professional assessment panels in order to explain and legitimate the removal to other sites of disturbing children, is part of the foundation, fabric and culture of education systems in England and France. It is interesting to note the frequency in the accounts in this study, provided by teachers, head teachers or governors, with which the idea of danger is associated with disability or difference. This bears out Sibley's (1995) argument that a fundamental requirement of boundary maintenance and the creation of separate and separating places is the production of stereotypes.

P.C. suggested ways in which the principles of integration which are 'generally accepted' conflict with teachers' attitudes and practices in ordinary schools:

> Of course, this is a period in which the education system is moving towards greater integration. In ordinary schools teachers are in general in favour of integration when the child's difficulties are compatible with the general running of the class. But at the coal face, this increases the workload of the teachers and quite a few teachers are questioning integration especially when integration is just an 'illusion'. There's a lot of talk about how some of these children disturb the rest of the class, but when they don't (disturb the class) nobody talks about them!
>
> There are a lot of contradictions surrounding integration. There is a shared desire that everybody is accepted by everybody else, but there are limits to this acceptance in reality.

P.C. argued that ordinary schools actually create barriers to learning for some children:

> There are children for whom it is very harmful to stay in the education system as it is. They don't feel at home in the system and this can lead to disruptive behaviour, and non attendance because the education system is not responding to what those children need.

Paradoxically, she suggested that the education system is dangerous ('very harmful') for some children who, in turn, become dangerous ('disruptive') to the system itself. In this symmetrical and mutually disturbing situation, 'removal' of the child is seen as rational. As we saw in Chapter Four, the emphasis is still placed on the requirement for the child to 'fit in', rather than on schools, curricula and teaching styles to change. In England, the effects of the national curriculum, testing, the publication of league tables and the culture of performativity in education over the recent period have encouraged a similar emphasis.

Young people can stay at the EMPRO until around the age of 20. In addition to basic education and workshop activities designed to prepare them for work, a range of sporting, social and therapeutic activities and therapies of various kinds ('where necessary') are built into the timetable. When they have reached the 'necessary level of maturity and self confidence' they begin to follow placements in various protected workshops or 'support through work' centres (centres d'aide par le travail – CAT). These are factories which are reserved only for disabled workers. As P.C. explained:

> To work there they have to have a level of productivity which is 30% below the normal. The business must of course make a little profit, but not on the same scale as an ordinary factory. It receives a government subsidy and gets a daily price per worker per day. The people who work there receive between 70%–100% of the SMIG (national minimum wage) which is made up of various sources of income – from their work, benefits for disabled adults and so on.

An important function of the EMPRO, then, is to prepare young people to take their place in a controlled and protected work environment in which remuneration for 'productivity' is merged with 'disability benefits' into a salary. The segregation of the special institution is a preparation for the segregation of the workplace, providing a structure within which the removal of 'impaired people' to a further 'social space of impairment' is assured. The description of the curriculum and rationale of the EMPRO with its emphasis on usefulness and productivity recalls the kind of ecosystems of the English workhouse discussed in Chapter Four. Writing about the role of nineteenth century workhouses in England, Gleeson refers to:

> the construction of 'powerful notions of corporeal normalcy/deviancy around the impaired/non-impaired dichotomy' ... These cultural material constructions – reinforced increasingly through state practices – served to stabilise and reinforce the political-economic devalorisation of impaired labour power. (Gleeson, 1999, p. 108)

Other political and economic forces, however, have had an impact on the purposes and nature of the 'protected workshops' and on the social construction of 'handicap'. As P.C. explained,

> Fewer and fewer of our young people are able to find a job because of the economic crisis. In the 'support through work' centres, for example, an increasing number of men and women who have been unemployed for a long time are being given jobs. In a sense they have become 'handicapped workers' because of the long time they have been out of work ... but it means there are fewer places for our young people. At the moment a lot of young people leave this kind of institution and do not find work because other people who have become 'handicapped' have taken the kind of jobs they might have had in the past.
>
> I've been in charge here for 20 years and when I started at least 75% of our young people got jobs when they left. But at that time there were lots of little businesses and workshops in the immediate area and many were employed just as ordinary workers – not as disabled people, but many of these little businesses have closed or relocated. Some people lost their jobs and couldn't find another one in an ordinary working environment so had go to a 'support through work centre'.

Just as disabled people have been recategorized as economically productive and socially useful in times of war, non-disabled people may become transformed into 'disabled' through unemployment in periods of economic recession. This transformation is brought about through the spatial practice of the allocation of people to places outside the ordinary areas of social and economic life. Again, this points to the irrational character of processes of selection and categorization and the social construction of disability. In the examples I have drawn on in this study, disabled people become 'productive' and unproductive people become 'disabled' in response to changing social and economic conditions. This represents a profound paradox in terms of dominant representations of 'disability' as being a scientifically verifiable medically based situation in which 'the difficulty' belongs to and is caused by individual impairment, requiring specific responses. The recognition that the labels assigned to people and the spaces they occupy in different times and contexts are contingent upon quite other conditions, is still – in terms of policy making and social practice – about as distant as the town of Doncaster is from the planet Mars.

CONCLUSION

In this chapter I have discussed the four principle research settings which have provided much of the raw material for the issues raised in the different chapters of this book. It was in these settings and in thinking about them in relation to each other that many of the ideas and questions in this study have been developed. In discussing the four settings I have tried to draw as far as possible on the accounts of people who are closely connected to them, but recognize that what I have achieved is a very personal set of reflections and questions, rather than 'insider accounts'. In Chapter Seven I shall focus more sharply on the role of discourse in policy making and the processes through which different discourses define and construct particular identities within particular spatialized contexts.

CHAPTER 7

DISCOURSE, POWER AND POLICY MAKING: UNCOVERING THE POLITICS OF SOCIAL PRACTICE IN ENGLAND

INTRODUCTION

Discourse – in its many forms – plays a powerful role in the construction or moving of conceptual and relational boundaries, in the formation of identities and the creation and interpretation of meanings. I have already discussed the idea that buildings, pictures and other landscapes are forms of discourse through which processes of spatialization, exclusion and inclusion take place and knowledge about places and those associated with them is created. In this chapter, through an analysis of material gathered during my field work in England, I shall look particularly at the role of language as discourse as it is used to influence others, create knowledge and inform policy struggles.

Over the past forty years there has been an explosion of interest in the role of discourse across disciplines. In her introduction to a Special Issue of *Urban Studies* devoted to 'Discourse and Urban Change', Hastings writes:

> ... the processes by which meanings are made, shared, negotiated or imposed
> are intrinsic to processes of social reproduction, contestation and change and
> are therefore actively involved in shaping economy and society ... (and) on
> the role of language use in determining meaning in the urban policy process
> (Hastings, 1999, p. 8)

Similarly and relatedly (because schools are part of social, including rural and urban, landscapes), discourse plays a pivotal role in the making and breaking and re-ordering of education policy at all levels. The language of policy is routinely treated as if it were a neutral medium in which issues and proposals can be discussed and represented in non-partisan ways (Darcy, 1999; Jacobs and Manzi, 1996). Corker explains how '... language is critically linked to issues of knowledge, and ultimately power, because particular forms of knowledge are privileged' (Corker, 1999, p. 193). She argues that:

> ... for new disability discourse to produce the kind of socio-cultural change
> which is its task, it must significantly increase both its *prestige* and its *status*
> by directly engaging with hegemonic structures and practices. (Corker, 1999,
> p. 193)

Such an engagement will involve challenging the discursive mechanisms through which disabling policies are made. A theorization of policy as being made in multiple arenas by a variety of different actors in different arenas (Ball 1990, Fulcher 1999), entails a recognition that an infinite number and variety of discourses may be used in policy making processes and to different ends. It is worth reflecting, for example, on the strangeness of the language used in various official, governmental or institutional forums when it comes to deliberation and decision making. This formal discourse encompasses multiple meanings, one of which is that it is 'neutral', standing outside and above individual and group differences and interests, and this is at the heart of its hegemony. In assuming neutral clothing, it facilitates the role of governance and social control. Of course, official discourses serve a number of purposes, but among these is the provision of mechanisms by which power is declared and maintained, and social values and practices hegemonised. This is one example of the way power is exercised through the codification of language.

Discourse mechanisms are part of the 'labyrinth of complex shapes and practices' which are 'taken for granted' as rooted in ordinary, common sense social behaviour. Language codes and values routinely operate by subterfuge through informal practices. Priestley observes:

> Students with special educational needs are frequently distinguished from their non-disabled peers by formal and informal practices, This kind of ritual, and very public, 'othering' reinforces powerful discursive messages in the minds of pupils. Based on a cumulative experience of small incidents, they begin to build discursive categories of 'special needs' or 'disability'. (Priestley, 1999, p. 96)

Informal practice may be used as a device for identifying and removing others. As Corbett argues:

> We need to listen to what we say. Unless we consciously hear our own words, we are unable and unwilling to question what feelings are revealed beneath ill-considered mouthing. (Corbett, 1996, p. 3)

We need, too, to listen to the discourses around us and in different contexts; we need to deconstruct what is said as part of a wider project of understanding the processes of exclusion and the entrenchment of prejudice. In this chapter I look specifically at how discourse was deployed in individual accounts or in meetings in a number of different research settings and situations and its interconnections with policy making and processes of spatialization in Greentown, England. I will examine the micro levels at which language works in, for example, the imposition of a particular notion of reasonableness or 'appropriacy' as a device for – or with the effect of – retaining the exclusion of some children and young people from ordinary schools. I shall examine how students were othered, or positioned as external to, or part of, the general community, through the choice and use of particular ways of speaking which create and sustain spaces and distances between 'the ordinary' and 'others' and draw on examples of the use of technical-bureaucratic language to high-jack the political agenda and close down debate. I discussed the range and diversity of settings and situations in which the material has been gathered in Chapter Three. Some of these situations were planned – such as interviews or discussions with teachers on pre-arranged visits to schools. Others have 'happened' on a car journey or over mugs of coffee before a meeting, providing examples of what Power has described as 'the opportunistic nature of ethnography' in which:

> ... the endless variety of data sources and the ability to scratch beneath the surface mean that insights can be derived from unexpected incidents. (Power, 1998, p. 14)

This inevitably poses the problem of how to manage the different kinds of material, how to select from it and how to analyse and present it. I feel, at this point, that I am poised like a pattern cutter, scissors in hand, ready to cut out the shape I want to work with because it is here, in this chapter, that the serious task of selecting material, and positioning it in relation to other material takes shape. It is here that some ideas or viewpoints will be made to stand out in comparison with others and hence it is here that my own values and world-view will be most fully at work in selecting and interpreting what others have said. Of course, this is no more or less than what has been going on throughout the research and writing processes, but at this stage I am dealing very directly with the ideas, feelings and utterances of others. I am again, acutely aware that I cannot hope to 'represent' all views equally. On the contrary, such an attempt would obscure the nature of the project in carrying out the research which is a personal-political one. Not only is there an insurmountable technical problem of representing all views of all participants equally, but to behave as if I believe the presentation of a balanced and neutral account is possible would be profoundly misleading.

In making my selections, I have focused on material taken from three interviews and three meetings, considering it more useful to include extended pieces of dialogue and observation from a small number of arenas than to flit between a large number. I am concerned with communication as a social process and the relationships and power struggles associated with how people talk to, and about, each other in different contexts; only longer stretches of dialogue would allow for this. The following section provides a brief critical analysis of the notion of 'policy-as-discourse' as a theoretical framework for analyzing the material and discussing the particular challenges which I have encountered in trying to carry out this kind of work. This is followed by a presentation and analysis of material gathered in interview situations and meetings during the research process, from a 'policy-as-discourse' perspective.

POLICY AS DISCOURSE

Bacchi argues that 'policy-as-discourse' theorists 'develop an understanding of discourse which suits their political purpose' (Bacchi, 2000, p. 46). Underpinning this argument is an implicit belief that theorizing can be 'neutral' or 'not political' which is unacceptable. Just as the conceptualization of research issues and the research process is infused by the values and perceptions of the researcher, so is the practice of theorizing. But Bacchi also highlights an important issue regarding the theorizing of 'the power to contest discursive constructions':

> Policy-as-discourse analysts ... are primarily interested in identifying the reasons progressive changes are so difficult to accomplish. Hence they tend to emphasise the constraints imposed by discourses, through meaning construction. In the process, the power to contest discursive constructions goes undertheorized. (Bacchi, 2000, p. 47)

Whilst identifying reasons why changes are 'difficult to accomplish' is one important reason for examining discourse in policy making, this is only part of my overall purpose which is to examine some of the processes and struggles which take place in policy making regardless of whether these are regarded as 'progressive' or not.

In her discussion of Fulcher's examination of the disempowerment of disabled people through the discourses adopted as part of the processes of policy making, Bacchi argues that according to this analysis, 'The only ones getting to 'use' 'discourse' in this approach, it appears, are those 'holding power' (Bacchi, 2000, p. 54)'. This is a mis-reading of Fulcher's argument in which policy making is seen as going on everywhere with multiple participants exerting power and power-as-resistance.

What I have found particularly interesting in reflecting on the material is that the same person or group can be 'those holding the most power' in one setting, but are removed to the outer spaces of debate and action, in another context. Thus, parent governors at Freelands were powerful contributors to debates in meetings held at their school, but were not invited to meetings of the governors of the mainstream primary school to discuss issues relating to the proposed creation of a resource base there. Similarly, the presence of the head teacher of Freelands was completely ignored by staff and governors at Hillbank School when she appeared as a member of a panel at a meeting to discuss the arrangements for the proposed change. In other forums she claimed, and occupied, a central place in the debate.

Arenas, actors and discourses are all involved in producing 'political states of play' (Fulcher, 1999) which are in a constant state of flux and realignment. This fluidity and the constant re-negotiation of power and the re-positioning of actors and arguments, is central to the view of policy making in my study. Related to this is the understanding that identities, values, discourses and policies are social constructions which occur in particular settings and historical moments. And, finally, while recognizing that in writing this account I am using my own voice, and no-one else's, I also want to emphasise the importance of listening to and understanding different perspectives.

These issues raise the question of relativism. One basis for the way I have approached my research is the belief that values, discourses and social practice can only be understood within the framework of particular spaces and their cultures at particular times. I have argued that policy making, routinely treated as rational and progressive, is irrational, unruly and often oppressive. I have tried to examine my own assumptions and values and to recognize that all I can hope for is to 'interpret' those of others. There are two possible criticisms of this approach. One is that the research I have carried out is personal and interpretative and contingent upon particular and unique situations and circumstances – and hence does not provide 'reliable knowledge about the world' (Hammersley, 1994). But, as Hammersley argues:

> Where once educational and political practice could be seen as open to 'rationalization' on the basis of scientific research founded on a method that guaranteed valid results, now we must recognise that politics and practice may be ontologically resistant to such 'rationalization', and also that the knowledge produced by research is always fallible. Furthermore, what research offers is not a God's eye view, but rather perspectives from particular angles, the appropriateness of which can be challenged. (Hammersley, 1994, p. 148)

I would add to this argument that research is as much concerned with the exploration and generation of new questions, insights and theories as it is with 'finding answers', and that these can inform or contribute to policy making. In the context of this study, for example, there are serious questions raised about the democratic processes involved in decision making which could lead to a re-assessment of processes and procedures. This will be more fully discussed later in the chapter and in the conclusion.

A second charge of 'relativism' concerns the question of values: if the arguments put forward are based on 'my own' values and these are 'mere constructions', then why should these values be privileged over anybody else's? Who is to say that 'democracy', for example, is any more desirable or legitimate than autocracy or anarchy? My response to this is that the present study seeks to provide a critical engagement with policy making and social processes and is concerned with a commitment to social justice. As Ozga and Gewirtz argue:

> Working within a critical frame places requirements on the researcher to pursue ethical-research principles and to assess research activity in relation to what might be broadly termed social-justice concerns. (Ozga and Gewirtz, 1994, p. 122)

In adopting this position, I am also claiming that research can make the world a better place by making it more equitable and more humane; how such a notion is interpreted in different cultures will vary, but interpretations of social justice and human rights will not embrace oppression and marginalization on the basis of difference.

THE CHALLENGE OF 'ANALYSIS'

The diffuseness and variety of the material generated in the research process present a major challenge in terms of its management and analysis, as well as in terms of any possible charges of 'relativism'. I have adopted an approach to discourse analysis which is borrowed from linguistics and social theory and informed by the work of social and cultural geographers some of which is discussed in Chapter Two. Discourse in this study is concerned with the ways in which language 'constructs objects, subjects and experiences, including subjectivity and a sense of self...' (Willig, 1999, p. 2). It conceptualizes language as 'constitutive of experience' as well as representational and reflective. The language we use to 'describe' does not reflect intrinsic and objectively constituted characteristics or processes, but 'brings into being the objects described'. Willig argues that

> ... there is always more than one way of describing something and our
> choice of how to use words to package perceptions and experiences gives
> rise to particular versions of events and reality. Discourse analysis, therefore,
> provides a clear alternative to the categorization of behaviours, measurement
> of variables and attempts to develop predictive models of human behaviour
> ... (Willig, 1999, p. 2)

My analysis of the material presented in this chapter is concerned with the constitutive and productive nature of discourse referred to by Willig. It is framed by Fulcher's theorization of discourse as an integral part of policy making (rather than a simple 'descriptor' or 'record' of it) and by Hastings' argument concerning the role of language use in determining meaning in policy processes. My analysis will seek out counter-discourses and examples of power being exercised through discourse wherever it occurs and, in doing so, I hope to respond to Bacchi's claim that '... the power to contest discursive constructions goes undertheorized'. My analysis does not separate 'discourse' from other processes in policy making. Thus, extracts from discussions or meetings which appear in this chapter may be deconstructed at a number of levels, including how language is used, by whom, in what contexts, with what purposes and ends, and in terms of what is 'said' as a piece of information and what is transmitted by way of connotation. On all of these levels, the contexts in which particular discourses are used are crucial.

FREELANDS: NAMING AND PLACING FROM THE INSIDE

When I began my visits to Freelands in the summer of 1996, my purpose was to follow the processes of policy making as preparations were made for its closure and absorption or transformation into other structures. I wanted to find out about the school and its background, but also about teachers' own perceptions of policy making and the process of change. In this section I have examined the material gathered in interviews with teachers to find examples of discourses which describe and position students at the school in relation to their education and social identity. In doing this, I am regarding 'ways of seeing' and discourses of representation as part of the wider cultural processes and framework in which policy is made.

During the course of the interviews at Freelands those interviewed, in most cases, tended to focus on the students' difficulties in relation to learning and 'access to the curriculum', and the complexity of those difficulties; they also spoke of their rights to equal opportunity in terms of the quality of education provided and the need for recognition of differences between students. This recognition involved, among other things, access to the curriculum as well as to specialist facilities and programmes, where necessary. The argument that 'equality' and 'inclusion' must encompass a recognition of individual medical, physical and learning requirements was powerfully stated by many of those interviewed.

Interview with J.M.

The headteacher, J.M. critically discussed the difficulties of transforming ordinary schools and the local College of Further Education exposing the 'normalizing gaze' of mainstream schools and the College of Further Education towards students who attend Freelands School.

> ... they (i.e. the college) can cope with straightforward learning difficulties even at moderate/severe borderline. They can cope with people who are basic literacy and basic numeracy. They (colleges) can cope with people who are coming out of severe learning difficulty schools who maybe want to do practical life skills courses as well. Things like a bit of cooking and a bit of hair and make-up – those 'caring for yourself' sort of courses. They are not able at the moment to grasp the complexity of the needs of some of our children and young people who need courses which are going to take them forward educationally or are going to give them interests outside of school or college in terms of leisure and the sort of equipment and the approaches they might need to do that and the communication needs of some of our children. We are really having a problem getting that message across ...

In trying to 'get across' her message, J.M. implicitly represented some groups of students as straight-forward, 'moderate/severe borderline', merely requiring a curriculum (at the College level) based on 'practical life skills'. In contrast, she adopted a discourse which challenged low expectations in terms of Freelands students, representing them as 'needing' a rich and varied curriculum in which courses 'take them forward' educationally. In arguing that the College of Further Education did not currently offer a curriculum and environment which takes into account the complexity of Freelands students' 'needs', J.M. implicitly raises the question of the rights of those students:

> The alternative site that is proposed for the seniors now, in common with most Greentown schools, doesn't have a sixth form provision so everybody leaves at 16 which means that if something doesn't happen through the college (i.e. 'appropriate provision') ... then our pupils are going to be the only ones on that site post-16.

This quotation introduces a further dimension in the maelstrom of policy making, that of the effects of one set of policies (i.e. the closure of Freelands) and the creation of a new situation in which disabled students may experience exclusion. At 16+ disabled students could find themselves stranded in mainstream schools while their peers go off to Colleges of Further Education, re-articulating existing exclusions. One implication of this is that the whole manner in which policies are conceived and implemented needs to be reconceptualized so that planning becomes multi-dimensional, rather than 'linear', involving multiple perspectives.

J.M. did discuss one group of students quite specifically; the 'grouping' was based on the social, physical and emotional consequences of having muscular dystrophy:

> **J.M.**: We have five children at the moment – five boys in the primary department with muscular dystrophy – and they whiz round together in their electric wheelchairs and they are great mates. If they were scattered right across Greentown in individual schools they would have nobody to empathize with because they don't need to spend a lot of time saying 'I can't do this anymore – my legs don't work anymore' – they *know*. They've known each other over the years. They've seen each other walking, then going into a wheelchair, getting less and less able and struggling physically. They know – and they can see it happening to each other. It's not just them – it's not 'Why me?', it's 'Well, you know, we've all got muscular dystrophy and this is what happens'. ... At least there are other kids that the same thing is happening to and they can get cross together, have a good old moan together and be obnoxious together. And there's that bond there and I think it's very important for those boys – and very important for their parents as well that they have an opportunity to know that there are others in school who actually understand because nobody else can. And one thing about this school, it does mean that children have opportunities for friendships with other disabled kids.

My response to this marks a point at which I began to re-examine my own preconceptions about 'what ought to happen' from a different angle. The transcript shows that I responded:

> **F.A.**: Yes ... that just underlines this whole question of entitlement. I mean, we talk about entitlement to a curriculum but we forget about all the other possible 'entitlements' ... when I say 'we', I don't mean you, I mean people like me who are always arguing for people going to schools in their local communities. What you've said has made me think that inclusion may not always be everyone going to their *local* school, it would be about a whole lot of different processes which might sometimes be contradictory. Inclusion could be a number of different things. This is why children's own views and wishes are so important. It's complicated, isn't it?

> **J.M.**: Yes. Very, very complicated I think, yes.

J.M.'s comments echoed those of by C.W. (in Chapter Three), but his were made from the perspective of an ex-student at the school. Special schools, then, may provide places in which relationships of support and solidarity can be formed which – if disabled students were dispersed across the wider school population – would not be possible *in the same way*. This raises important issues concerning the rights of disabled people and the need to critically examine assumptions about what constitutes 'inclusion' from a number of perspectives. It would be important to try to maintain support and solidarity within and between groups of students in education, regardless of the characteristics which make them a group or a 'minority', but this does not mean preserving special schools. It might mean giving some groups of children opportunities to choose a particular setting but it is hard to see why this could not be part of an ordinary school. One issue here is the extreme fear some people in mainstream schools may have about the presence of children who are ill. Far from this being a reason for maintaining segregated settings, this is yet another reason why inclusion involves a process of cultural transformation on all levels in terms of values, processes and organisation and, above all, in terms of the way people understand and relate to each other. Another issue is the possible conflict between 'focusing on individuals' experiences of physical or intellectual restriction arising directly from impairments, of pain, and of facing and fearing death' (Closs, 2000, p. 3) and the kind of transformative action which is needed to bring about inclusive education. But, Shakespeare and Watson (1998, quoted in Closs, 2000) argue for, 'a balance between understanding disabled people as individuals and members of a disadvantaged group, and between realizing the commonalities and respecting the differences' (Closs, 2000, p. 13).

J.M. saw the students at Freelands as being a 'minority group' and as 'having difficulties'. Her discussion of the choice of a possible secondary school as a site for the secondary aged students from Freelands was revealing:

> **J.M.:** The secondary school chosen for our young people to move to is a school which we may have some PR difficulties with as far as some parents are concerned in that it is an inner city school and is viewed as being not a high achieving school but in some ways that may actually help our pupils in that they may not be quite so unusual in having difficulties. They won't necessarily be the only minority group. There are other racial minority groups at that school, so the staff and the school have had to work round those sorts of issues which, in principle, are fairly similar once you've got your head round dealing with a small racial group and the problems that can cause and the curriculum problems that can ensue from that, and behavioural problems and how will the children relate and how everybody gets along in a community ...

J.M. is arguing implicitly in favour of a school which already has a diverse population as a site for students and staff from Freelands to move to, but there is an uneasy tension between a suggestion that 'minority groups' may be seen as the cause of problems (relating to 'curriculum', 'behaviour' 'how children relate' and 'how everybody gets along as a community') and the necessity of school transformation. The discourses used here, such as '... the staff and the school have had to work around' and '*dealing with* a small racial group' suggest that difficulties arise because of the presence of that group rather than in relation to the wider social context of the school. In general, J.M. thinks that mainstream school would be '... a much better, a more real sort of setting for a lot of our pupils.' but she is apprehensive about the ability of schools to 'meet their needs'. This is explained by her in terms of the 'complex difficulties' of the students concerned as well as in terms of the entrenchment of attitudes and practices of schools themselves.

It emerged later in an interview that although initially the LEA's proposal (not apparently supported by J.M. herself) was for all members of Freelands to move to the proposed resource bases, later there would be a selection process.

> **J.M.**: So there is a gradual shift going on and it may be that once the initial group of children have gone to the secondary placement, then as children come up to 11 in the primary resource base there will be a reassessment and maybe they'll be moved to another sector before they actually reach secondary age.

> **F.A.**: What, like Maynard School (school designated for students 'with severe learning difficulties' on the same site as Freelands), for example?

> **J.M.**: Yes

Far from the proposals being a determined move by the LEA to challenge the exclusion of all disabled students, the preservation of a 'fall-back' school designated for 'students with severe learning difficulties' could lead to the intensification of selection and spatializing processes, rather than reducing them. It would be possible for students to be decanted out of the mainstream resource base into a segregated setting when their presence 'in mainstream' is deemed 'inappropriate'. This would entail attaching an 'SLD' label to the students transferring to Maynard School in place of the 'physical impairment' label they started out with. This is an example of the complexity of the processes involved in policy making. While one group of students were to be 'promoted' to resource bases in ordinary schools, another group will be later re-categorized and relegated to a different special school from the one they first came from. Such a scenario in which students are shunted from one setting to another and then on again, raises very serious questions about whose interests and what agendas are paramount in the whole exercise. Some of the possible implications of a move of some children to Maynard School will become clear when I discuss extracts from an interview with another teacher, G.B below. The change in label, the repackaging of students, is part of a blurring of boundaries between professional assessment and technical-bureaucratic processes which can be used to mask exclusions. These processes – which are endemic in the English education system – are all part of the spatial shifting and movement involved in the maintenance of separate sites for specified purposes. Many of these 'purposes' are closely linked to veiled bureaucratic agendas or political ones concerned with 'raising standards' and the struggle between schools for markets and are based on goals which are the antithesis of principle of inclusion and equality.

Interview with A.J., teacher

The population of Freelands has been transformed in recent years in response to successive government policies concerning, for example, 'integration' during the 1980s and 1990s, and the introduction of the national curriculum.

A.J., who has taught at the school for a number of years, described the students at Freelands:

A.J.: They have physical difficulties, mainly, multiple and complex. I think we're bordering on the *severe* learning difficulties now because as I see it anyway – most of the moderate learning difficulties with the physical disability are out in mainstream.

When I started here 13 years ago we'd got 120 students, although the majority of them shouldn't have been here, they should have been in mainstream – it was your thalidomides and polio victims .... They were literally physically disabled and that was it and that's how we're still seen. The special learning needs are not seen still – we are just seen as bodies in wheelchairs and it's not like that at all.

While A.J.'s account suggests that she was not against *some* disabled children going to ordinary schools – far from it – some students and some degrees of impairment require specialist provision. She did accept that segregation could take place in a different way, as a 'unit attached' to a mainstream school because of:

... the need for role models, basically. They would be the most important thing because there is nothing for them to latch on to.

A.J. saw a unit 'attached to' a mainstream school as being physically and organizationally separate. Central to this view is A.J.'s notion of 'specials' which is used to denote a homogenized group of others requiring different and separating treatment from 'ordinary' students. (It is intriguing to note how persistent the notion of 'the normal' is, even though the term is not used explicitly in any of the material gathered in England. This suggests that concepts can hang around very successfully in new guises.) At the same time, A.J. implicitly condemns the homogenizing gaze which sees her students (which she aligns herself with discursively) as 'bodies in wheelchairs' rather than individual learners and members of the community.

Interview with G.B.

In contrast to A.J., G.B., part of whose autobiographical account given in Chapter Three, had a long history of teaching in different segregated settings. His accounts of his experiences in posts held at different stages of his career were sometimes lurid and shocking:

So in 1972 or 73 I got a twelve month contract at L. School for maladjusted kids and they were extremely violent. You used to gather a heap of bodies on the playground and say 'Whose hair is that blowing across the playground?' and things like that. Another lass there had seen three girls who had got better leather jackets than hers and stabbed the three of them.

The discourse of mayhem and violence adopted by G.B. and the lumping together of children apparently on the basis of their perceived 'violence', positioned both the schools and the young people as 'beyond the pale'; pupils became 'others' in places and times past in which unspeakable things happened. This is an example of the merging of place and identity as discussed in Chapter 2. An interesting example of the way in which disabled children in a different school on the same site (Maynard School) as Freelands were 'othered' arose:

F.A.: Tell me about Maynard School.

G.B.: I don't know! Violent! All sorts of problems but more than physical handicaps.

F.A.: Do you mean they experience learning difficulties perhaps as well? Will those children be 'integrated' eventually?

G.B.: All sorts of things. No, I never go in the place. The first Christmas they were here some of our 16+ pupils went in with a big Christmas card we had made for them. Three girls went in, two in wheelchairs and one walking; coming out again, they were attacked by their pupils.

Here, the 'site' is outlawed and those who frequent it are constructed as danger-ous others. Paradoxically, I was later to come across similar repudiating discourses applied to the students at Freelands and deployed by a parent governor of the primary school initially chosen to receive the primary-aged Freelands children.

I was present in a lesson which G.B. was teaching. It seemed interesting and stimulating; G.B. responded with enthusiasm and respect to students' questions and observations and I reflected that he could have been working with any group of students aged 12–13 in an ordinary school. His equitable and respectful teaching style contrasted curiously with the way he represented students as 'other' in the way he spoke about them in the context of his earlier teaching experience. G.B.'s social practice in terms of the discourses he used placed disabled children (known in earlier contexts) outside and beyond 'the normal'. Yet his social practice as a teacher situated the children as respected learners. In reading over these examples and others (not quoted) in the interview material from England and France, I notice a tendency by some of those interviewed, to provide 'colourful' descriptions of particular settings and groups of students located in their own professional histories, or in relation to other sites. I can think of examples from situations in which I might have held forth with anecdotes about the strange and challenging characteristics of pupils or their parents, perhaps wanting to evoke curiosity and awe in my audience. Perhaps, descriptions located in other times and other places and of people now long out of our own orbit, are seen as liberating us from ordinary concerns about the language we use. Or, is it possible that in speaking about periods and contexts in the past we casually slip into an unreconstructed vernacular on the assumption that the language we used *then* does not require reframing *now* in the light of an (assumed) greater awareness of the implications of 'bad-mouthing'?

There was one occasion when G.B. implicitly took a position which challenged the rationale of applying the label 'educational subnormal' to a group of students at a residential special school (his first teaching post, described in Chapter Three):

They were all educationally subnormal and they were educationally subnormal because they had never been to school. I mean these kids were from gypsy families and it was jolly hard to get hold of them and they were smashing kids really. Absolute crackers at first until they calmed down, because they had never been to school before.

This is revealing. First, that G.B. does not, on all occasions, accept the use of labels unquestioningly. Secondly, the extract presents evidence of the othering of children belonging to a minority group and their exclusion through bureaucratic mechanisms of labelling and removal and G.B. is clearly aware of this. Thirdly, the quotation exemplifies the contingent and opportunistic use of categorization and segregated sites for those who are 'difficult to place' or regarded as threatening others.

These reflections on some of the issues raised in relation to the interviews, suggest that teachers – people – have complex, contradictory ways of seeing and of representing the work that they do and the communities they work with. In this context, therefore, the task of analyzing discourse is not one of identifying and isolating individual strands such as 'labelling' or discourses of social justice, and of making simplistic value judgments on the basis of these, but of putting these together and trying to understand their complexity and meaning.

NAMING AND PLACING: THE STRUGGLE FOR SPACE

The discussion in this section is based on selections from material gathered during three meetings at which I was an observer. These meetings were all concerned with the wider 'consultation procedures' which were set in motion by the LEA in connection with the proposed closure of Freelands School. The meetings were part of the process of policy making, in that they provided arenas in which different values and positions were adopted and struggled over. A key feature of the composition of the meetings – in terms of those who were invited to attend – was that different groups were either kept apart or there was an extreme imbalance in terms of their levels of representation. This made it possible for strongly represented groups in particular meetings to occupy more 'floor space' and express views more vehemently than might have been the case if other interests had been more strongly represented in the same forum. Of course, these three meetings were only part of a whole range of procedures involving all kinds of meetings in different settings. They are not necessarily representative of all those other meetings. I have chosen to focus on these, however, as they provide examples of the role of discourse as tactic in policy and of the importance of space and place in constructing identities.

In general it was not possible to make audio-recordings of the proceedings and I was obliged to try and write everything down in a notebook. At the beginning of each meeting I was generally introduced by the chairperson and sometimes asked to explain what I was doing. I explained to the meeting that I was following policy making processes in relation to the proposed closure of Freelands School and asked their permission to make notes of what was said.

The first meeting was set up at Hillbank School by the LEA, and presented as part of a 'consultation process' concerning the proposed move of primary aged children and their teachers and support staff from Freelands School to Hillbank School.

Meeting 1: At Hillbank School (March 1998)

The meeting was called to discuss the proposed move of the primary section of Freelands school to Hillbank School where, according to the LEA, there was 'spare capacity', making the mainstream school an 'ideal choice'. It was attended by the following:

A.M. (an ex headteacher, appointed as temporary advisor by the LEA to see through the consultation period); B.J. (Head Teacher of Hillbank School); P.F. (teacher governor); J.W. (LEA Officer from personnel, who remained silent throughout the meeting); P.H. (Education Officer for Capital Programmes); J.M. ('acting' head teacher of Freelands School (who was not given an opportunity to speak during the meeting)); F.A. (researcher); 15 teachers, 4 support staff.

The start of the meeting was delayed because the teachers did not want the meeting to go ahead without their union representative being present. Questions were asked about whether the union had been informed of the meeting. It was eventually agreed that a further meeting would be called with the union official present. There was an uneasy atmosphere as A.M. opened the meeting and it was immediately clear that any outstanding issues concerning the meeting and consultation process were to be dismissed.

> **A.M.:** Thank you for coming. I am sorry for the course of events. The Union representatives did not inform the office that they couldn't attend. We feel that we ought to do our best to accommodate your needs in the right setting and with your representatives.
>
> We have already had a one month extension for you to air your concerns, talk to each other. I hope you have all seen the consultation document. J.M. is present as acting head of Freelands School. We are here to discuss premises issues and I would like to introduce you to P.H. who is going to rehearse some of these with you.

In this opening, the advisor appointed to manage the consultation process with the schools involved informed the meeting that they had already been given plenty of time (with a 'one month extension') to discuss issues and raise concerns and that this was not part of the purpose of the present meeting. The space in which teachers could 'air their concerns' lay outside this formal arena in which powerful key figures were in control. The advisor thus imposed boundaries around what could be talked about in the meeting, and – by inference – what couldn't.

The proceedings of the meeting were illustrative of the use of discourse 'as tactic and as theory' (Fulcher, 1999, p. 11; Macdonnell, 1986). The 'tactic' is to control and manipulate the agenda and manage the debate (via a 'consultation process') as a means of maintaining power and closing down discussion. The 'theory' is that there is a legitimate disconnection of particular issues such as those relating to buildings, the use of space and capital expenditure from issues relating to inclusion, teaching and learning, and rights. Thus, the deployment of particular tactical ways of constructing issues and interests via discourse is deeply political, especially when it concerns struggles over who has control over what may, and may not, be legitimately discussed.

The chair of the meeting introduced P.H. (Education Officer for Capital Programmes):

> **P.H.**: Good evening. My department has a duty to bring in as much capital as possible to improve our buildings. Once we get the money, we can press on with the architecture. My team picks up a lot on planning issues. We have to rely heavily on custom and practice and national guidelines and building regulations, but we also like to discuss with practitioners.
>
> Our starting point is the question: How do we make effective and efficient use of our buildings? We do look at schools to see where there is over provision and inefficient use of resources, space.
>
> We have to ensure an efficient and equitable use of resources.
>
> New school buildings cost money.

These statements exemplify the political nature of discourse and the ways it can be used to define certain agendas as legitimate, outlawing others. They imposed a particular construction of issues relating to possible important changes in the use and distribution of space in the school, at the same time as positioning alternative perspectives as illegitimate. P.H. framed the issues within a discourse of economic rationality and 'reasonableness' in relation to the use of resources, legitimated by reference to national guidelines and building regulations which teachers and others involved in education may not be familiar with. She asserted her 'expert' and (by implication) disinterested status through a 'language of rigidity, imperviousness and defensiveness' (Corbett, 1996, p. 40) which:

> ... achieves its control firstly through its use of language and secondly, because this discourse and its associated practices have two key institutional bases: bureaucracy and professional and paraprofessional training ... (Fulcher, 1999, p. 247)

Embedded in the professional discourse and specialist training (the first of which is legitimated by the second) is an assumption that there is an 'expertise' which is separate from, and superior to, other kinds of knowledge. This is marked by, for example, the higher salaries received by bureaucrats and 'experts' of all kinds in comparison with teachers.

P.H. places the 'consultation' in contrast to overriding important financial concerns. She adds, however, 'but we also like to discuss with practitioners' suggesting that 'discussion with practitioners ' is only taking place because 'they' (the Education Planning Office for Capital Building) agree to it, thus positioning the 'consultation process' as procedurally optional and not, therefore, a procedural requirement concerned with democratic representation.

P.H. moves on briskly to outline a possible vision for rationalizing the use of space in the school which would include the move of students from Freelands:

> 75 pupils in each year group ... This may affect the infrastructure ... So lets think about the Freelands resource base ...
>
> The proposal is: equivalent space: 3 classes plus access – Lift – toileting provision doors internally.

> Externally, there is a need to provide adequate space for turning round
> the vehicles – and the wheel chairs – getting the children off site etc.

The discourse is one of managing a problem, which is about fitting a new group
of different people (referred to only in terms of technical challenges which they
presented to planners) into existing structures in order to 'rationalize the use of
resources'. No space is made for a discussion of wider issues about relationships,
equity and the need for cultural transformation at all levels of policy making and
practice.

P.H. was challenged by a number of questions from teachers present at the
meeting, some of whom were becoming increasingly agitated. She was ready with
the answers:

> **Teacher 1**: If the Freelands project hadn't been introduced, we'd have merrily
> gone on with all this space, wouldn't we?
>
> **P.H.**: We would have been looking at the building in terms of rationalizing
> the space.
>
> **Teacher 1**: What area would you have been looking at? What savings would
> you be making?
>
> **P.H.**: Alternative use of the building as a Youth Centre or Housing Office.
> Or even demolishing half of the building.

The meeting is, in effect, being told to accept disabled children and the transformation in the use of space that will involve or else part of the school will be taken
over for other uses which, by implication, would involve the presence of possibly
'disruptive' groups such as teenagers or members of the public seeking housing
('the homeless') coming onto the site. And of course, half the building could be
'demolished'. This was interpreted by many of those present (I later discovered in
the course of a conversation) as 'threatening' and 'intimidating'.

A group of teachers sitting in one part of the hall were clearly becoming angry
and their manner of asking the questions was challenging. The questions themselves
were an attempt at resistance by moving the debate away from the professional-
bureaucratic discourse deployed by P.H., to another arena – that of the impact of
a change of the use of space in the school on 'the curriculum'.

> **Head Teacher**: I don't think you made this clear that the main loss will be
> the infant hall. We might not worry too much about the principle of having
> a specialist area. But the HALL!
>
> **Teacher 2**: Yes, the hall is fully timetabled.
>
> **P.H.**: We are looking at trying to improve the staff room and to have a studio
> and a whole variety of things.
>
> **Teacher 4**: When you move facilities like the hall you're altering our cur-
> riculum.
>
> **P.H.**: The context of where I'm coming from is straightforward: my role is

justifying to the committee and the ratepayers – that we are making efficient use of resources.

Teacher 2: You say there are benefits for all the children. What will be the benefits for the children here?

P.H.: As part of the disabled toilets, hopefully there would be refurbishment for all toilets. It's early days. I'm only talking about buildings. Not all the other issues to do with inclusion.

A.M.: It's not a fait accompli. I would like you to keep an open mind because there are definite benefits for the children, for other children and the Freelands children.

P.H.: When we do a consultation like this I am in a Catch 22 situation. If I'd brought ready made plans you'd have said 'You've jumped the gun. We weren't consulted'. But I've come here without a plan and you're saying we've no answers to your questions.

The assertion by P.H. that she has 'come without a plan' is surely disingenuous; no 'plan' perhaps, other than framing the debate so that the financial interests of the local authority override other concerns as far as possible. In these extracts of sections taken from the transcription of this meeting (but not reordered sequentially or relationally) the struggles taking place between the competing discourses are evident. LEA officers and teachers square up to each other in a 'no holds barred' battle. Threats to 'demolish' half the building or the moving onto the site of potentially threatening others (teenagers, social services client groups) made by the LEA officers, wrestle with teachers' implicit questioning of the integrity of the officers. When challenged to say what benefits will be enjoyed by all children in the school, P.H.is only able to suggest 'hopefully a refurbishment of all toilets'. For staff, she suggests 'improving the staff room'.

One tactic which was frequently deployed in order to keep control or exclude challenging questions and perspectives from the arena, was that of ignoring or re-interpreting a question. In one exchange (not quoted) a teacher asks a straightforward question concerning the time scale for the building programme. This question was ignored by P.H., who irritatedly tried to make the questioner appear irrational and unreasonable in contrast to her own pretended ordered and 'democratic' way of handling the 'consultation' process.

At no time were questions relating to rights and equality raised by anybody present. It came as a surprise, then, when at the end of the meeting a teacher who had remained silent said to me:

We don't all think like this. Some of us would welcome these children into the school. That's the way education should be going.

'Why didn't you say this now in the meeting?' I asked. She replied,

There's a small group who are very powerful and they've taken over. It's got very nasty.

Until this point, my interpretation of the proceedings of the meeting was that the LEA 'Education Officer for Capital Programmes' flanked by the Chair of the meeting who had been put in post temporally to 'manage the consultation', had successfully imposed an agenda on the meeting and deflected questions which might undermine their purpose – which was to close down Freelands school and move the primary aged children from there to Hillbank. Using her professional-bureaucratic position, P.H. had tried – mainly successfully – to keep the discussion on the level of rationalizing resources, through a redefinition of the use of space at Hillbank. This 'redefinition' would, argued teachers, threaten existing practices and arrangements in the school relating to the curriculum and the teachers' questions seemed to me reasonable and legitimate.

The teacher sitting next to me offered me a lift into the city centre. During the journey she explained that the teachers who had raised the questions and some of the governors who weren't present, adamantly opposed accepting a group of disabled students into the school on the grounds that 'it would change the character of the school' and 'it would not be in the interests of "their" children'. She explained that underpinning questions raised about the loss of space in the school and the effect this could have on the curriculum, were unstated issues regarding assumptions and attitudes concerning disabled children. In effect, the teachers who spoke in the meeting had masked these concerns under a professional counter-discourse concerning the curriculum.

This fresh perspective on what had taken place was reinforced in the following meeting held a week later in which governors from Hillbank formed a wall of opposition to the LEA. In addition to concerns expressed about the possible 'effects' of having Freelands children in the school in terms of teaching loads and performance tables, discursive devices were deployed which positioned the community of Freelands School (children, parents, teachers, governors) as undesirable others. The contrast in the choice of arguments put forward by some of the same people in the two meetings is particularly revealing.

Meeting 2: Meeting of governors at Hillbank School (April 1998)

The stated purpose of the meeting was to discuss proposals that primary aged children and staff working with them at Freelands should move to Hillbank School.

Present at meeting: A.B. (Senior LEA Officer for Special Educational Needs); A.M. (Retired Head Teacher, temporarily employed by LEA to manage the consultation process); R.W. (Chair of Governors of Hillbank School); B.J. (Head Teacher Hillbank School); L.C. (Parent Governor); T.F. (Teacher Governor); four other governors; F.A. (researcher).

A.M., who I had already interviewed and who chaired the previous meeting, opened the governors' meeting:

> **A.M.:** The thought of integrating pupils with SEN is of course nothing new
> in Greentown, nor is it new to the national framework. Some children have

been integrated very successfully into mainstream schools ...

The staff at Freelands feel that their pupils should be alongside their able-bodied peers – and that with the range of ability among the children, they feel they are segregating their folk more than they should from the social and intellectual experience needed by their pupils. There is of course, the question of finding a school where they could integrate without detriment to their able-bodies peers.

Again, the opening to the meeting set the tone and the boundaries within which the issues could be discussed, and rehearsed the discourses which could be used. Students at Freelands School are positioned as 'pupils with SEN'; thus, any problems which may arise are somehow derived from these pupils themselves because it is they who *have* the 'special needs' .

The grammatical use of the passive voice positions disabled students as having things done to them – i.e. 'having integration done to them', rather than being involved as ordinary members of communities participating in projects of social transformation with other young people. By noting that *some* pupils ... have 'been integrated successfully', there is an implication that this is by no means a certainty and there have also been 'failures'. The responsibility for *wanting* 'their' pupils to move to Hillbank is placed firmly with the teachers at Freelands (who are not represented at the meeting) and, A.M. suggests, arises from altruistic concerns about equity. This contrasted with my own experience, at that stage, of sitting in meetings – including one organized by the local teachers' unions – and listening to the serious reservations expressed by staff at Freelands about both the ability of future provision to respond to the diversity of learners from Freelands School and about their own professional position in relation to their future employment prospects and role if Freelands were closed down.

Furthermore, the suggestions that the 'integration of disabled students' should not take place if it were deemed to be to the 'detriment of their able-bodied peers' sanctions the highly discriminatory position that the presence of disabled students could somehow be harmful to non-disabled students, implying that the interests of non-disabled students are different from, and should naturally take precedence over, those of disabled students. This suggests that there are 'two groups' of students whose interests are potentially in conflict, and for whom the allocation of separate spaces may be desirable.

It is interesting to note that A.M. opened the meeting by making placatory references to an issue raised by the hostile teachers in the previous meeting – namely, concerns that there should be no 'detriment' to 'able-bodied' children. Once again, there is an implicit framing of disabled students as people to be wary of, who are potentially 'dangerous' to the normal, legitimate members of the school. The language of 'able-bodiment' asserts the hegemony of the ordered, normal body.

The next group to be singled out was the parents of children at Freelands School:

R.W. (Chair of Governors): Am I right that the parents of these children will be more directly involved and concerned for the education of *their* children

> and do we have to take this into account? I mean, will they expect to come along and be on this board of governors?
>
> **A.B.**: That would be for the governors to decide, but we would think that it would be helpful to have a co-opted member.

In this quotation the Chair of Governors implied that the parents of children from Freelands would be selfishly interested only in the education of 'their own' children and that that it would therefore be unreasonable for them to expect to be represented on the governing body. The most senior LEA officer for 'special needs' area, timidly appealed to the need to be 'helpful' rather than defending the right of all parents to representation on the governing body. This was at first surprising as in an earlier interview A.B. had expressed a clear commitment to the rights of disabled children and their families to be included and to be treated equitably in relation to their education. Such contradictions between positions adopted in different arenas has been as a recurring feature in the material gathered. It may be evidence of the struggles and contradictions which are at work in policy making, as played out through the dilemmas faced by different groups and individuals as they attempt to comply with conflicting agendas which are personal, professional and political. At this stage in the governors' meeting the LEA officer felt, perhaps, the need to adopt a tactic of conciliation and appeasement in order to try and win over the meeting to the LEA perspective. In taking on the role of implementing government policy which is opposed to the values and perceived interests of, say, governing bodies or groups of parents, LEA officers may be positioned as legitimating values and practices which may be in opposition to those they believe in.

One of the teacher governors tried a different tack:

> **Teacher governor**: Unfortunately the world has become very competitive and we are now in the business of performance related league tables which parents and OFSTED take note of. So will their SATS be included in our performances?
>
> **A.B.**: Well, the current government is very anxious about this. What they want is to look at progression, not just bald figures.
>
> **R.W.** (Chair of Governors): Some of us have had leaflets from the C of E (Church of England) School pushed through our letter boxes saying they've got 100% in their SATs. I think its important that staff should not feel their efforts are being subverted.
>
> **A.M.**: There is a concern that there will be a new focus on individual progression.

It is suggested here that the children from Freelands (referred to as 'they') will 'lower the standards' in the school, making it less competitive (in comparison to the local C of E, school) and will 'subvert' the 'efforts' of staff. The LEA representatives distance themselves from the issues raised by not answering the questions directly, instead hiding behind reputed government policy.

The teacher governor turned her attention to staff from Freelands, first implicitly suggesting that some teachers might not be properly qualified teachers with formal 'Qualified Teachers Status' (QTS).

> **Teacher Governor**: Could we know how many staff with QTS (qualified teacher status) will be coming from Freelands?
>
> **A.M.**: No, we'll know that tomorrow.
>
> **Teacher Governor**: Can you give us a rough idea?
>
> **A.M.**: No, it's rather complicated.
>
> **Teacher Governor**: Can I ask if they get the special schools allowance?
>
> **A.M.**: Yes
>
> **Teacher Governor**: When they come here, will they lose it?
>
> **A.B.**: There's a big discussion going on about whether teachers should get special school's allowance.
>
> **Teacher Governor**: But the teachers in mainstream won't get it when those children are in the school?
>
> **A.B.**: A lot of discussion is going on at the moment but the Freelands teachers would be treated the same as other teachers in Integrated Resources. (i.e. they would get the 'Special Schools' allowance).
>
> **Teacher Governor**: What is the teacher-pupil ration at Freelands?
>
> **A.M.**: 5 to 1
>
> **R.W.**: Will this be maintained? Presumably you will be able to give us information about the number of staff coming?

In this exchange a number of discursive devices are adopted which serve to frame the teachers at Freelands as possibly not 'proper teachers' and of being especially privileged in receiving more money for their work than teachers at Hillbank. This privilege will continue, adding further injustice to the existing situation because 'those children' will also be taught by ordinary teachers at Hillbank. The question of teacher-pupil ration is a two-edged sword. The ratio of 1–5 sounds ludicrously generous in contrast to the 1–32 referred to in the previous meeting as standard at Hillbank (not quoted here). When pressed, the LEA representatives later reveal that it is not planned to maintain the 1–5 ratio, but that teachers newly appointed to the school will be expected to be able to 'work with disabled children'. By implication, this emphasizes the apparent injustice concerning the Special Schools allowance not being paid to mainstream teachers. In this meeting, 'insiders' from Hillbank School turned the tables on LEA representatives, positioning them as 'unrealistic' and 'irrational'.

A further issue relates to the unexamined assumptions informing the 'special' allowance for 'special' school teachers. Implicitly the equation is made between the *presence* of disabled children and extra remuneration because of their 'specialness'.

As Corbett argues:

> What does 'special' mean? If we detach this word from its anchor in 'edu-
> cational' (*or 'allowance', 'school' or 'teacher'*) we can see that 'special'
> does not mean especially good and valued ... It is linked to 'needs' which
> implies dependency, inadequacy and unworthiness. (Corbett, 1996, p. 3, my
> additions emphasized in brackets)

'Special' then, is a label to do with 'abnormality' and 'not as good as' and
where 'special' is present, additional moneys need to be handed over to those
responsible for dealing with this 'specialness' because it is onerous or repugnant.
If 'special' teachers are getting paid to deal with 'those children' then so should
'we' the 'normal', legitimate teachers if 'those children are in the school'. Here,
the distribution of additional payments is spatialized; it is dependent upon *where*
disabled students are, not on what additional expenditure might be needed if the
school's population is expanded.

Discursive practices which undermine open and respectful discussion call into
question the whole process of 'democratic consultation'. In the two meetings quoted,
issues of teaching and learning, for example, were never properly addressed because
they were obscured by a more powerful discourse of labelling and exclusion. In
addition, uncomfortable questions about rights and equality simmered just below
the surface of the debate waiting to erupt – which they did, quite unexpectedly,
in the second meeting.

> **Parent Governor**: I visited Freelands and saw that very few children could
> communicate.
>
> **A.M.**: Some can speak.
>
> **Parent Governor**: Yes, but look at all the time it will need ... I mean,
> while they're trying to communicate, what will be happening in the rest of
> the classroom. It's the academic integration I have a problem with, not the
> social.
>
> **A.B.**: It's about *tolerance* and the kind of society ...
>
> **Parent Governor** (interrupting): Isn't it all being driven by the parents of
> special needs children?
>
> **A.B.** (vehemently): NO! I *do* believe that we are trying to build a better
> society. And these kids exist. We can't just shove them away.

This exchange represents a real struggle over values and over who controls the
discourse – and hence the agenda – of the meeting. It shows the multiple levels at
which wider issues and struggles are being fought out in this meeting. Suddenly,
there are a number of different kinds of discourse taking place; the repudiating gaze
of the parent governor comes into direct conflict with the 'social justice' stance
adopted by the LEA officer. The content of the dialogue is inseparable from the
discursive devices used to impose one set of values over another. An interesting
feature of the struggle going on here is its spatial dimension. The Parent Governor

is focusing on issues relating to the specific situation of the proposed move of Freelands students to Hillbank and the kinds of issues which might arise in relation to 'academic integration'. A.B. takes the discussion outside the boundaries of the school gates and into a different value and discourse arena, that of 'tolerance' and the 'kind of society' we want to live in. The discourse of appeasement deployed by A.M. at the beginning of the meeting and the discourse of 'concerned professional' are, for the moment, sidelined only to be re-introduced later as a way of moving the meeting on and masking conflict. The sudden introduction of a social justice agenda temporarily put the meeting into confusion and a difficult silence ensued. This was a critical moment in the meeting and in the wider framework of the 'consultation' process because it was the first time that resistance had been mounted to the deficit-driven arguments and language; these had gone unchallenged in the previous meeting. What would happen?

This was also a critical moment in my research in that the above exchange exposed the ethical and political nature of the struggle in sharp relief. Fulcher (1999) explains:

> ... no discursive practice ... is ever purely technical. It is located in a moral
> system of values and in a political system which has established a hierarchy
> of values. (Fulcher, 1999, p. 11)

The discursive practices in this meeting relate to conflicting values about the kind of society we live in, but the parent governor and the LEA officer are envisaging quite different and opposing kinds of societies. In adopting a language of social justice to counter moves to 'shove these kids away' as she strategically put it, A.B. temporarily reduced the meeting, including the parent governor, to a shocked silence.

One insight which emerges from an examination of the discourses and tactics used in these two meetings is that individuals and groups vary in the amount of power they are able to exert in different contexts. The two meetings discussed here have taken place in the same place, only a few days apart. In the first meeting, the LEA representatives appear to hold the power from the outset by adopting a professional-bureaucratic discourse, while in the second meeting the LEA officer's opening to the meeting is placatory, seeming to acknowledge that the 'detriment to other children' is a legitimate concern. The teachers in the first meeting appeared to focus primarily on the use of space at Hillbank and how any loss of space would affect the curriculum and teaching in the classroom. The LEA representative responsible for capital programme expenditure manipulated the meeting, imposing a veto on issues outside 'the rational use of resources'. In the second meeting teacher governors (two of whom had been principle protagonists in the first meeting) and the parent governor initially adopted a different set of tactics which involved asking questions which positioned members of the Freelands community in negative ways. The discursive representation of groups, including teachers, parents and students, as undesirable and unattractive, exemplifies attempts to exploit existing mythologies through discourse as a way of influencing or controlling policy making. When the

LEA officer, A.B., introduces a social justice challenge, they revert to other tactics, invoking issues associated with the classroom and the curriculum, as well as 'the amount of work that would be created'.

The following section focuses on a meeting of governors at Freelands school, held eight months later. The meeting is chaired by P.D., a newly appointed special needs advisor who has picked up the job of managing the planning of alternative provision to Freelands. A discussion of this meeting provides an interesting contrast with the meetings in the above section in terms of the attitudes of governors towards the kinds of relationships they would like to form with the mainstream school community. In addition, it allows for an exploration of ways in which governors 'see' the students in their own school and the hopes and expectations that they have for them.

Meeting 3: Meetings of the governors at Freelands School (November 1998)

Present: B.S. (parent governor); B.B. (parent governor); J.S. (Chair of governors, father of ex-pupil); J.M. (head teacher); C.M. (Nursery teacher); M.B. (teacher); P.D. (Adviser for 'SEN' development and planning, LEA); F.A. (researcher).

> **P.D.**: I was appointed in September as an advisor for SEN and Strategic Development and Planning. I have 18 months experience leading an SEN team in B. I intend to be here to see the development through
>
> **B.B.** (parent): Where have all the others gone?
>
> **J.S.**: Why has it taken 13 years for the changes to take place?
>
> **P.D.**: I've read all the background ... there are more files on this project than any other.
>
> **J.S.**: Previous meetings have been called to suit officers. When they had already got their plans made. But this is different. We're in at the beginning.

In this meeting, people appear to want to listen to each other. From the outset, P.D. positions herself as coming from the outside with some experience but not with a fixed idea of what was going to happen, or even what issues could be discussed in what way in the meeting. She appeared to be feeling her way, as a newcomer, through the history and events and amongst the different players surrounding the proposed closure of Freelands. J.M., the head teacher, also appeared to want to encourage an open discussion. The meeting was quite unlike the meetings at Hillbank where people seemed to hide their feelings and their fears and 'real' questions by adopting professional discourses or blocking off certain avenues of exploration with a variety of discursive tactics.

P.D. had come to discuss a new proposal with the governors of Freelands School. The plan to move the primary aged section of the school to Hillbank has 'fallen through', because of difficulties concerning the link with the proposed secondary school identified to 'receive' the secondary aged children at Freelands. It appeared that LEA officers concerned were 'unaware' that Hillbank was not a 'feeder' school for the proposed secondary school, so that disabled children would be separated from their friends when they left primary school. It was apparent (to me) that another reason why Hillbank was 'no longer an option' was because of the organized hostility and resistance on the part of a group of teachers and governors at the school. Some of the different ways in which this resistance worked its way through the 'consultation' debate were apparent in the transcriptions of the meetings (above). Freelands parents and governors had not been formally told about this resistance, but there were some indications in the meeting that they were aware of it.

P.D. explained that there was a new proposal to establish a campus site at Boxwood School, a model she described as:

> ... a particularly attractive one because it is an expansionist model. The primary and secondary schools are already all on one site. They see each school as being complementary to each other and making a good contribution to the community. Within their own schools they have an interest in children with SEN. It is a bit of opportunism because there is new building going on. The nursery and primary school are being completely re-built.
>
> First of all, we have in mind a Disability Living Centre which will house specialist equipment, not just for a small population but for all sorts of people. It will have a training aspect, involving parents and teachers working with children ...

This represents a radical departure from the original proposal which was that primary aged children from Freelands would move to a 'resource base' which would be part of an ordinary primary school (Hillbank). Secondary aged children would be members of an ordinary comprehensive school (Marshfield) which would also have a resource base. In the new proposal, Freelands would be transformed into a Disability Living Centre on a campus site on which there were already established two ordinary schools covering the full age range, and there were also plans to build a nursery. At this stage of the meeting it looked as if the idea of 'school' was being marginalized. The chair of governors, said:

> **J.S.:** My view is that this shouldn't be another LEA school. I'm disappointed that Health is falling behind ... It should be a centre for integrated resources ... so that parents don't have to do what I had to do – run round all over the city looking for equipment. Health and Social Services should be together if it's going to be of use to our students, but it's got to be sustainable. I see it as a *regional* centre for the area. It should be a sustainable project.
>
> **P.D.:** Regional development is certainly the government's preference for SEN.

This exchange introduced an emphasis on the perceived 'health' and 'social service' requirements of students and their families as being at the centre of the project. Far from moving nearer to schools for all, there was now a suggestion that some new kind of centre should be created for a whole region as the 'government's preferences for SEN'.

The term 'SEN' was used as a large 'hold-all' category with a spatial dimension articulated through the 'regional' development in 'SEN', homogenizing difficulties in learning and disabilities into a globalized category, positioned as exterior to ordinary educational structures. This is very different from a perception of responses to diversity as located in ordinary schools and as part of a cultural shift in relation to wider processes of exclusion. Suddenly 'education' receded as the main concern, and 'health' and 'welfare' issues were brought to the fore. The notion of a 'Disability Living Centre' suggested a social and political structure which both spatializes and segregates on the basis of impairment.

Paradoxically, the next issue to be raised was concerned with 'inclusion'.

> **P.D.**: If I can raise another issue which the education committee was concerned with, there is little mention of inclusion in the proposal but this authority is committed to inclusion. We are looking for possibilities. A problem-solving approach is more effective than drawing up a plan ... or a blueprint that says '*This* is inclusive'.

P.D. had just taken up a post in a Local Education Authority which stated that it was 'committed to inclusion' but acknowledged that she had 'no idea' what this might mean in practice in that particular LEA. She was faced with the task of interpreting this position in the context of discussions with parents and teachers and governors. 'Inclusion' has become a 'movable feast' – a piece of discourse tossed into the general mêlée of issues. But 'inclusive education' is concerned with challenging values and cultures; it is concerned with displacing 'solid structures' whether these are buildings, attitudes, practices or discourses. In the meeting under discussion, there was no evidence of the 'bad mouthing' which characterized the two previous meetings described, but the 'solid structures' such as the discourse of 'SEN' and the spatialized notion of 'disability living' which pose traditional barriers to overcoming segregation, were firmly embedded.

P.D. reports that when the idea of the campus was raised with head teachers,

> some exciting things were suggested. For example, 'virtual classrooms' for disabled secondary students.

Paradoxically, this idea suggests that disabled young people could be 'included' while being physically segregated from other learners. Underpinning the 'excitement' about the possibilities opened up by technology and the use of buzz words such as 'virtual', is a commitment to the idea of 'the modern' as being equivalent to 'progressive' and hence 'more humanitarian'. This 'excitement' denotes misunderstandings about the relationships involved in learning as a social activity, in contrast with those in which learning is 'virtual' or 'simulated'. The 'virtual' classroom separates the learner from the social processes and interactions of learning and is, therefore, the opposite of 'inclusive'.

The following section shows some of the different ideas and concerns that parents had about 'inclusion' and the discourses they used to talk about them.

> **B.B.** (parent): I'm not against inclusion at all, but I am concerned that inclusion is done because it's cheaper.

P.D.: This is not because of cost-cutting. If we wanted to go down that road, we'd have chosen the integrated resources.

P.D. had not been in post when the meetings discussed above had taken place. It was quite conceivable that she was unaware of the undisguised financially driven framework in which the debate had been set by the LEA. It is interesting to reflect on the 'knowledge' that P.D. has acquired that if cost-cutting had been a major concern, then the 'integrated resource' model would have been adopted. In fact, this model had been the one which the LEA sought to introduce – and the principle reason they gave was that there was a need to 'rationalize resources' – but opposition to the idea from a powerful group at Hillbank had successfully contributed to such a policy being abandoned.

Parents, governors and teachers seemed to be cautiously positive about the new proposal. J.S., the Chair of Governors, was anxious that Freelands should continue as a separate school. In order to emphasize the 'separate identity' he saw as essential, he quickly gave the site a new name 'Boxwood Special School' – a discursive device which provided the meeting with a way of talking about the new development which expresses its separate identity. Freelands became 'Boxwood Special School' for the duration of the rest of meeting.

J.S.: Our concern would be if the resource was just a bolt on. But as long as the Freelands School – or Boxwood Special School – were to be able to continue as a separate base – but able to integrate – or include – children as and when they can ...

P.D.: If you put children *on the site* there is an expectation that will happen ...

The idea that 'being on the same site' will lead to 'integration' or 'inclusion' just 'happening' sounds attractive. Nobody made the observation that Freelands and Maynard School already shared a site and – indeed – were physically joined, yet, far from having positive social contacts, the two school communities appeared to have no contact whatsoever.

Those present at the meeting were enthusiastic about establishing friendly relations between students in different sites on the proposed campus and this was usually referred to as 'integration', but sometimes as 'inclusion', showing a catch-all use of both terms which masked issues concerning different possible interpretations about the kinds of social and learning experiences all those on the campus might develop.

B.B. (parent): Will it be integration both ways because I think it will be advantageous for children from the main school to come over to our site?

P.D.: It will all be on *one* site

J.M. (parent): Children can come down from the local primary school to attend playtime. It would be so easy to arrange if we were all on one site. We do have children that could integrate.

B.B.: I have to say that this is the most exciting proposal we've had yet. In the past, I don't think we felt we were consulted at all.

P.D.: It's funny isn't it, but during the years when children should be learning to live together, they don't have the opportunity of mixing …

Again, confusion was evident about what 'sharing the same site' might mean. P.D.'s comment suggests that in the new campus situation things would be different because children 'will have the opportunity of mixing', but what was actually proposed was a new way of organizing existing segregations based on separate sites and spatialized identities. There was ambivalence and nervousness on the part of those attending the meeting about how much and what kind of sharing would be desirable and what it would mean.

J.M.: An extra heated swimming pool. If it's to be part of the campus, then we should have a proper pool so the other children can use it.

J.S.: I would look at the possibility of having a divided pool, one part cooler than the other.

J.M.: welcomed the idea of sharing, recognizing that a swimming pool would benefit all students, regardless of difference. This contrasted powerfully with the position taken by some Hillbank teachers who were vehemently opposed to any sharing of space or facilities.

The meeting turned its attentions to the use and organization of space.

C.M. (Nursery Teacher): Can I ask … We kept stressing, can we be involved in the planning and we were told 'Oh yes'. Then what happened was we got a plan presented to us, with doors opening up to the outside, walking through communal areas to toilets, and so on.

P.D.: Tomorrow we'll give them a bare outline. It will have to wait until we know what the involvement of health will be. The technical details can be worked out by the experts.

J.S.: I don't know about 'experts' … but it's got to be done <u>with</u> us – not <u>to</u> us. We must be involved in the very early days.

P.D.: There are planning requirements which we cannot overcome. They are dictated by regulations. When I was a head, I could influence a number of things but you never get all the things you want and you may not understand why.

Of course, You can't do everything by committee. You've got to give the designer a bit of leeway.

C.M. (Nursery teacher): Last time, nobody even came and asked us: what are you doing with these children? With these plinths? What is needed? WE know how high wheel chairs are (in relation to) the height of the table. Half an inch may seem very small, but the difference may mean a child can't get their legs under the table.

P.D.: It's got to be cost effective.

On one level, there were a number of different lines of argument taking place which individuals put forward regardless of whether there was a dialogue or common exchange of views. The 'arguments' were articulated in ways which avoided conflict, each interlocutor 'riding their own bicycle'. C.M. was concerned that they – the teachers – should be consulted about the architectural design for any new development especially in terms of the use of space and the organization of the physical environment. Underpinning his comments were issues of equality and dignity and the right of disabled children and young people to enjoy full access to the environment and a sense of well-being. There were also issues about consultation and the importance of listening to those who occupied particular roles in particular spaces (teachers and learners, for example) but who were traditionally excluded from the decision making processes relating to the structure and organization of those spaces. In this sense, the notion of 'expertise' was being challenged as well as underpinning concerns about democracy and the right to participation. At another level still, C.M. was engaged in a power struggle over values and how these are expressed through the use of space.

J.S. stressed the power relations involved in a shift from doing things *to*, to doing things *with* 'us'. Again, this raises important issues relating to democracy and power. The spatial dimensions of the struggle were also present, although they were not overt. As professional, J.S. explained (extract not quoted here) that in his work context, he was able to make his views known to architects because they shared a common professional space, providing a forum and framework for discussion. In the context of the plans for Freelands, however, there was no common arena in which architects, 'experts', parents, teachers, governors, students and advisers can exchange views and debate issues. P.D. referred to a meeting which was to take place the following day when, I surmised, issues relating to the physical organization of the new site would be discussed. Nobody raised any questions about the composition or purpose of the meeting and no connections were made – at least explicitly – to the challenges raised in the meeting about expertise and the arguments put forward about participation and consultation. The meeting P.D. referred to was to take place 'elsewhere', in another arena from which they – the parents and teachers and students at the school who had crucial knowledge and experience – would be excluded. This raises important questions concerning democracy and representation in decision making processes about policy.

One particularly noticeable feature of this meeting was the enthusiasm and excitement generated by all concerned by the proposed changes. At the same time, there seemed to be an assumption among some of those present that 'Freelands' would continue to exist as a distinct and separate place.

> **J.S.:** If we look at our children with integration – I want to ask – When will the first able bodied child come to Freelands?
>
> **P.D.:** How would you feel about having a big jamboree with the teachers and governors to discuss the plan?
>
> **J.M.:** I think it would be nice to start together.

B.S. (parent): It would be a bit of an ice-breaker.

B.B. (parent): We must have the input of parents. As a parent of a disabled kid, it's not nice feeling your kid's going to a school where other parents don't want it ... My main concern is that (last time) it was dropped on parents from above.

P.D.: If you've got confidence in the plan ...

B.B. (parent): It would be nice to think we can invite governors and parents to a Christmas Show.

P.D.: The pupil voice in this *must* have a place.

B.B.: The only thing is, it would be awful if it fell through.

B.S. (parent): It is scandalous that some children have had all their secondary education in this building with the lack of space ... and my son probably won't benefit from this opportunity.

Far from wanting to preserve things as they are, governors, including parents, *were* willing to embrace change and looked forwarded to being part of a wider community and contributing to it. There was excitement about inviting 'governors and parents' to a Christmas Show, at the same time as real fear that the proposed plan might 'fall through'. One father stressed the importance of involving parents and the hurt that can occur in a situation where 'other parents don't want your kid'. There was regret and anger, too, on the part of another parent, that children have had to receive all their education in 'this building with the lack of space' as he contemplates the possibilities which might become available on the new campus site. There was sadness that his son 'probably won't be able to benefit from this opportunity'.

In this meeting governors felt able to express their feelings in ways which were very personal, but also in ways which looked towards the future positively. The revelation of the pain experienced by parents at the attitudes of other parents was powerful. If governors from, say, Hillbank School had been present, would they have had cause for self-reflection in the light of what they heard? Would they have had their 'world view' disturbed if they had been able to listen to other perspectives? This question highlights the wider issue already discussed of how policy making is compartmentalized in terms of the segregation of arenas in which discussion takes place. This prevents all those concerned from considering issues from a number of angles.

Although the importance of the 'pupil voice' was raised once by P.D., the question of listening to the perspectives of children and young people was rarely considered by anybody in any of the interviews I was involved in or in any meeting I attended, in any context, apart from one public consultation meeting organized by the LEA to discuss its draft policy on inclusion for the education service. At this meeting there was a small number of young people on the platform representing some marginalized groups (young people 'being looked after' and students who experience learning or behavioural difficulties). Again, this raises serious issues for democracy.

CONCLUSION

In studying the pieces of dialogue in this chapter, a number of themes emerge. An important one concerns the spatial organization of the decision making processes which entailed discussions about 'inclusion' taking place in different sites. Within these sites, particular interest groups struggled over values and policies, deploying particular discourses to assert agendas and to achieve political ends. In saying this, I am not arguing that these policy agendas and tactics were cynically and consciously worked out (although this cannot be automatically ruled out either), but that different players in different sites adopted roles and attitudes which were mediated by wider social and political conditions and concerns. Histories – personal and political – interacted with conflicting structures, images, professional interests and discourses in ways which were profoundly spatialized. Questions concerning what language was used by whom, in the presence of which audience and to what ends are integrally related to the situation and where and when these occurred.

In the above exchanges, there are a number of examples of these relationships between time, place and context. G.B. allowed himself to speak about students historically 'elsewhere' in ways which constructed them as dangerous, irrational and 'apart' from ordinary human society. In the first meeting described at Hillbank the professional role of P.H. the LEA officer for capital programmes, legitimated a use of technical-bureaucratic language which she adopted to endorse her 'rational' arguments concerning 'cost effectiveness'. Teachers adopted professional discourses and concerns relating to the use of space and the curriculum to mask additional or other antagonisms and preoccupations in relation to t the population of Freelands. At the second meeting at Hillbank a number of governors constructed the population of Freelands as undesirable, including statements and innuendo about students, parents, teachers and governors who were variously presented as deviant, only interested in 'their own' children, self seeking and having unreasonable expectations of participation.

In contrast, those present at the meeting of governors at Freelands showed no hostility towards the teachers and students of the schools on the proposed campus development; on the contrary, they envisaged 'sharing' their resources and having friendly exchanges. Far from focusing on their own situation in terms of whether teachers would continue to get the special schools allowance, or how much teaching they would have to do and how difficult it all might be for them, they appeared positive and excited about the change. At the same time, they also appeared to want to preserve the 'special' status of their students and maintain a spatialized identity on the campus. I should point out, of course, that these exchanges took place at an eight month interval when the proposal had changed from a 'resource based' model to a 'campus' model in which Freelands would be recreated as a 'Disability Living Centre' separate from the schools themselves.

My purpose in including discussion of meetings at these different stages is to look at the processes of policy making and the discourses used in particular situations, not to present a gradually unfolding story. The material presented does suggest, however, that the fragmentation of the consultation process did not allow for an open debate about fundamental issues concerning the rights of all learners and the possible outcomes, limitations and opportunities of any proposed changes for all concerned. If meetings had brought together all interested parties, then these difficult issues could have been seriously debated. Conflicts and prejudices could have been brought out into the open, and stereotypes challenged. Different kinds of issues were raised in particular ways in different arenas and this meant that 'knowledge' about what was happening, who wanted what and why – (political states of play) – was not shared between all interested parties. This leads me into a further theme which has emerged from my analysis, that of democracy.

The meetings described were all part of a 'consultation process'. While the term 'democracy' was never used explicitly in any of the meetings, the term 'consultation' was frequently used by LEA representatives as a means of naming what was going on. Embedded in the notion of 'consultation' is the idea of democracy – in the sense that all those concerned shall be 'consulted' and all voices listened to. In deconstructing the discursive practices and processes in the three meetings, what emerges is something very different. A discourse of 'consultation' was used to embellish or disguise a very different set of processes – those generated in an attempt by some LEA officers to impose a particular policy on a complex and highly charged situation, across diverse sites and among diverse groups who knew very little about each other. Indeed, a common feature of the exchanges which took place in the two meetings at Hillbank was the presentation by different parties of stereotypes and prejudices as 'factual' and hence uncontested. People who were not present were represented as having particular characteristics, 'needs', attitudes and agendas in the struggle to gain ground in policy making struggles.

In the meetings, LEA officers adopted discourses associated with their particular professional roles and agendas which closed down creative exploration and controlled debate as well as obscuring or mystifying the location of power in the policy making process. The kinds of discourse used by different groups represent a struggle between professionalism or other 'vested interests' and democratism (Fulcher, 1999, pp. 178–80). Just as discourse is an integral part of policy making, so it is equally embedded in processes which promote or suppress democracy.

In this chapter I have tried to uncover some of the complexity of the interactions involved in policy making. I have argued that far from accepting that it is only those who 'hold power' who 'get to use discourse', discourse is not 'possessed' by one group but is an integral part of social processes. Furthermore, although the structural, cultural and economic imbalance of power in societies must never be underestimated, 'power' is not static and does not reside only among those who are endowed with it by the state or by accumulated capital or control of the media, for example. Power can be claimed by different groups and individuals and is exercised in multiple arenas in diverse ways. Power can 'belong' to opposing factions at the same time, and that is why there is struggle. In the context of this study, though, a crucial issue is how discourse is used to claim and exert power and with what outcomes in terms of the spacing and placing of disabled children and young people.

I am deeply aware that there is no examination here of the processes and procedures through which the students themselves have been excluded from the opportunity to claim any voice, any power, in the policy making processes discussed.

In the next chapter I examine some of the structures and processes of spatialization relating to education in France. My purpose is not to compare the two national settings for the reasons already outlined, but to explore related issues of spacing, placing and difference from a number of different angles. The analysis of *'structures'* is yet another exploration of discourse. 'Structures' here refers to the physical and social spaces which are the literal and symbolic constructions through which 'settings' are created and 'values' diffused. In this chapter I have focused first on language-as-discourse and its role in mediating policy making in a particular context. In Chapter Eight I shall adopt a number of different vantage points relating to some of the structures and procedures at work in the French context. I shall examine ways in which the language used by professionals maps on to these structures and procedures and the extent to which 'language', 'structures' and 'procedures' are all part of the same set of discourses relating to identity, bureaucracy and social ordering.

CHAPTER 8

LANDSCAPES OF NAMING AND PLACING:
STRUCTURES AND PRACTICES OF SELECTION
AND SORTING IN FRANCE

INTRODUCTION

In the last chapter I suggested that a critical analysis of discursive practices deployed by different groups in the English context support the notion that the 'spatial' is an important dimension in policy struggles. These spatialized discourses relate to wider social processes which produce and reproduce differentiation between groups in which power relations fluctuate but are unequal. The style, content and context of discourse is crucially implicated in spatializing processes. The arenas in which discourses occur affect and are involved in the kinds of things people say, the way they say them and what they remain silent about. The segmentation of arenas in policy making processes prevents different groups speaking directly, and listening, to each other. Thus, the continued existence of segregated settings and bounded departments at local authority level contribute to a fragmentation of 'consultation' processes and to closure in terms of exchange of knowledge, experience and perspective. The highly compartmentalized roles and discourses of different professionals and the particular interests they represent are also deeply implicated in processes of spacing and placing. All of these factors are part of a wider landscape in which – in the context of this study – some groups of children and young people are constructed as other and as having different 'needs' from their 'ordinary' peers and this is used as a rationale for exclusion and marginalisation.

In this chapter I explore processes of spatialization associated with structures and procedures in relation to education and difference in France. This exploration is informed by material gathered in the research settings (discussed in Chapter Six) but I shall also draw on material taken from other situations. More specifically, I shall focus on two areas which, in different ways, inform practices of spacing and placing: the structures of provision and management of difference in the French system and the role of professionals in the construction of exclusions. In considering different perspectives presented in the material, I have started to make connections with some of the issues which emerged in Chapter Six, particularly in relation to spatiality and exclusion.

In Chapter Seven I focused primarily on the language used in different contexts to 'make', or influence policy. In this chapter, I will begin to explore the role of professionals and their relationships to educational structures and procedures in identifying and placing children and young people in the labyrinth of structures which make up the different systems of 'education', 'health' and 'social security'.

INTERPRETING 'THE FOREIGN'

The difficulties involved in deconstructing 'foreign' landscapes or analysing a 'foreign' language in terms of their possible meanings cannot be underestimated. Scott is right in saying:

> The difficulty for the participant observer is that either they have to find a solution to the problem of translation, or they have to accept that they will use concepts, categories and ways of seeing which may be alien to participants in the social setting being studied. Therefore they cannot in this sense participate fully, as they are involved in the act of translation and at the same time are making judgments (utilising their value system) about a society which must forever remain tantalisingly out of reach. (Scott, 1996, p. 148)

Stone (1999) has illustrated the many layers of complexity involved in trying to unravel cultural meanings embedded in language through her research into the Chinese language of impairments and the way the characters have 'played their part in communicating and consolidating dominant perceptions of impairment and disability' (Stone, 1999, p. 146). Of particular interest is her discussion of the language of 'normalcy' and 'non-normalcy' and what we can learn from it in terms of cultural perceptions of disability and difference. In Chapter seven I tried to show how language was used in a 'policy war' between different groups in relation to a particular setting in England. Different discourses relating to 'normality' and 'difference' were deployed to inform debate in attempts to bring about certain outcomes. In examining these I found they revealed much about attitudes and values of the different parties involved. I decided that my knowledge of French is not sufficiently deep and broad enough to attempt a similarly close interpretative analysis of discourse in relation to the French material (Armstrong, Belmont and Verillon, 2000). Instead, I shall look at a broader sweep of structures and relationships which relate to space and place.

Both Scott's and Stone's observations could be applied to settings within the same broad national framework. Groups and communities of all kinds, including those associated with schools, represent an enormous range of linguistic diversity within one country. Of course, I never imagined that I could 'participate fully' in any of the contexts I have studied – either in England or France. I recognize the inevitable pitfalls in 'the act of translation' and the impossibility of divorcing my own values and culturally situated knowledge from the analytic process. Far from being discouraged by these difficulties, it is the processes involved in travelling between different concepts, structures and discourses which are the most revealing in terms of shaking out old preconceptions and taken-for-granted knowledge about familiar and unfamiliar contexts.

In the previous two chapters there are many instances of the use of discursive devices, including labels, which create boundaries and exclusions. In the French context, the language used appears more likely to refer to medical categories and institutions, than is the case in the English contexts, although there were wide differences between the French settings. In England, characteristics of students were described in rather vague ways such as 'not ordinary children', 'very complex difficulties', 'in a wheel chair'. However, the research process and material gathered in the two national settings is quite different, and it would be a mistake to make any simple comparisons between the use of language in the two contexts.

STRUCTURES AND PROCEDURES: 'MAKING COMPARISONS'

It is not easy to describe or make blanket statements about 'special education' in France (or, indeed, in any other national setting). Firstly, there is the problem of terminologies which are embedded in the multiple transactions of social and cultural life. There are important differences in the way in which disabilities are understood, categorized and labelled in different cultures (Armstrong, 1999a; Plaisance, 2000), and there is the additional problem of finding a match in English for the terms used in French which do not carry the same values and meanings as in English. This became apparent when I tried to find a school or other setting in France which 'matched' Freelands in terms of the 'criteria for entry' for pupils. There were also many occasions during the research when confusion arose about the meanings and values attached to words. In French, for example, the term 'handicapé' has, I was assured, none of the negative connotations of the word 'handicapped' in English. This begs the question of how, and by whom, the use of language is arbitrated and whether hegemonic linguistic practices in France have been challenged by the development of new disability discourse as a means of 'resisting negativity' (Corker, 1999). Secondly, and linked to this first problem, the structures and institutions which 'serve' the various categories of disability or 'levels of academic attainment' are different from those in England or elsewhere. Thirdly, not all provision is made within the national education system and some young people attend hospitals or institutions controlled by the Ministries of Health and Social Security rather than 'schools'. It is therefore not possible to talk about 'special education' as if it were a unified service or idea. This is true in England too, in that 'special education' can refer to segregated schools (such as Freelands) but can also be present as overlapping with the processes and practices concerned with 'special educational needs' in ordinary schools.

The differences lie in the levels of complexity in terms of terminology and meanings, as well as in terms of the different government ministries implicated, the range of professional roles and voluntary organizations involved, the highly diversified categorization of impairments, the enormous range of schools and institutions outside the ordinary education system and the bureaucracy involved in managing and maintaining all of these. The many special classes, schools and institutions are material and symbolic places which play a physical, bureaucratic and spatializing role in terms of assessing, separating and ordering groups of children and young people; in doing so they produce and reproduce images and values which perpetuate social exclusions. They create a series of landscapes in which boundaries are drawn between 'the ordinary' and 'the other'. These landscapes are shaped by the histories, mythologies and practices associated with them as well as by the geographical location and physical characteristics which differentiate 'ordinary' spaces and settings from those 'elsewhere'.

Special institutions in France, including those 'inside' the education system, and like those in England, are often quite unlike ordinary schools in atmosphere and appearance. The institutional 'froideur' of the hospital setting, or the dilapidated grandeur of what used to be a nineteenth century bourgeois family residence, have little in common with ordinary schools. The populations of special settings look and behave differently from populations of 'ordinary' schools, not because of impairments or any physical characteristics but because of other, socially created factors. For example, unlike ordinary schools, the populations of special institutions often include children and young people of all ages – from the very youngest children to young adults. Frequently children of different ages are in the same class (the Externat Médico-Professionel discussed in Chapter Six was an example of this) and classes are small. Secondly, perhaps because of the relatively small numbers present, relationships between staff and children appear more informal. This informality is often reproduced in some settings in terms of environments which appear less 'institutional', more homely than those of an ordinary school. This was the case in the third French setting – the Externat – where the whole atmosphere was intimate and personal. (The example of the cook coming out to see if everybody was enjoying their meal and giving a group of young people a recipe, would be difficult to imagine in an ordinary school).

The ways in which segregated institutions are visibly distinctive in terms of physical characteristics, organization, population and atmosphere are not, first and foremost, related to impairment, but to the social fact of being separate, smaller, and away from the centre of communities. As Massey points out, 'the spatial organization of society – makes a difference to how it works' (Massey, 1994, p. 254).

MANAGEMENT AND CONTROL OF SPECIALIST PROVISION

In France, the systems for identifying and categorizing disability and difficulty and allocating children and young people to particular settings are clearly laid down in law, but these 'systems' are mediated by policy making practices, some of which will be discussed below. An estimated 1.38% of the total school age population are educated in establishments funded by the Ministry of Social Security and run by associations (voluntary bodies). The French system, which is highly differentiated, is based on two distinctive paradigms, education and health, which function as separate and clearly identifiable cultures. The majority of disabled children (enfants handicapés) are enrolled in 'special education classes' of one kind or another but fewer than half – 43.8% – are registered in schools or classes run by the Ministry for Education. The remaining 56.2% attend institutions funded by the Ministry for Social Affairs (Fablet, 2000) and managed by one of the many 'associations' in France. The associations have their historical roots in an Act of Parliament passed in 1901 to encourage community and neighbourhood solidarity and humanitarian action in support of people who experienced hardships such as sickness, homelessness and poverty (Hanet-Kania, 1996). This initiative did not arise so much out of a benevolent humanitarianism on the part of central government as being the expression of the cultural experience of solidarity and struggle of local communities during the Paris Commune of 1871 (Michel, 1970).

Associations are bodies with their own statutes and management structures which, in the case of the major national associations resemble large benevolent companies. (It is quite usual for an association to organize a conference with over 1,000 delegates, including parents, professionals and representatives from other organizations.) There are also small local associations which run perhaps only one institution. Exceptionally, there are institutions run by the local city council through the 'mairie' (the town hall). Most associations relating to disability were originally set up by groups of parents to provide support for and campaign on behalf of their disabled children. These organizations have a lot of power and autonomy. They are invariably set up with one purpose in mind: to protect and advance the perceived interests of a particular group such as 'children with an intellectual impairment', 'children and young people with a motor disability', 'widows and children of fishermen'. The origins, histories and practices of the associations are, therefore, both impairment or 'deficit' based *and* rooted in French social and revolutionary history. New associations are still being created, such as one set up recently to enhance the treatment of 'autistic' children which is based in two hospitals. The majority of institutions which are outside the education system are run by one of these associations and this may be an explanation for the wide differences between them in terms of their cultures and practices. In general, such institutions have a powerful medical or therapeutic orientation, usually employing far more medical and therapeutic or psycho-social professionals than qualified teachers. It is one of the paradoxes of the history of special education, perhaps, that organizations and practices whose antecedents emerged as part of a progressive or revolutionary struggle are – 120 years later – playing a conservative role. Or is it that simple? The associations in France are implicated in the perpetuation of segregated structures, but they are also at the forefront in political struggles for equal rights to access to the environment, to jobs and to a reasonable standard of living. Their role is not comparable to the traditional charity movement in England because the emphasis is often overtly political, emphasizing the rights and requirements of groups and individuals rather than their 'deficits' and 'needs'. Disabled people (or whatever group is the focus of the work of the organization) are invariably represented among the leading figures of the associations themselves.

Legislation passed in Parliament (1975, 1989) designed to reduce exclusion in the educational provision for disabled children and young people with disabilities or difficulties in learning has not reduced the importance of the complex and diverse network of the specialist institutions in France. The 1989 'Loi d'orientation sur l'education' declared:

> The right to education is guaranteed to everybody in order that they may develop their personality, achieve a higher standard of initial and continuous training, participate in social and professional life and exercise their rights and duties as citizens.
>
> The acquisition of a general culture and a recognised qualification is guarantied to all young people whatever their social, cultural or geographical origins. Educational integration of young handicapped people is to be encouraged. (my translation from French)

However, systems of segregation, including the material places and cultures of specialist institutions, have remained and exercise a conservative role on new initiatives. In addition, teachers are often reluctant to abandon long established practices and traditions, and curriculum reform in schools has been slow. Chauvière and Plaisance (2000) explain the apparent failure to fulfil the promise of 'integration' embodied in the 1975 and 1989 Acts in terms of the pervasive contradictions which run through the systems which manage education and in terms of the role of different and powerful 'associations' and groups of professionals in perpetuating segregative practices. In addition, they argue that the 'space' of the school has become transformed by an invasion of professionals from 'the outside':

> The hallowed space of the school, originally created as a protection for children against social inequalities, has become porous in relation to 'the outside'. At the same time, in the space of special education and of special institutions managed by 'associations' professional or strategic interests have created a system of mini-ghettos for a target population (Chauvière and Plaisance, 2000, p. 5) (my translation from French)

It is through a study of the relationship between the different structures, practices and cultures of the education system and the diverse institutions, professional bodies and categories of disability and difference that a spatialized construction of difference emerges. The 'special institutions' which were discussed in Chapter Six do not exist 'in a vacuum' apart from other structures and practices. On the contrary, it could be argued that institutions such as the Externat Médico-Professionel exist so that 'ordinary' schools can remain as they are, perpetuating a hegemony of 'the normal'.

Crucially, institutions and practices outside the education system continue to provide 'services' to children and young people who are seen as having medical, physical, intellectual, psychiatric and even 'social' difficulties rather than primarily educational needs. This means that widening participation in education to include disabled students in ordinary schools is limited by structures and statutes outside the education system itself as well as by other factors internal to the education system such as the processes of examination and selection which underpin it. As will be seen later in the chapter, some children and young people are implicitly treated as 'ineducable' in that they attend institutions in which little or no teaching is made available to them. This may be the result of a decision made by a team of medical professionals such as psychologists and psychiatrists on the grounds that there is 'no point' in trying to teach a particular child or young person or that it might be harmful to them. Such a decision may also be made by default if there is a shortage of teaching staff employed in an institution. These issues relate to the question of the rights of children and young people to education. They raise questions about the roles of professionals in deciding on the identity of individual children in terms of whether they are 'patients' or 'pupils'. This has implications for their social and physical location and expectations about 'who they are' and what opportunities they may be offered.

THE ROLE OF PROFESSIONALS AS BROKERS IN PROCESSES AND PROCEDURES OF EXCLUSION AND INCLUSION

Bélanger's (2000) critical analysis of the privileged position of medicine and psychiatry in the field of special education traces the role that professionals have played in creating categories of difficulty and impairment. Bélanger and Garant (1999) challenge the notion that educational psychologists were 'necessary' for the development of a compulsory education system for all by 'dealing with' children who presented 'difficulties'. Under the Langevin-Wallon Plan (1947) educational psychology was, they argue, concerned:

> to help all children to maximise their chances of success at school, and not merely children who were experiencing difficulties at the school. ... in accordance with principles of social justice and equality of opportunity, to enlarge educational opportunities to include all children. (Bélanger and Garant , 1999, p. 139)

Instead, educational psychologists became crucially implicated in the work of the 'Commissions médico-pédagogiques' whose role was to make decisions about which pupils should be moved to special schools, who should attend special classes and who could stay in ordinary schools. They exercise a similar role on the present 'Commissions d'éducation spéciale' which:

> ... tend to ratify the request for exclusion from mainstream educational settings according to the availability of special provision in each geographical department, thus matching 'needs' to 'resources' and consequently applying the break to the policy of integration. (Bélanger and Garant, 1999, p. 140)

Educational psychologists are, therefore, instrumental in sorting and placing children and young people, including their removal from 'ordinary' settings to 'special' ones. As already explained many of these settings are not run by the education ministry, but come under the financial umbrella of the ministries for health and social security and are often managed by one of the associations referred to in the previous section. The commissions and the professionals who contribute to their work provide the bureaucratic framework within which technologies of removal can be brought into play. These 'technologies' and their instruments include testing and assessment, 'observation', the creation of 'new identities' through the writing of reports and the assigning of labels, and, finally, the removal of children and young people from ordinary settings to places 'elsewhere'.

Historically, as Chauvière remarks:

> The ... treatment of the 'irregular' child gradually replaced the repression and banishment metered out in the nineteenth century. But this orientation strengthened differentiation between the various State sectors, and ... this led to an increase in the separation between the specialized treatment of children 'with problems' from the ordinary school 'for all'. (Chauvière, 2000, p. 54) (my translation from French)

This analysis implicitly makes the link between the existence of a system of different specialized sectors, a bureaucracy to maintain it and, crucially, the existence of sites 'on the margins' and away from the ordinary central site of education, to which those who were deemed 'irregular' could be removed. The role of the educational psychologist (or other professionals) is to collaborate in this process and assist in moving children and young people who are regarded as 'irregular' onwards – and outwards.

THE COMMISSIONS AND SPECIAL EDUCATION

Local commissions are 'bipartite' with equal representation from the Ministry of Education and Ministry for Health. Parents are also represented on this commission which makes decisions about the future placement of a child. Apart from the cost of any teaching which takes place, running costs for institutions outside the national education system are met by Social Security.

I sat in on the proceedings of a Commission and later interviewed two women – the Director of the Commission and a teacher from a local primary school – to find out how the legal entitlement of parents worked out in practice. I expected that the argument that a child was 'a danger' would be used to remove them from their school. In the following piece of dialogue between myself, the teacher and the Director, some important issues emerged.

> **The Director of the Commission (DC):** The role of the commission is to consider all the reports – medical, social, psychological and then make a decision. This is presented as a report to the parents and when they sign the necessary paper work, there is a legal document which moves a child to a special class attached to an ordinary school, for example, or moves them out of the education system into a special institution. If the parents don't agree with the decision then they send the papers back to us. That is their right. But we try and avoid this situation. The different professionals work very closely with the families so that there will be a successful outcome. They try to take into account what parents feel and what they want for their child.

> **Teacher (T):** I've seen cases where the parents have refused the decision of the Commission and their child has stayed in school. It's rare, but not insignificant.

DC: Usually we don't issue papers until we have got the agreement of the parents. But sometimes they start having doubts or change their minds. We are talking about a legal document here which can remove a child from the education system. To get out of the specialist setting and back into the education system the case has to come back to the Commission with reports from all the specialists.

FA: What if parents don't want their child to go to a special institution?

DC: They have the right to refuse.

T: They stay in the ordinary school. The state school system is legally obliged to provide education between the ages of 6–16.

There seems to be a clear understanding here on the part of the Director of the Commission and the primary school teacher that the decision to move a child out of the Education system is a major one and that parental legal rights must be respected if they do not want their child to be removed from ordinary education. I found two aspects of this discussion particularly interesting. First the role of professionals in preparing the ground or persuading parents about a proposal concerning their child's future which raises questions about the power relations, and, in particular, how easy or difficult it might be in practice for parents to resist the power of professional opinion. Secondly, parents have a legal right to insist that their child stays in their local school (provided, presumably, that they are not declared 'dangerous').

THE PRACTICES OF REMOVAL

The commission is the key mechanism through which children are 'spaced out' of the education system. This frequently takes place at the transfer stage from école maternelle (nursery school) to primary school, or from primary to secondary education. The number of children in segregated settings increases considerably at the primary-to-secondary transfer stage (OECD, 1995).

What is clear is that in general there is very little expectation that young people who have 'complex difficulties', psychological or health problems will stay in the ordinary education system at secondary level. Furthermore, few secondary schools are designed to be accessible to people with mobility difficulties.

M.F., an educational psychologist, described the situation:

Integration works quite well at the nursery level and at primary school until around the age of 11–12 years. After that, around the time when children are transferring to college, there's a change. You suddenly get the aristocratic handicaps and the non-aristocratic handicaps. Many teachers will have no problem with integrating a blind child or a physically disabled child. The teachers are happy to accept anyone who can follow the curriculum provided they have a support teacher and they can get around the building. But a child who has Downs Syndrome or a disruptive child, nobody wants them.

There are two additional factors which might encourage commissions to move young people out of the education system. One is the view that they will experience increasing difficulties in terms of 'keeping up' with the curriculum and expected pace of learning. This, it is argued, would be discouraging for the young person concerned and would hold the rest of the class back. Secondly, the special education settings within the ordinary education system have a reputation for having a high proportion of young people who experience difficulties in learning because of 'social problems'. Young people who are reported as being 'fragile' or 'sickly' or deemed 'too trusting' and 'too friendly', may be considered to be 'at risk' in an ordinary school. In the complex processes involved in selection and removal, the population of the special education sector in the education system and the young people who are channelled into segregated special institutions outside the education system are both constructed as 'deviant'.

The decisions made by the commissions have major educational implications for the young people concerned. In two of the three research settings discussed in Chapter Six, young people received full-time teaching and followed the ordinary national curriculum. Both settings were within the education system, although one was actually a centre within a hospital, and the other had medical facilities and staff who were an integral part of the education programme. In the third situation – the Externat Médico-Professionel, young people received 12 hours teaching, based on a reduced version of the French primary school curriculum, but this was not obligatory.

Teachers, and directors in particular, have extensive and pervasive power in terms of their control over the curriculum provided for young people who attend specialist institutions. P.C. was proud of the educational provision and staffing levels at the Externat which compare favorably with those in some other settings. This was borne out by my visit to an Institut Médico-Professionel (IMPRO) (discussed below) where some young people did not attend lessons at all. A further consequence of removal from structures within the education system is the closing down of opportunities to participate in post-compulsory education. For many young people who attend specialist institutions, choices of 'where to go next' will be limited to a Centre d'aide par le Travail.

SPECIALIZED STRUCTURES INSIDE THE EDUCATION SYSTEM

There are important 'specialized' structures within the education system. These include the *Réseaux d'aide specialisée aux élèves en difficulté – RASED* (specialist support networks for pupils who experience difficulties) which are usually based in a primary school but serve a group of primary and nursery schools in an area. These networks are made up of special teachers, rééducateurs specializing in psycho-pedagogy or psycho-motricity and an educational psychologist. This group meets regularly to discuss progress and intervention relating to individual pupils and works closely with class teachers and heads of schools. Parents and other professionals such as speech therapists and social workers are not invited to these meetings although a member of the network may liaise with them. Difficulties and intervention strategies are identified after classroom observation of the pupil concerned by one or more of the professionals involved with the pupil after discussion with the class teacher. A member of the network with an 'appropriate specialism' will take responsibility for working with the pupils on a weekly basis, usually in one-to-one withdrawal sessions. M.F., the psychologist I interviewed, explained that there are not enough RASEDs and many children who need help don't get it. He said:

> They remain at the back of the class and wait for the lesson to be over. Teachers are most anxious to get the ones causing problems removed from the class for 'extra help'. The teacher tells the specialist 'I'm not getting anywhere with this child. He has a lot of problems and he's lazy. You can certainly take this child out for special help. In fact, you can take two or three others like him at the same time. Once you get them up to the standard, you can bring them back to me'

There are also the *Classes for Educational Integration – the 'CLIS'* which were introduced by the Jospin Law (1989). These are 'special' classes attached to ordinary schools for pupils with physical disabilities, auditory or visual impairments or – in some cases – psychological difficulties. The CLIS are not for pupils regarded as having 'serious difficulties in learning'. One criteria for admission to such a class is that the pupil should be able to 'benefit from the experience of ordinary school life'. There is no question, here, of adapting 'ordinary school life' in response to pupil diversity. Although these classes are for 'educational integration', pupils who belong to them are taught separately for much of the time by teachers who have specialized in a particular disability. There is little evidence yet of a move towards the organization of schools and the reform of the curriculum so that students with disabilities can be included in ordinary classes as a matter of course.

M.F., educational psychologist, explained the increase in numbers of students being moved from the ordinary education system to structures outside it at the age of transfer from primary to secondary as 'one of the failures of the French system'. This 'removal' occurred, he said, because:

> ... there is very little support in the collèges (lower secondary schools) for pupils in difficulty. A small number of schools have some special classes attached – known as the Section d'Education Specialisé (SES, or SEGPA) – which only have 15 students in a class. They are not really part of the school and have their own specialist director. A major difference is that the students in the SES are taught by 'instituteurs' – primary school teachers – while other students have 'professors' – secondary teachers. The attitude is: these young people in college need a 'professor' – but a primary teacher is good enough for students experiencing difficulty. The training of primary and secondary teachers is very different.
>
> Most of the young people who attend the SES (or SEGPA) in the big cities are from disadvantaged backgrounds. You don't get disabled students going there – it's the children of immigrants from the third world – Tunisian or Algerian. If you go and visit a SEGPA you will see black kids, Arab kids. Some children are from French families – but they'll usually be gypsies, or

into alcoholism or prostitution – that sort of thing. Statistically, only young people from socially disadvantaged families will go to the SEGPA and boys are massively over-represented.

From this account, the SEGPA appears to be a separate institution, co-existing alongside a college (ordinary secondary school) but whose function is to provide a 'place' to hold disturbing or disturbing others. Like institutions outside the education system, the SEGPAs exist so that a hegemony of 'the normal' can be maintained. Segregated institutions are themselves part of this hegemony which requires that some groups of students are constructed as different from the standard, 'legitimate' students. This divide is expressed through the standard practice at the SEGPA of providing a version of a primary curriculum rather than the ordinary secondary curriculum, and by the employment of primary school teachers instead of teachers who are trained to work with adolescents and young adults. This may construct the young people who attend the SEGPA (aged 12–16) as immature and childish, and inferior to their peers in the ordinary college.

M.F.'s description of the population of the SEGPAs suggests a population which is seen as both undesirable and even potentially dangerous – and already marginalized. Some months after this interview took place, I visited a SEGPA in one of the most economically deprived areas beyond the 'péréphérique' of Paris. This was where the old shanty towns had been put up by migrant factory workers from the former French African colonies and from Portugal in the 1960s and 70s. These were demolished in the late 1970s and 80s and tower blocks built to house the same population, but now there are second and third generations of young people who, unlike their parents, face severe unemployment. One teacher I spoke to – a young Moroccan woman – had a very different view of her students than the one presented by the psychologist (above). She recognized the social and educational difficulties experienced by her students but explained these in terms of unemployment, racism, poverty, poor housing and the cultural divergence between school ethos and curriculum and the local community. This offers a further example of the importance of seeking out different perspectives in the research process.

In France children and young people who are disruptive in school cannot legally be removed from ordinary settings on the grounds of their behaviour. M.F. explained,

> They can be highly intelligent and function normally – but they are not accepted in the 'collectivité scolaire'. There are special institutions for children and young people who have psychiatric problems. A young person whose behaviour in school is very bad can be moved to one of these institutions, after a decision by a district commission based on psychiatric reports and so on. Even then, the parents have to agree – unless they are a 'danger' to themselves or others.

Is it possible that a child or young person whose behaviour is a manifestation of rebellion against intolerable social conditions or an oppressive and irrelevant curriculum in a setting where there is virtually no support for them in overcoming their learning difficulties could be re-invented as a young person with a psychiatric illness? This is a further example of the practices associated with 'special education' and 'difference' in which decisions and labels associated with particular children follow a hidden rationale, that of removal, so that ordinary schools are not disturbed and do not have to change, rather than being based on the rights and interests of the children themselves. This system has an internal and circular logic of its own. As one teacher commented,

> Frequently the young people who come from a college or SEGPA to an Externat, Internat or wherever, seem to get happier and more confident. They develop positively, socially and emotionally. They are able to work in small groups and are involved in activities they can relate to in a friendly environment in which their voice is heard.

Not surprisingly, teachers and psychologists cite such apparent progress as 'proof' that a particular young person 'needs', or is benefiting from, a segregated setting. This is part of the same set of beliefs as those surrounding 'protection' and 'fragility' of students and the 'dangerousness' of ordinary schools. This shows how the concept of 'danger' can move around and assume different identities. Children can be removed from ordinary schools because they are 'dangerous' to others or to themselves. Paradoxically, the 'dangerousness' of ordinary schools (or of the SEGPA) is used as a justification for keeping children and young people in segregated settings and for preserving special institutions. Stereotypes are necessary for maintaining the separation of different groups on the basis of their 'deficiencies', their 'fragility' or their 'dangerousness'. Thus, when I asked P.C. why the young people left the Externat with no form of certification to show what they had achieved, she responded:

> Because they are incapable. They can't achieve even the lowest level of certification

She did not make any connections in terms of the 'capability' of the young people and the fact that they followed a very restricted primary curriculum and only spent twelve hours a week in lessons. Certification is used as an instrument in a wider set of mechanisms to distance the 'capable' from the 'incapable', contributing to the stereotype of young people who attend the Externat as 'less than' ordinary young people. The Externat provides a 'signifier of imperfection and inferiority' (Sibley 1995), a place in which deficient identities are confirmed. As Sibley argues:

> Stereotypes play an important part in the configuration of social space because of the importance of distanciation in the behaviour of social groups, that is, distancing from others who are represented negatively, and because of the way in which group image and place image combine to create landscapes of exclusion. (Sibley, 1995, p. 14)

M.F.'s description of the students who attend the SEGPA could be interpreted as creating distance from them, in that the language he uses suggests deviance and marginality. In itself, of course, to refer to 'Algerians' or 'Tunisians' is not 'negative'. However, by attaching these descriptors to a marginalized place which is associated with educational failure and disaffection and by discursively placing them among groups which are constructed as 'socially deviant' ('prostitutes', 'alcoholics', 'gypsies') – to be 'Algerian' or 'Tunisian' is to be part of a negative group image and place image which 'combine to create landscapes of exclusion'.

INTEGRATION AS EXCLUSION

To summarize, 'special education' inside the education system at the primary stage in France consists of the following: some limited help from specialists who withdraw children from classes, or Integration Classes for disabled children and those with sensory impairments who are able to follow the ordinary curriculum and which function separately from ordinary classes. Disabled children may become part of an ordinary school on an integration programme (Berthe-Denoeux and Leoni, 2000) but:

> The integration of a disabled child in a class (is seen as) a highly complex operation requiring a great deal of preparation by those involved and is often regarded as a concession made to the family, rather than a question of the child's rights. (Berthe-Denoeux and Leoni, 2000, p. 189) (My translation)

If the child 'being integrated' is unable to follow the ordinary curriculum or does not have adequate support, they will be returned to a specialist setting. At secondary level, students who are failing in school or are disaffected may attend a SEGPA – which draws in all those adolescents in the area who pose problems in the ordinary classroom, sometimes on the same site as an ordinary collège. The SEGPA is not designed for disabled students or for those with other impairments. Young disabled people and those who are identified as having difficulties in learning, will usually be moved to a specialist institution outside the education system.

The existence of structures outside the education system has profound implications for disabled children and those with learning difficulties, as a teacher at the Lycée Bresson pointed out to me:

> As soon as the child moves outside the structures of the National Education System, there is no certainty that they will receive an education in the normal sense of the word. This means, of course, that there is no real chance of them returning to a school in the future. If they've missed too much school, the chances of catching up are negligible. So, once outside the system they usually stay out.

The 'National Education System' is both a place and a discourse of normality. 'Staying out' is not only about being other but also about being denied the possibilty of re-entry into the hemisphere of the normal. The 'normal' hemisphere encompasses rights to education – although these are unevenly distributed. Outside 'rights' are interpreted in an ad hoc manner, embedded in the agendas and the gaze of professionals, and the power of their 'expertise'.

'PATIENT' OR 'PUPIL' ?
THE INSTITUT MÉDICO-PROFESSIONNEL

Settings outside the Education System vary a great deal in terms of the emphasis placed on 'scolarisation' (schooling). In the case of one institution I visited, an Institut Médico-Professionnel (IMPRO) which is designated for children and young people aged between 5–19 'with psychological and psychiatric difficulties and associated learning difficulties', some young people do not receive any formal teaching in the sense of following a curriculum or having lessons with a qualified teacher. There are three primary trained teachers for 74 children and young people. Only 51 of these receive teaching. Z.P. is in charge of the 'school' section of the institution.

> **Z.P.**: All children and young people here belong to different groups which are run by a psychologist or psychiatrist and an 'éducateur'. An éducateur isn't a teacher – their training is different. Their role is to help the child develop socially and emotionally and this will include their intellectual and creative development as well, but they don't follow a school curriculum. There are lots of activities and outings and working individually and in groups.
>
> There are two classrooms here where we do the teaching and I've written 'school' above them so that's our school! Nobody attends the school on a full-time basis – they go to workshop activities and receive therapy of different kinds. The amount of time a child spends in school here varies; some just come for two and a half hours a week, but at least they are getting some schooling. This year our Director has said that all those between the ages of 6–14 must attend the 'school' on a part-time basis and follow the primary curriculum in ordinary schools as far as possible.

The emphasis placed on education is less important than the therapeutic work provided for the young people who come to this institution and some receive no 'teaching' at all. The implications of removal from the ordinary education system are far-reaching. Z.P. pointed out that in 'ordinary structures' specialist help is 'not available' to children and young people with complex psychological difficulties and the emphasis placed on 'getting through the curriculum' and 'reaching levels of required attainment' leads to their removal to settings outside the education system.

The IMPRO is housed in a large, homely and ramshackle building which used to be a nineteenth century private home of some grandeur, and now has the appearance of neither a school nor institution. I spent two mornings with a class of young people aged 14–19 who were studying French grammar based on materials used with 11 year olds in primary school. In one session we put the work aside and had a discussion about 'young people in England' and what they wanted to do when they left school. My impression was that the young people were happy to be there and enjoyed their work and the relationships in the small class. Those over the statutory school leaving age (16) were there 'by choice', although I had the impression that social workers were involved in making the decisions about 'placement' of two of them who were 'in care'. Members of the older age group also have opportunities for work experience and some are currently serving part-time apprenticeships with sympathetic local firms.

Z.P. explained later that most of the group experienced 'severe psychological difficulties' for one reason or another; two had 'communication problems', another 'mild cerebral palsy' and one 'suffered from anorexia'. One girl, S.F., was moved to the institution from a college when she was taken into care. A young man, Y.L., had been moved out of his college on the grounds that he was too disruptive to remain there. I was told that all the young people in the class now came to the IMPRO willingly and were regular attenders. While many of the children at the IMPRO spend all their school-age years there, the group I spoke to had all arrived at, or after, the transfer stage from primary to secondary school.

The professional gaze

Z.P. described the struggles which arise between her view of the young people and the deficit 'gaze' of one of her colleagues – a psychologist.

> There are two different ways of understanding the role of support. One is liberating and it is based on a perception of one's role which says 'This student is progressing. She's going forward because she understands what she is doing'. The other view of support is about control and says: 'she's making progress because I am there. Her progress is because of me'.
>
> I want to support the young people by opening out new experiences for them. That is why I have developed the integration programme with the local college and it's going well. But I've met a lot of resistance from some others, and from this psychologist in particular. When S.F., one of the young people in my class, said to us 'I want to try and be part of that.' The psychologist said to me: 'Be careful. She's very fragile. Anything might happen'. Well, I'm an institutrice not a psychologist and perhaps what I say is rubbish, but when I hear the psychologist say 'she is fragile' that means he is saying 'she is incapable. Anything can happen! She might go completely crazy. She needs protection' and it opens up all sorts of fantastic scenarios. It's very dangerous. These two views of 'support' are totally opposed and they are played out like night and day in the institution.

These comments illustrate two quite different perceptions of the young people at the IMPRO and of the relationship between their development and progress and the role of the teacher and the psychologist concerned. The notion that the psychologist is 'necessary' for a student to change and progress, is part of a construction of *his* power and *her* dependency. It is about disciplining the 'other' and exerting his control over her. This contrasts with the view of the teacher, Z.P., who sees her role as creating situations which 'open up new experiences' to the young people. There is also a tension between the relative power and status of the teacher and the psychologist in which the latter attempts to undermine the teacher's professional knowledge and right to make decisions relating to her students' education. This may be one consequence of education being 'optional' and given less importance than therapeutic and psychological 'intervention'. In such a situation, the teacher's role may easily be devalued.

The psychologist constructs S.F. as 'fragile' and as someone who is potentially dangerous or out of control, capable of precipitating chaos and anarchy at the same time as being 'in need of protection'. As Z.P. rightly remarks, his construction 'opens up all sorts of fantastic scenarios'. There is a struggle going on here over space and identity, as well as over professional and gender issues. In order to keep S.F. inside prescribed boundaries and in order to prevent her from violating the hierarchical organization of groups in space, which he and other professionals preside over, the psychologist tries to produce a feeling of fear *of* S.F. and anxiety about taking responsibility for her safety if she crosses those boundaries. Such tactics are deeply rooted in wider pathologising practices and cultural stereotyping of difference. In this particular example, there is a powerful, unspoken fear of the unruly female who needs to be contained which is attached to a construction of 'S.F.' on the part of the psychologist but encompasses the woman teacher who is challenging his professional status and patriarchy.

CONCLUSION

In this chapter I have discussed the structural, procedural and professional relationships and processes which contribute to a system which is based on a notion of 'the normal'. Children and young people who do not conform to the particular version of 'normality' which underpins the education system are the focus of professional and bureaucratic attention which works to remove them to other sites on the edges ef, or outside, the education system. Alternative sites, often financed by the Ministry for Social Security and managed by Associations whose raison d'être is, in most cases, special provision on the basis of impairment, provide arenas which are both physically and symbolically landscapes of exclusion. The role of professionals as brokers in identifying and removing young people on the grounds that they are 'incapable' or 'fragile' has been discussed and questions raised about the implications of such removals for their rights to education.

I have tried to tease out some of the relationships which exist between a number of levels in the social systems surrounding education and difference. By focusing on a small number of situations, I have tried to make some links between wider issues concerning exclusion and its consequences in relation to education in France. I have included some discussion of discourses which are implicated in identifying and distancing disturbing others, and I have linked these to structural and procedural features and processes which separate and exclude individuals and groups of young people from education. 'Professionals' play a pivotal role in processes of spatialization. In the final chapter I shall try to draw together some ideas and questions which have emerged in the study in relation to my original research questions concerning theories of space, place and identity and the role of history.

CHAPTER 9

CONCLUSION: SPACE, PLACE AND THE PRODUCTION OF THE OTHER

Critical Reflections (and a Symphony)

INTRODUCTION

In this final chapter I shall return to some of the issues and questions raised in earlier chapters and discuss them in the light of the research experience and some of the theoretical ideas put forward.

I will highlight questions and 'discoveries' which I consider particularly important in the light of a stated commitment to social justice and in particular, consider the extent to which I have drawn attention to, or challenged 'the assumptions informing policy …', or thrown some light on how injustices and inequalities are produced, reproduced and sustained …' (Ozga and Gewirtz, 1994, p 122).

One difficulty with trying to bring all the main themes and arguments together in a conclusion is the temptation to tidy them all up neatly in a set of homogenised statements. This difficulty is exacerbated by the ambitious and multi-disciplinary nature of this study, in which questions and issues emerge along the way. While recognising the complexity and multi-dimensional nature of social relations and struggle, there is inevitably an unevenness in terms of this engagement both within and across the questions and issues discussed.

In the beginning, I set out to do a straight-forward comparative study of education policy making in relation to disabled children. Returning to an entry in my early notebooks already cited in Chapter One, I saw my task as exploring:

> … how and where education policy is made in France and England in relation to disabled pupils, and the ways in which it impedes, or promotes, their inclusion in ordinary schools …
>
> My 'hunch' is that *educational opportunities for disabled young people are shaped and structured in complex and sometimes contradictory ways by different policy making interests, structures, procedures and practices* which disregard equality and human rights issues. My study will investigate the relationships between these different areas and the roles they play in producing and reproducing inequalities, in the context of two specialist institutions, one in France and one in the UK.

Re-reading this in the final stages of the writing process, I am struck first, by how much more complex and messy the research process has been than I anticipated, and secondly how useful my 'hunch' was in setting me off on a number of pathways. At the same time, in those early stages I did not fully appreciate the complexity of the relationships involved in the multiple levels of 'policy making interests, structures, procedures and practices' which I would have to grapple with.

The research approaches I adopted were diverse, and the strategies used often emerged during the research process itself, rather than being planned and applied in an orderly way. I referred to concepts such as 'inclusion' and 'rights', 'deconstruction', 'landscape' and 'discourse' in ways which are fluid, providing a challenge of interpretation. I moved, often shakily, between ideas and images, from one setting to another and backwards and forwards across different historical periods. The multiple levels of the enquiry and shifting character of the use of terminology and research arenas emerged through the 'wild profusion' of the structures, processes and practices which formed the body of my enquiry. In trying to draw these all together, I am not attempting to tidy things away and 'sign off', but to tease out and clarify some issues which are fundamental to questions of equality and justice.

THEORIES OF SPACE AND PLACE

One of the main questions which I have tried to address concerns the extent to which theories relating to space and place can contribute to our understanding of processes of exclusion in education, especially in relation to disabled children. I have briefly examined the relationship between the use of space, the erection of boundaries, the creation of places for particular purposes and the construction of identities and linked these to a critical analysis of policy making in a small number of sites in relation to processes of exclusion and inclusion. While much of the discussion has focused on 'disability', during the research process I found the edges between 'exclusion' on the grounds of disability and 'exclusion' associated with wider processes of sifting and sorting were blurred and overlapping. At this stage, I am curious to re-examine some of the ideas which I discussed in Chapter Two in the light of the research experience.

First of all, there is the overarching argument that 'an important dimension through which social systems produce and reproduce power relations is the spatial' (Chapter Two). In reflecting on the analysis of the events and processes connected with the different research settings in the light of this proposition, I find that there is 'evidence' to support this statement. My analysis of the positioning and distancing of disabled students at Freelands School in the policy making processes surrounding its proposed closure, by teachers, governors, 'professionals' and LEA officers, revealed some of the embeddedness of the mechanisms and multiple layers at which exclusions take place. These exclusions are connected with the identification of a group of people (in this case, disabled children and young people) with places and cultures outside the ordinary spaces which are used, frequented, and occupied by 'ordinary' people.

The existence of segregated sites usually situated on the peripheries of towns and cities with their different 'special' appearances, cultures and discourses, creates and perpetuates a set of spatial and place relationships which construct groups as different on the basis of 'not being like the majority'. It is interesting to draw comparisons between the placing of special schools in England with those of specialized institutions in France (putting aside, for a moment, earlier assertions that it is 'not possible' to make comparisons between different cultures). In both national contexts these sites are on the edges of communities, up a hill, beyond the reach of the 'centre', behind walls, set well back – very well back – from the road. Of course, so are many other schools and institutions, but a special school at the centre of a village or a town is a very rare thing indeed. A notable exception to this is the Institut National des Sourds-Muets on the rue St Jacques in the heart of the Latin Quarter in Paris. It has been there since 1794; students and teachers from the Institut crowd the local cafés in nearby streets at certain times of day, creating an unusual situation for tourists. On one occasion, I watched a group of tourists from North America stop in their tracks as they were about to enter a café, gazing in apparent bewilderment at the numbers of people sitting outside on the terrace, drinking coffee, playing chess, reading Le Monde or le Figaro ... and *signing*. The tourists hesitated: was this a café just for deaf people and were they 'out of place'? They left to find another café, feeling uncomfortable with the ambiguity. This example raises issues about the relationship between 'place', 'behaviour and 'identity', which has emerged as one of the principle themes in the study.

In this study I have tried to explore the role of social and geographical location in constructing difference and deviance through a number of examples. In Chapter Seven, for example, governors of an ordinary school referred to students, teachers, governors and parents associated with Freelands special school in a variety of negative ways based on assumptions made about the relationships between a 'place' and those who are seen as belonging to it. Separate sites, removed from daily social exchanges between different groups, perpetuate place myths and stereotypes. This was illustrated in the comment made by one parent governor about the children ('others') at Freelands ('elsewhere'):

I've been up there and seen them and they're not like our kids at all.

In the same meeting it was suggested that teachers might not have 'qualified teacher status', and that parents would be 'only interested in their *own* disabled children'.

In both the French and the English contexts there were examples of many different ways in which groups were homogenised into a dependent, incapable or threatening mass of 'others' who were identified on the basis of particular segregated sites. This demonstrates some of the ways in which 'spaces ... are ascribed meanings and convey meanings' (Kitchen, 1998, p. 349) and how '...the spatial organization of society ... makes a difference to how it works' (Massey, 1994, p. 254).

Teachers and professionals 'inside' segregated settings also position children and young people as having particular characteristics and needs associated with their impairments or difficulties. The removal of children and young people from ordinary settings which do not recognise diversity to settings in which they receive 'different treatment' and in which they are perceived as 'making progress', 'safe' or 'getting the therapy they need' provides a framework within which segregated schools and institutions can be seen as 'doing good' and addressing the particular needs of individuals, legitimating the expertise of specialists and professionals. Paradoxically, some settings such as Freelands in England and the Institut Médico-Professionnel (IMPRO) in France (referred to in Chapter Eight) are prepared for, or exist for the purpose of dealing with, a particular version of 'diversity' in the sense that children and young people who attend these settings are aged from the pre-school years to the post-compulsory years. At Freelands the students were described as having a very wide range of physical impairments, medical conditions and learning difficulties. At the IMPRO there were children and young people who were described as having psychiatric and social problems which have affected their learning. There were also some who had physical impairments or conditions. The SEGPAs also exist as places in which diverse populations can be gathered together on the grounds that they do not 'fit' into the shape and culture of ordinary educational institutions. In this way, segregated settings exist as part of a wider hegemony of 'the normal' because they allow the central, visible educational spaces to be occupied by ordinary, legitimate students for whom 'real' education is intended.

The populations of segregated institutions are, therefore, 'diverse' in a number of different ways. However, the logic of creating outer zones to which disturbing others can be removed is being undermined by the transformation of the populations of ordinary schools. This paradox illustrates Lefebvre's argument discussed in Chapter Two, that:

> Socio-political contradictions are realized spatially. The contradictions of space thus make the contradictions of social relations operative. In other words, spatial contradictions 'express' conflicts between socio-political interests and forces ...' (Lefebvre, 1991 p. 365)

In my study a number of examples of conflicts and contradictions have emerged between 'socio-political interests and forces' and their relationship to processes which change the boundaries surrounding categories of difference and the re-interpretation of identities. In this context I have considered the following examples:

- the effects of war on the economy and supply of labour in terms of the reinvention of 'useless' people as productive and necessary workers;
- the relationship between the evacuation of children and young people from cities and the inclusion of disabled children in ordinary schools;
- the assigning of the informal temporary label of 'disabled by long-term unemployment' to people who had been out of work for a long time, allowing them to take up places in the segregated 'help through work' factories set up as centres for the employment of disabled people and those who have difficulties in learning;

- the use of professional-bureaucratic procedures to assign 'medical' labels to disturbing young people in order to remove them from ordinary schools;
- the creation of new groupings of children and young people described as having a wide range of impairment, medical conditions, possible 'behavioural' problems and other difficulties, (described by one teacher as 'the ones no-one knows what to do with') and their placement in a setting designated for one 'traditional' category (e.g. children with physical impairments).

This 'discovery' of the wide ranging and routine ways in which people are 're-bottled' and freshly labelled, or homogenised so that they 'fit' into an existing category is, for me, one of the most interesting (and significantly offensive) aspects of the research to emerge. It underlines the argument that categories of difference are socially constructed and contingent upon broader contexts. Of course, there is nothing new in the 'social construction' argument or in the observation that labels are used to 'deal with people' and dictate 'settings' and 'treatment'. What is illuminating in the context of this study, perhaps, are the ways in which these processes are linked to a) wider economic and social processes, b) the role of professionals in presiding over these, and c) their relationship to the practices and consequences of spacing and placing.

The relationship between social and economic processes, the practices of professionals, and processes of spacing and placing which I regard as one of the most important issues raised in this study, require further research across disciplines. For example, an exploration of the relationship between social and economic conditions, the identification and the placing of children in foster care or 'children's homes' and the roles of different professionals in processes of removal would provide the basis for an important piece of further research.

Some of the issues raised so far relate to part of the discussion in Chapter Two concerning the relationship between the production of capital, labour and productivity, and processes of spatialization. Both Lefebvre and Scull link the industrialization of the means of production and the need for a controlled and effective supply of mass labour, with the growth of large scale and highly differentiated institutions such as asylums, prisons and hospitals. The economies and technologies of scale established in the factories of capitalist industry provided a model for the vast institutions which were established in Victorian times. The relationship between social-political responses to differences, and care, control and productivity has emerged as a theme in some of the material discussed in this study. Greater understanding is needed of the inter-relationship between the principle of social 'usefulness', economic interests and the involvement of representatives of the State in imposing definitions of normality and the role these play in producing exclusion and marginalization. This leads me to a further question concerning the relationship between assumptions and beliefs about place and identity and the ways in which disabled children and young people may be perceived.

Many issues relating to this question have already been raised in the previous sections, especially concerning the connections made between the characteristics ascribed to children and young people and the spaces they are assigned inside (or beyond) the education system. There are still some closer links to be made with my analysis of the material in the study.

One observation that has emerged is that there is often 'agreement' between professionals and others associated with 'special' settings and 'ordinary' settings that those assigned to sites outside the mainstream are different from those 'inside'. I have discussed examples in which teachers or governors associated with 'ordinary' and segregated settings (in England and in France) described children and young people in terms of their 'difficulties' and 'dependency' and what made them 'different' from other children and young people. Descriptions included references to 'complex difficulties', 'being in a wheel chair', 'being too friendly and too trusting', 'severely disabled', 'fragile', 'specials', 'from disadvantaged backgrounds' and so on. What was particularly striking was the persistent failure by some commentators – apart from those connected to the Lycée Bresson, the head teacher and parents at Freelands – to refer to other attributes of children and young people who attended segregated settings, to their individuality and what they shared in common with their peers, what they enjoyed doing and what they contributed to their communities. This 'failure' attached itself to the identities of dependent, fragile, sometimes dangerous 'others' who belong in special places where they can be managed. There were many situations during the research in which disabled children's identities were merged with a set of homogenised features, and there were times when 'visual difference' became implicitly associated with the identities of disabled children and particular settings (especially in the meeting of governors at Hillbank School discussed in Chapter Seven). But there were many other 'marks of difference', which were ascribed to excluded others relating to dependency, unpredictability, vulnerability, strangeness, and even dangerousness. All of these were merged at different times with the identities of particular groups or individuals associated with particular places. A crucial issue relating to human rights arises from the study concerning the consequences of the construction of identities (and assumptions and beliefs associated with them), in terms of the spatializing processes of children and young people in relation to education.

This brings me to a further set of issues which has emerged during the study relating to the possibility of subverting the processes of identity formation and procedures which mark out and marginalize, and the possible contradictions involved. The Lycée Bresson presented an unusual example of institutional counter culture expressed through the multiple discourses of the physical environment, curriculum, practices and organization of the school and the language used to talk about its population and purposes, demonstrating the possibilities and opportunities for overcoming disabling practices and barriers to participation. At the same time, the Lycée Bresson was highly selective in that only young people deemed 'capable' of following the academic curriculum, as well as fulfilling other criteria relating to disability or golf playing. The 'academic criteria' were imposed as part of the broader criteria of selection which operated in the wider education system as a whole. The paradox lies in the 'overcoming' of one set of hegemonic and oppressive practices and values while 'enforcing' and reproducing another set. This raises issues which are under explored and under theorized in the study, but ones which would provide important areas for future research in terms of examining the possible contradictions of 'radical' practices within wider political and social contexts.

An important focus for discussion in earlier chapters concerns the important and pervasive question of 'discourse', especially in terms of the ways in which spatializing discourse relating to space and place inform the processes and practices of policy making. In Chapter Seven I referred to the 'shifting meanings' of discourses surrounding 'inclusion' and how these express the 'complexities of the processes of displacement and movement involved in widening participation in ordinary settings'. The 'slippage' and disguise which characterizes the use of language as tactic and strategy, is part of wider systems relating to conflicting values and interests. I have discussed the role of discourse in the multiple levels of policy making and examples of the stealth and subterfuge of the different power-discourses used in the struggles over what kind of society we live in, and who shall be included and who removed from common spaces and participation. I have tried to examine some of the possible implications of the role of discourse in terms of policy making, social justice and the impact and anchorage it has in all aspects of our thinking and social life.

A further set of issues which emerged during the research process relates to the obscured political meanings and purposes surrounding practices of 'consultation' and the implications of these for democracy and social justice. I am referring to the systematic segmentation and compartmentalization of 'meetings' and other forums which took place in different territories, involving particular groupings of actors. Crucially, some groups and individuals who were profoundly affected by decisions and outcomes of 'the consultation process' were absent, or only appeared as silent trespassers. (In the example of the meeting of teachers and LEA officers at Hillbank, the head teacher of Freelands was not asked for her opinion or her perceptions on the issues under discussion). The most disturbing example in the English context is the complete and systematic absence of children and young people from discussions about what kind of school they would like to belong to or how they would like their school to change. It is a paradox that while it is technically a requirement under the (UK) Code of Practice (1994) and the revised Code, that individual students should be fully involved in decisions about their education, groups of students who have been homogenised under the same category (e.g. 'physical impairment', 'emotional and behavioural difficulties' and 'learning difficulty') do not participate in decision making processes in terms of their future educational and social life.

The possible consequences and implications of the compartmentalization of different perspectives on issues such as the proposed closure of a special school are far-reaching. Groups with opposing views were, in general, kept apart. In the case of the Freelands 'consultation' process, separate meetings were arranged for teachers, governors and parents connected to different sites. This meant that they did not have the opportunity of listening to all the different issues at stake being discussed in a common forum. It is difficult to believe, for example, that the teachers and governors at Hillbank would not have begun to reflect on the values and implications involved in excluding children on the grounds of disability and difference from 'their' school if they, and students at the school, had been able to meet naturally and informally with parents, teachers, governors and students at Freelands. It is also hard to imagine that the views expressed and the discourses used would not have been modified in the presence of a wider audience. It is highly significant that legislation (however inadequate) is in place which makes illegal the expression of views and language which are racially discriminatory, but that people can express views in meetings which are implicitly or explicitly discriminatory to disabled people. In a consultation process, then, all those concerned including children and young people and the wider community, should meet together and listen to each other's voices. Current practices prevent this from happening – an example, surely, of the enactment of the 'Habit of Exclusive Thinking' (Corbett, 1996).

The bureaucratic dividing up of the 'consultation process' also allowed local education authority officers to 'manage' the different groups of teachers, governors and parents separately, enabling them to 'offer assurances' to one group in one situation, which were not mentioned or openly discussed in another setting. This also made it possible for the views of one group to be misrepresented in forums from which they had been excluded.

The question of 'representation' relates to all aspects of the use of discourse. In Chapter Eight there were a number of instances cited in which individuals and groups were represented as having particular characteristics which were used as a rationale or justification for removing them from ordinary educational settings, as well as creating and sustaining stereotypes. The young people concerned were not present to challenge the identities assigned to them or to express their interests and points of view.

To summarize, discourses relating to the language used, what is said, by whom and in what context permeate all levels of policy making. The separation of different venues for the discussion of policy making allows consultation processes to be manipulated and prevents different groups from listening to each other. This raises important questions concerning democracy in the context of practices relating to 'consultation'. Secondly, the use of discourse as a mechanism for othering groups and individuals as part of wider bureaucratic and political processes of exclusion is endemic in systems in France and England and represents a denial of the human right to be heard and to be treated with dignity and justice.

A serious limitation in terms of the research underpinning the study mirrors the exclusion of children and young people from the 'consultation process'. Although I wanted to find out the views of young disabled people and those excluded from ordinary education settings, in general their voices are only faintly heard and are marginalized from the main arena of the study. There is the important exception of the contribution of C.W. and his analysis of his education and policy making issues. Insights from his account permeate the study in many guises, especially in terms of the relationship between the mapping of personal history onto wider structural, procedural and discursive processes. C.W. also raised some crucial issues which are usually absent from debates on education and about the possible consequences of 'inclusion' for some students, suggesting that we need to engage with the meanings and implications of different interpretations of inclusion from multiple perspectives. However, I did not manage to discuss policy issues and 'consultation' with the children and young people concerned in this study. This was because it was difficult to create situations in which an informal discussion could take place in conditions in which all concerned felt comfortable. There was also an assumption on the part of some professionals and teachers (for example, at the Hôpital Sainte Thérèse and to a lesser extent at the Lycée Bresson) that I would not be interested in discussing issues with the young people concerned. On reflection, only one setting – the IMPRO – made it possible for me to form a relationship with the small group of students I met, by inviting me take the class!

Finally, I want to return to the question of history, and the ways in which we might reconsider dominant accounts of the development of special education. I discussed the importance of challenging traditional historical accounts quite extensively in Chapters Four and Five. Here I shall make a few additional connections with other material in the study and add some general statements to draw the ideas together. I argued in Chapter Four that traditional historical accounts which construct a homogenised, developmental unfolding landscape in which increasing 'humanitarianism' accompanies the 'steady march of progress' are misleading. Traditional accounts must be challenged by the enormous range of possible evidence which suggests not 'rationality' but irrationality, not 'orderly progress' but struggle, contradiction, serendipity and contingency. In many ways, this contested view of history mirrors the policy making processes I have been researching and the relational and contextual mechanisms which inform them.

I have drawn briefly on images, paintings, and architecture to suggest different possible ways of interrogating and interpreting the environment and social exclusions. These are linked to a critical approach to history in terms of representations and social responses to difference and disability and the questions these raise. My reflections on different pictures and other historically situated materials are extremely tentative, but represent an attempt to open up possibilities of finding fresh sources and perspectives, rather than providing explanations or a polished alternative 'history'.

A further issue which has arisen, which I have already touched upon, is the importance and uniqueness of individual histories as they interweave with the major historical landmarks and fine personal-historical details in broader social landscapes. It is the relationships between levels of personal experience against what else is going on in the broader social historical picture and, conversely, what the broader picture means in terms of the lives of individuals and what these relationships mean in terms of issues of equity and inclusion, which are important.

NO CONCLUSION

I will end this piece of writing with a last reflection on a critical moment in my research when the idea took hold that spaces, places, people, events, time, power and experience are all drawn together in extraordinary ways to make an infinite number of histories. Policy making is like that too, in that it occurs everywhere, all the time and in multiple arenas. This realization gradually became embedded in my thinking and the way I was planning and interpreting what I was doing, but I can point to an 'event' which was critical in bringing this about. In the early stages of writing this thesis, I came across *Different Trains*, a symphony composed by Steve Reich in 1988, and I kept on listening to it and reading over what Reich had written about it. It became my inspiration as I began to make the connections between Reich's own story and his research which is explored in the symphony, and the kinds of demands I was making on my own research material.

This is what he wrote:

> The concept for the piece comes from my childhood. When I was one year old, my parents separated. My mother moved to Los Angeles and my father stayed in New York. Since they arranged divided custody, I traveled back and forth by train frequently between New York and Los Angeles from 1939 to 1942 accompanied by my governess. While these trips were exciting and romantic at the time, I look back and think that, if I had been in Europe during this period, as a Jew I would have had to ride very different trains. With this in mind I wanted to make a piece that would accurately reflect the whole situation. In order to prepare the tape I had to do the following:
>
> 1. Record my governess, now in her seventies, reminiscing about our train trips together.
> 2. Record a retired Pullman porter, Lawrence Davis, now in his eighties, who used to ride lines between New York and Los Angeles, reminiscing about his life.
> 3. Collect recordings of Holocaust survivors Rachella, Paul and Rachael – all about my age and now living in America – speaking of their experiences.
> 4. Collect recorded American and European train sounds of the 1930s and '40s.
>
> The piece thus presents both a documentary and a musical reality ... (Reich, 1988)

Reich created a historical text linking and exploring personal history and the clamour of universal conflict and oppression – a text which is formed through autobiography and biography as they interweave with time, place and space. *Different Trains* is a piece of interpretative ethnography which shapes and holds together a 'symphony' in which the self is at the centre of the writing of history. It is a symphony in which the voices of real people become part of orchestral music. In this study, while the 'symphony' is unfinished and is unequivocally 'mine', I have tried to bring the voices of people from different places into the centre of the research process and the telling of their different stories.

REFERENCES

Adelman, C., Kemmis, S. and Jenkins, D. (1980) 'Rethinking case study: notes from the Second Cambridge conference' in Simon, H. (ed.) *Towards a Science of the Singular*, Norwich: Centre for Applied Research in Education, University of East Anglia.

Ainscow, M. (1999) *Understanding the Development of Inclusive Schools*, London: Falmer Press.

Albert, E. M. (1960) 'My "Boy", Munty.' in Casagrande, J. B. (ed.) *In the Company of Man: Twenty Portraits of Anthropological Informants*, New York: Harper Torchbooks.

Apple, M. (1990) *Ideology and Curriculum*, London: Routledge and Kegan Paul.

Arendt, H. (1959) *The Human Condition*, Chicago: University of Chicago Press.

Armstrong, D. (1995) *Power and partnership in education: parents, children and special educational needs*, London: Routledge.

Armstrong, F. J. (1995) 'Appellation Controllée: Mixing and sorting in the French education system', in Potts, P., Armstrong, F. J. and Masterton, M. (eds) *Equality and Diversity in Education: National and International Contexts*, London: Routledge.

Armstrong, F. (1996) 'Special Education in France' in Corbett, A. and Moon, B. (eds) *Education in France: Continuity and Change in the Mitterand Years, 1981–1995*, London: Routledge.

Armstrong, F. (1999a) 'Comparative perspectives on difference and difficulty: a cross-cultural approach', in Barton, L. and Armstrong, F. (eds) (1999) *Difference and Difficulty: Insights, Issues and Dilemmas*, Sheffield: University of Sheffield.

Armstrong, F. (1999b) 'Inclusion, curriculum and the struggle for space in school' in *International Journal of Special Education*, Vol 3: no 1, 75–87.

Armstrong, F. (2002) 'Managing difference: inclusion, performance and power' in Brighton, A. (ed.) 'The Rise and Rise of Management Discourse, Part 2', *Critical Quarterly*, 44 (4), 51–56.

Armstrong, F., Armstrong, D. and Barton, L. (2000a) (eds) *Inclusive Education: Policy, Contexts and Comparative Perspectives*, London: David Fulton.

Armstrong, F. and Barton, L. (eds) (1999) *Disability, Human Rights and Education*, Buckingham: Open University Press.

Armstrong, F., Belmont, B. and Verillon, A. (2000) '"Vive la différence?" Exploring context, policy and change in special education in France: developing cross-cultural collaboration' in Armstrong, F., Armstrong, D. and Barton, L. (eds) *Inclusive Education: Policy, Contexts and Comparative Perspectives*, London: David Fulton Publishers.

Armstrong, F. and Booth, T. (1994) *'Learning for All': Unit 16*, Buckingham: Open University Press.

Armstrong, F., Clarke, M. and Murphy, S. (1995) '" … some kind of bampot." Young people in care and their experience of the education system' in Potts, P., Armstrong, F. and Masterton, M. (eds) *Equality and Diversity in Education 1: Experiences of learning, Teaching and Managing School*, London: Routledge.

Armytage, W. H. G. (1965) *Four Hundred Years of English Education*, Cambridge: Cambridge University Press.

Atkinson, P. and Hammersley, M. (1998) 'Ethnography and Participant Observation' in Denzin, Norman A. and Lincoln, Yvonna S. (eds) *Strategies of Qualitative Enquiry*, London: Sage Publications.

Bacchi, C, (2000) 'Policy as Discourse: what does it mean? where does it get us?' in *Discourse: studies in the cultural politics of education*, 21 (1), 45–55.

Bailey, R. (1994) 'A Tale of a Bubble' in Keith, P. *Mustn't Grumble: Writing by Disabled Women*, London: The Women's Press.

Ball, S. (ed.) (1990) *Foucault and Education: Disciplines and Knowledge*, London: Routledge.

Ball, S. J. (1994) *Education Reform: A critical and post-structural approach*, Buckingham: Open University Press.

Ballarin, J-L. (1994) *Enfants difficiles,structures specialisée*, Paris: Nathan.

Barnes, C., Mercer, G. and Shakespeare, T. (1999) *Exploring Disability: A Sociological Introduction*, Cambridge: Polity Press.

Barthes, R. (1973) *Mythologies*, St Albans: Paladin.

Barton, L. (1996) 'Sociology and disability: some emerging issues' in Barton, L. (ed.) *Disability and Society: Emerging Issues and Insights*, London: Longman.

Barton, L. (1998) 'Markets, managerialism and Inclusive Education' in Clough, P. (ed.) *Managing Inclusive Education: From Policy to Experience*, London: Paul Chapman Publishing.

Barton, L. and Armstrong, F. (1999), 'Introduction' in Armstrong, F. and Barton, L. (eds) *Disability, Human Rights and Education*, Buckingham: Open University Press.

Barton, L. and Slee, R. (1999) 'Competition, selection and inclusive education: some observation' in *International Journal of Inclusive Education*, Vol 3: no 1, 3 –12 (Special Issue).

Bassey, M. (1999) *Case Study Research in Educational Settings*, Buckingham: Open University Press.

Becker, H. (1963) *Outsiders: Studies in the Sociology of Deviance*, New York: The Free Press.

Bélanger, N. (2000) 'Entre psychologues et politiques. Le tournant des années 1960 en France' in Chauvière, M. and Plaisance, E. (2000) (eds) *L'École face aux handicaps: éducation spéciale ou éducation intégrative?*, Paris: Press Universitaire de France.

Bélanger, N. and Garant, N. (1999) 'Educational opportunities and polysemic notions of equality in France' in Armstrong, F. and Barton, L. (eds) *Disability, human rights and education: cross-cultural perspectives*, Buckingham: Open University Press.

Berger, J. (1972) *Ways of Seeing*, London: Penguin.

Berthe-Denoeux, M-F. and Léoni, V. (2000) 'le regard des enfants valides' in Chauvière, M. and Plaisance, E. (eds) *L'École face aux handicaps: éducation spéciale ou éducation intégrative?*, Paris: Press Universitaire de France.

Booth, T. (1981) 'Demystefying Integration' in Swann, W. (ed.) *The Practice of Special Education*, Oxford: Blackwell.

Booth, T. (1987) 'Labels and their consequences' in Lane, D. and Stratford, B. (eds) *Current Approaches to Down's Syndrome*, London: Cassell.

Booth, T. (1995) 'Mapping Inclusion and Exclusion: Concepts for all?' in Clark, C., Dyson, A. and Millward, A. (eds) *Towards Inclusive Schools?*, London: David Fulton Publishers.

Booth, T. (1999) 'Viewing inclusion from a distance: Gaining perspectives frcm comparative study' in *Support for Learning*, 14: 4, 164–-8.

Booth, T. (2000) 'Inclusion and exclusion policy in England: who controls the agenda?' in Armstrong, F. , Armstrong, D. and Barton, L. (eds) *Inclusive Education: Policy, Contexts and Comparative Perspectives*, London: David Fulton Publications.

Booth, T. (2003) 'Inclusion and Exclusion in the city: concepts and contexts' in Potts, P. (ed.) *Inclusion in the City: Selection, Schooling and Community*, London, RoutledgeFalmer

Booth, T. and Ainscow, M. (eds) (1998) From Them To Us: An International Study of Inclusion in Education, London, Routledge.

Booth, T., Ainscow, M., Black-Hawkins, K., Vaughan, M. and Shaw, L. (1999) *Index for Inclusion: developing learning and participation in schools*, Bristol: Centre for Studies on Inclusive Education.

Bronte, C. (1994) *Villette*, Oxford: Oxford University Press (First published in 1853).

Burgess, R. G. (1982) 'Multiple Strategies in Field Research' in Burgess, R. G. (ed.) *Field Research: a Sourcebook and Field Manual*, London: Allen and Unwin.

Chartier, R. (1994) 'The Chimera of the Origin: Archaeology, Cultural History, and the French Revolution' in Goldstein, J. (ed) *Foucault and the Writing of History*, (p 171).

Chauvière, M. (2000) 'L'école et le secteur médico-social. Naissance d'un contentieux' in Chauvière, M. and Plaisance, E. (2000) (eds) *L'École face aux handicaps: éducation spéciale ou éducation intégrative?*, Paris: Press Universitaire de France.

Chauvière, M. and Plaisance, E. (eds) (2000) *L'École face aux handicaps: éducation spéciale ou éducation intégrative?*, Paris: Press Universitaire de France.

Closs, (ed.) (2000) *The Education of Children with Medical Conditions*, London, David Fulton Publishers.

Coffey, A. (1999) *The Ethnographic Self: Fieldwork and the Representation of Identity*, London: Sage Publications.

Cohen, A. and Hugon, A. (1995) *Nouveaux Lycées, Nouveaux Pédagogues*, Paris: Harmattan, CRESAS.

Cole, T. (1989) *Apart or A Part? Integration and the Growth of British Special Education*, Milton Keynes: Open University Press.

Copeland, I. (1999) *The Making of the Backward Pupil in Education in England 1870-1914*, London: Woburn Press

Corbett, J. (1996) *Bad-Mouthing: The Language of Special Needs*, London: The Falmer Press.

Corbett, J. (2001) *Supporting Inclusive Education: A Connective Pedagogy*, London: RoutledgeFalmer.

Corker, M. (1999) 'new Disability Discourse, the principle of optimisation and social change' in Corker, M. and French, S. (eds) *Disability Discourse*, Buckingham: Open University Press

Cosgrove, D. (1987) 'New Directions in cultural geography' in *Area* 19. 2 , 95–101.

Cresswell, T. (1996) *In Place/Out of Place: geography, ideology and transgression*, London: UCL Press.

Darcy, M. (1999) 'The Discourse of "Community" and the reinvention of Social Housing Policy in Australia'. *Urban Studies*, 36 (1) 13–26.

Defoe, D. (1697) 'Of Fools' in 'An Essay on Projects' republished in Morley, H. (1889) The Earlier Life and Works of Daniel Defoe, The Carisbrook Library.

Denzin, N. K. (1970) *The Research Act*, Chicago: Aldine.

Denzin, N. K. (1978) *The Research Act: A theoretical introduction to sociological methods*, New York: McGraw-Hill.

Denzin, Norman A. and Lincoln, Yvonna S. (eds) (1998) *Strategies of Qualitative Enquiry*, London: Sage Publications.

Department for Education and Employment (DfEE) (1995) *A brief guide to the Disability Discrimination Act, Disability on the Agenda*, Bristol.

Department for Education and Employment (DfEE) (1996) *The 1996 School Premises Regulations*, Circular number 10/96, London: The DfEE Publications Centre.

Department for Education and Employment (DfEE) (1997) *What the Disability Discrimination Act (DDA) 1995 means for schools and LEAs*, Circular number 3/97, London: DfEE Publications Centre.

Department for Education and Employment (DfEE) (1999a) *Building Bulletin 91: Access for Disabled People to School Buildings: Management and Design Guide*, London: The Stationary Office.

Department for Education and Employment (DfEE) (1999b) *Final Report of the Disability Rights Task Force*, London: DfEE Publications Centre.

Department of Education and Science (DES) (1978) *Special Educational Needs* (The Warnock Report), London: HMSO.

Derrida, J. (1989) 'Jacques Derrida in Discussion with Christopher Norris" in Papadakis, Andreas, C. (ed.) *Deconstruction 11*, London: Academy Editions.

Dickens, C. (1998) *Nicholas Nickleby*, Oxford: Oxford University Press (First published in 1839).

Doll, E. A. (1962) 'A historical survey of research and management of mental retardation in the United States' in Trapp, E. P. and Himelstein (eds) *Readings on the Exceptional Child: Research and Theory*, New York: Alfred J. Knopf.

Donald, J. (1992) 'Metropolis: the city as text' in: R. Bockock and K. Thompson (eds) *Social and Cultural Forms of Modernity*, Cambridge: Polity Press.

Dutton, T. A. (1996) 'Cultural Studies and Critical Pedagogy: Cultural Pedagogy and Architecture' in Dutton, T. A. and Hurst Mann, L. (eds) *Reconstructing Architecture: Critical Discourses and Social Practices*, Minneapolis: University of Minnesota Press.

Emihovich, C. (1995) 'Distancing passion: narratives in social science' in Hatch, Amos J. and Wisniewski, R. (eds) *Life History and Narrative*, London: The Falmer Press.

Fablet, D. (2000) 'Une comparaison des modes de professionalisation' in Chauvière, M. and Plaisance, E. (eds) *L'École face aux handicaps: éducation spéciale ou éducation intégrative?*, Paris: Press Universitaire de France.

Foucault, M. (1967) *Madness and Civilization: A History of Insanity in the Age of Reason*, London: Tavistock.

Foucault, M. (1971) 'Nietzche, Genealogy, History' in Rabinow, P. (ed.) (1991) *The Foucault Reader*, London, Penguin Books.

Foucault, M. (1974) *The Archeology of Knowledge*, London: Tavistock.

Foucault, M. (1976) *The Birth of the Clinic: An Archeology of Medical Perception*, London: Tavistock.

Foucault, M. (1977) *Discipline and Punish*, Harmonsdworth: Penguin.

Foucault, M. (1980) *Power/Knowledge*, Brighton: Harvester.

Foucault, M. (1982) 'The Subject and Power', in Dreyfus, H, and Rabinow, P. (eds) *Michel Foucault: Beyond Structuralism and Hermeneutics*, Chicago: University of Chicago Press.

Foucault, M. and Rabinow, P. (1994) 'Space, Knowledge, and Power' Interview with Michel Foucault conducted by Paul Rabinow, published in Rabinow, P. *The Foucault Reader: An Introduction to Foucault's Thought*, London: Penguin Books.

Fulcher, G. (1993) 'Schools and Contests: A Reframing of the Effective Schools Debate?' in Slee, R. (ed.) *Is there a Desk With My Name On It? The Politics of Integration*, London: Falmer Press.

Fulcher, G. (1999) *Disabling Policies? A comparative approach to education and disability*, Sheffield: Philip Armstrong Publications. (Originally published in 1989 by The Falmer Press).

Galton, M. and Blyth, A. (1989) *Handbook of Primary Education in Europe*, Exeter: David Fulton.

Gans, H. J. (1962) *The Urban Villagers*, New York: The Free Press.

Gewirtz, S. (2002) *The Managerial School*, London, Routledge.

Giddens, A. (1981) *A Contemporary Critique of Historical Materialism, Vol 1: Power Property and the State*, London: Macmillan.

Giroux, H.A. (1996) *Fugitive Cultures: race, violence and youth*, London: Routledge.

Gleeson, B. (1999) *Geographies of disability*, London: Routledge.

Goffman, E. (1968) *Stigma: Notes on the management of Spoiled Identity*, London: Penguin Books.

Grosvenor, I., Lawn, M. and Rousmaniere, K. (Eds) (1999) *Silences and Images: The Social History of the Classroom*, New York, Peter Lang: 1 published as part of the series *History of Schools and Schooling*, edited by Alan R.Sadovnik, and Susan F. Semel.

Guthrie, D. (1945) *A History of Medicine*, London: Thomas Nelson.

Hall, J. T. (1997) *Social Devaluation and Special Education: The Right to Full Inclusion and an Honest Statement*, London: Jessica Kingsley Publishers.

Hammersley, M. (1994) 'Ethnography, policy making and practice in education' in Halpin, D. and Troyna, B. (eds) *Researching Education Policy: Ethical and Methodological Issues*, London: The Falmer Press.

Hamilton, D. (2001) 'Notes from Nowhere. (On the Beginnings of Modern Schooling) in Popkewitz, T.S., Franklin, B., Pereyra, M.A. (eds) (2001) *Cultural History and Education*, London: RoutledgeFalmer

Hanet-Kania, N. (1996) 'L'État et les associations humanitaire en France', in Paugam, S. *L'exclusion: l'état des savoirs*, Paris: Éditions La Découverte.

Harris, S. (1992) 'A Career on the Margins? The position of careers teachers in Schools' in *British Journal of Sociology of Education*, 13 (2), pp. 162–76.

Harris, S. (1999) *Careers Education: Contesting Policy and Practice*, London: Paul Chapman/Sage.

Harris, S. (2003) 'Inter-agency practice and professional collaboration: the case of drug education and prevention' in *Journal of Education Policy*, (forthcoming).

Harvey, D. (1996) *Justice, Nature and the Geography of Difference*, Oxford: Blackwell.

Hastings, A. (1999) 'Discourse and Urban Change: Introduction to the Special Issue', *Urban Studies*, 36 (1) 8–12.

Hayden, D. (1996) *The Power of Place: Urban Landscapes as Public History*, Cambridge, Massachusetts: The MIT Press.

Hetherington, K, (1997) *The Badlands of Modernity: Heterotopia and Social Ordering*, London: Routledge.

Hevey, D. (1992) *The* Creatures *Time Forgot: Photography and Imagery*, London: Routledge.

Heywood, I. (1997) *Social Theories of Art: A Critique*, London: Macmillan Press.

Humphries, S. and Gordon, P. (1992) *Out of Sight: Childhood and Disability 1900–1950*, Plymouth: Northcote House.

Hurt, J. S. (1988) *Outside the Mainstream: A History of Special Education*, London: Batesford.

Imrie, R. (1996) *Disability and the City: International Perspectives*, London: Paul Chapman Publishing.

Imrie, R. (2000) 'Disabling Environments and the geography of Access' in *Disability and Society*, Vol. 15, No 1: 5–24.

Jacobs, K. and Manzi, T. (1996) 'Discourse and policy change: the significance of language for housing research' in *Housing Studies* 11 (4): 543–60 .

Jameson, F. (1991) *Postmodernism, or, The Cultural Logic of Late Capitalism*, Durham: Duke University Press.

Janesick, V. J. (1998) 'The Dance of Qualitative Research Design: Metaphor, Methodolatry, and Meaning' in Denzin, Norman A. and Lincoln, Yvonna S. (eds) *Strategies of Qualitative Enquiry*, London: Sage Publications.

Kenway, J. (1990) 'Education and the Right's discursive politics: private versus state schooling' in Ball, S. (ed.) *Foucault and Education: Disciplines and Knowledge*, London: Routledge.

Kitchin, R. (1998) '"Out of Place": Space, power and the exclusion of disabled people' in *Disability and Society*, Vol. 13, No. 3: 343–56.

Knight, J., Smith, R. and Sachs, J. (1990) 'Deconstructing hegemony: multicultural policy and a populist response' in Ball, Stephen J. (ed.) *Foucault and Education: Disciplines and Knowledge*, London: Routledge.

Lantier, N., Verillon, J-P, Aublé, B., Belmont, B. and Waysand, E. (1994) *Enfants Handicapés À L'École: Des instituteurs parlent de leurs pratiques,* Paris: L'Harmattan.

Lazerfeld. P. F. (1972) 'Forward to the English edition: forty years later' in Jahoda, M., Lazerfeld, P. F. and Ziesel, H. *Marienthal: The Sociography of an Unemployed Community*, London: Tavistock.

Lefebvre, H. (1972) *Espace et politique*, Paris: Éditions Anthropos.

Lefebvre, H. (1991) *The Production of Space*, Oxford: Blackwell.

Lévi-Strauss, C. (1966) *The Savage Mind* (2nd edition) Chicago: University of Chicago Press.

Macdonell, M. (1986) *Theories of Discourse: An Introduction*, Oxford: Basil Blackwell.

Malinowski, B. (1922) *Argonauts of the Western Pacific*, London: Routledge and Kegan Paul.

Markus, T. A. (1993) *Building and Power: Freedom and Control in the Origin of Modern Building Types*, London: Routledge.

Massey, D. (1994) *Space, Place and Gender*, Cambridge: Polity Press.

Mencher, S. (1967) *Poor Law to Poverty Program: Economic Security Policy in Britain and the United States*, Pittsburg: University of Pittsburgh Press.

Merleau-Ponty, M. (1964) *L'Oeil et L'Esprit,* Paris: Gallimard.

Michel, L. (1970) *La Commune: Histoire et Souvenirs* vols. 1 and 2, Paris: François Maspero. First published in Paris 1898 by Stock (éditeur).

Middleton, L. (1999) 'The Social Exclusion of Disabled Children: the role of the voluntary sector in Contract Culture' in *Disability and Society*, Vol.14, No.1,:129–139.

Miller, I. (1993) 'Guerilla artists in New York City', *Race and Class*, Vol 35: No 1: 27–40.

Moore, M., Beazley, S. and Maelzer, J. (1998) *Researching Disability Issues*, Buckingham: Open University Press.

Morgan-Klein, B. (1985) *Where am I going to stay?: A Report on Young People Leaving Care in Scotland*, Edinburgh: The Scottish Council for Single Homeless.

Morris, J. (1995) *Gone Missing? A Research and Policy Review of Disabled Children Living Away From Their Families*, London, Who Cares Trust.

Norwich, B. (2002) *Inclusion trends in England: 1997–2001*, Bristol: CSIE.

O'Hanlon, C. (1993) *Special Education: Integration in Europe*, London: David Fulton.

O'Hanlon, C. (ed.) (1995) *Inclusive Education in Europe*, London: David Fulton.

OECD (1995) *Integrating students with special needs into mainstream schools*, Paris: OECD.

OFSTED (1996) *Exclusions from Secondary Schools 1995–1996*, London.

Okely, J. (1983) *The Traveller Gypsies*, Cambridge: Cambridge University Press.

Okely, J. (1991) 'Defiant Moment: Gender, resistance and individuals' in *Man* 26 (1): 3–22.

Okely, J. (1992) 'Anthropology and autobiography: Participatory experience and embodied knowledge' in Okely, J and Callaway, H. (eds) *ASA Monographs 29. Anthropology and Autobiography*, London: Routledge.

Okely, J and Callaway, H. (eds) (1992) *ASA Monographs 29. Anthropology and Autobiography*, London: Routledge.

Oliver, M. and Barnes, C. (1998) *Disabled People and Social Policy: From Exclusion to Inclusion*, London: Longman.

Ozga, J. and Gewirtz, S. (1994) 'Sex, Lies and Audio tape: Interviewing the Education Policy Elite' in Halpin, D. and Troyna, B. (eds) *Researching Education Policy: Ethical and Methodological Issues*, London: The Falmer Press.

Peim, N. (2001) 'the history of the present: towards a contemporary phenomenology of the school', *History of Education*, 30:2, 177–190

Peters, S. (1995) 'Disability baggage: changing the educational research terrain', in Clough, P. and Barton, L. (eds) *Making Difficulties: Research and the Construction of SEN* London: Paul Chapman Publishing..

Plaisance, E. (2000) 'Les mots de l'éducation spéciale' in Chauvière, M. and Plaisance, E. (eds) *L'École face aux handicaps: éducation spéciale ou éducation intégrative?*, Paris: Press Universitaire de France.

Poppleton, P. (1992) 'The Significance of Being Alike: the implications of similarities and differences in the work-perceptions of teachers in an international five-country study', *Comparative Education*, 28(2) 215–23.

Porter, R. (1987) *Disease, Medicine and Society in England 1550–1860*, London: Macmillan.

Potts, P. (1992) 'Approaches to interviewing' in Booth, T., Masterton, M., Swann, W. and Potts, P. (eds) *Learning for all 1: Curricula for Diversity in Education*, London: Routledge.

Potts, P. (1995) '"What's the use of History" Understanding Educational Provision for Disabled Students and those who Experience Difficulties in Learning' *British Journal of Educational Studies* 43(4), 398–411.

Potts, P. (1998) 'Knowledge is not enough: An exploration of what we can expect from enquiries which are social' in Clough, P. and Barton, L. (1998) *Articulating with Difficulty: Research Voices in Inclusive Education*, London: Paul Chapman Publishing.

Potts, P. (1999) 'Human rights and inclusive education in China: a Western perspective' in Armstrong, F. and Barton, L. (eds) *Disability, Human Rights and Education*, Buckingham: Open University Press.

Potts, P. (ed.) (2003a) *Inclusion in the City: Selection, Schooling and Community*, London, RoutledgeFalmer

Potts, P. (2003b) 'A great learning city' in Potts, P. (ed.) *Inclusion in the City: Selection, Schooling and Community*, London, RoutledgeFalmer

Power, S. (1998) 'Researching the "pastoral" and the "academic": An Ethnographic Exploration of Bernstein's Sociology of the Curriculum', Walford, G. (ed.) *Doing Research About Education*, London: Falmer Press.

Priestley, M. (1999) 'Discourse and identity: disabled children in mainstream high schools' in Corker, M and French, S. (eds) *Disability Discourse*, Buckingham: Open University Press.

Pritchard, D. G. (1963) *Education and the Handicapped*, London: Routledge Kegan Paul.

Rabinow, P. (1984) *The Foucault Reader: An Introduction to Foucault's Thought*, London: Penguin Books.

Rée, J. (1999) *I see a Voice*, London: Harper Collins.

Safford, P. L. and Safford, E. J. (1996) *A History of Childhood and Disability*, New York and London: Teachers College Press, Columbia University.

Said, E. (1991) *Orientalism*, London: Penguin.

Saint, A. (1987) *Towards a Social Architecture: The Role of School-Building in Post-War England*, New Haven and London: Yale University Press

Sanjek, R. (1990) 'Fire, Loss and the Sorcerer's Apprentice' in Sanjek, R. (ed.) *Fieldnotes: The Makings of Anthropology*, London: Cornell University Press.

Scott, D. (1996) 'Ethnography and education' in Scott, D. and Usher, R. (eds) *Understanding educational research*, London: Routledge.

Scott, D. (1999) 'Endpiece: Researching an Agreement about rationality', in Scott, D. (ed.) (1999) *Values and Educational Research*, London, Institute of Education Bedford Way Papers,

Scull, Andrew T. (1979) *Museums of Madness: The Social Organization of Insanity in Nineteenth-Century England*, London: Penguin Books.

Shakespeare, T. (1993) 'Disabled people's self-organisation: a new social movement?', in *Disability, Handicap and Society*, 8:3, 249–63.

Shakespeare, T. (1994) 'Cultural Representation of Disabled People: dustbins of disavowal?' in *Disability and Society*, 9:3 pp. 283–300

Shakespeare, T. (1999) 'Art and Lies? Representations of disability on film', in Corker, M. and French, S. (eds) (1999) *Disability Discourse*, Buckingham: Open University Press

Shakespeare, T. and Watson, N. (1998) 'Theoretical perspectives on research with disabled children', in Robinson, C. and Stalker, K. (eds.) *Growing Up with Disability*, 111–28, London, Jessica Kingsley Publishers.

Shields, R. (1991) *Places on the Margin*, London: Routledge.

Sibley, D. (1995) *Geographies of Exclusion*, London: Routledge.

Skeggs, B. (1994) 'The constraints of Neutrality: The 1988 Education Reform Act and Feminist Research' in Halpin, D. and Troyna, B. (eds) *Researching Education Policy: Ethical and Methodological Issues*, London: The Falmer Press.

Slack, S. (1999) 'I am more than my wheels' in Corker, M. and French, S. (eds) *Disability Discourse*, Buckingham: Open University Press.

Slee, R. (1999) 'Special Education and Human Rights in Australia: how do we know about disablement, and what does it mean for educators?' in Armstrong, F. and Barton, L. (eds) *Disability, Human Rights and Education: Cross-cultural Perspectives*, Buckingham: Open University Press.

Soltan, M. (1996) 'Deconstruction and Architecture' in Dutton T. A. and Hurst Mann (eds) *Reconstructing Architecture: Critical Discourses and Social Practices*, Minneapolis: University of Minnesota Press.

Stake, R. E. (1998) 'Case Studies' in Denzin, Norman A. and Lincoln, Yvonna S. (eds) *Strategies of Qualitative Enquiry*, London: Sage Publications.

Stiker, Henri-Jacques, (1999) *A History of Disability*, Michigan: The University of Michigan Press.

Stone, E. (1999) 'Modern slogan, ancient script: impairment and disability in the Chinese language' in Corker, M and French, S. (eds) *Disability Discourse*, Buckingham: Open University Press.

Sultana, R. G. (1989) 'Transition education, student contestation and the production of meaning; possibilities and limitations of resistance theories', British Journal of Sociology of Education, 10 (3), 287–309

Sutherland, G. (1981) 'The origins of special education' in Swann, W. (ed.) *The Practice of Special Education*, Oxford: Basil Blackwell.

Taylor, J. (1991) *Hospital and Asylum Architecture in England 1840–1914: Building for Health Care*, London: Mansell Publishing Ltd.

Thomson, T, (1996) 'Family, Community and State: The micro-politics of mental deficiency' in Wright, D. and Digby, A. (eds) *From Idiocy to Mental Deficiency: Historical Perspectives on People With Learning disabilities*, London: Routledge.

Thrift, N. (1996) *Spatial Formations*, London: Sage.

Tomlinson, S. (1982) *A Sociology of Special Education*, London: Routledge and Kegan Paul.

Usher, R. (1996) 'Textuality and reflexivity in educational research' in Scott, D. and Usher, R. (eds) *Understanding Educational Research*, London: Routledge.

Utting, W. (1997) *People Like Us: the report of the review of the safeguards for children living away from home*, London: DOH/HMSO.

Valentine, J. (1997) 'Skirting and suiting stereotypes: representations of marginalized sexualities in Japan', *Theory, Culture and Society*, 14 (3), pp. 57–85.

Valentine, J. (2001) 'Disabled Discourse: hearing accounts of deafness constructed through Japanese television and film', *Disability and Society*, Vol. 16, No. 5, pp. 707–721.

Van Cleve, J. and Crouch, B. (1989) *A place of their own*, Washington, D. C.: Gallaudet University Press.

Vlachou, A. (1997) *Struggles for Inclusive Education*, Buckingham: Open University Press.

Ware, L. (2000) 'Sunflowers, enchantment and empires: reflections on inclusive education in the United States' in Armstrong, F., Armstrong, D. and Barton, L. (eds) (2000) *Inclusive Education: Policy, Contexts and Comparative Perspectives*, London: David Fulton .

Wedell, K. (1990) 'Children with Special Educational Needs' in Evans, O. and Varma, V. (eds) *Special Education: Past, Present and Future*, Basingstoke: The Falmer Press.

Whitty, G. (2002) *Making Sense of Education Policy*, London: Paul Chapman.

Willig, C. (ed.) (1999) *Applied Discourse Analysis: social and psychological interventions*, Buckingham: Open University Press.

Wilmot, F. and Saul, P. (1998) *A Breath of Fresh Air: Birmingham's Open-Air Schools 1911–1979*, Chichester: Phillimore and Co. Ltd.

Wright Mills, C. (1959) *The Sociological Imagination*, Harmondsworth: Penguin.

Wright, D. and Digby, A. (eds) (1996) *From Idiocy to Mental Deficiency: Historical Perspectives on People With Learning Difficulties*, London: Routledge.

Yin, R. K. (1993) *Applications of Case Study Research*, London: Sage.

Newspaper articles.

Liberation (25.7.02) 'La France ouvre les yeux sur ses handicapés', p. 2, article by Sandrine Cabut.

The Independent (24.9.98) 'Butlin's "evicted" deaf partygoers', article by Ian Burrell, p. 7.

The Times Educational Supplement (31.12.99) 'If only we had known then … .', article by Baroness Warnock, p. 27.

On-line material

Opinion, The Times Online (5.10.02) *This asylum-seekers Bill is repugnant*, report by Bill Morris.

BBCi News FRONT PAGE (5.12.02) Article on Sangatte by Jon Sopel

Recorded music

Steve Reich, *Different Trains*, Kronos Quartet.

Index